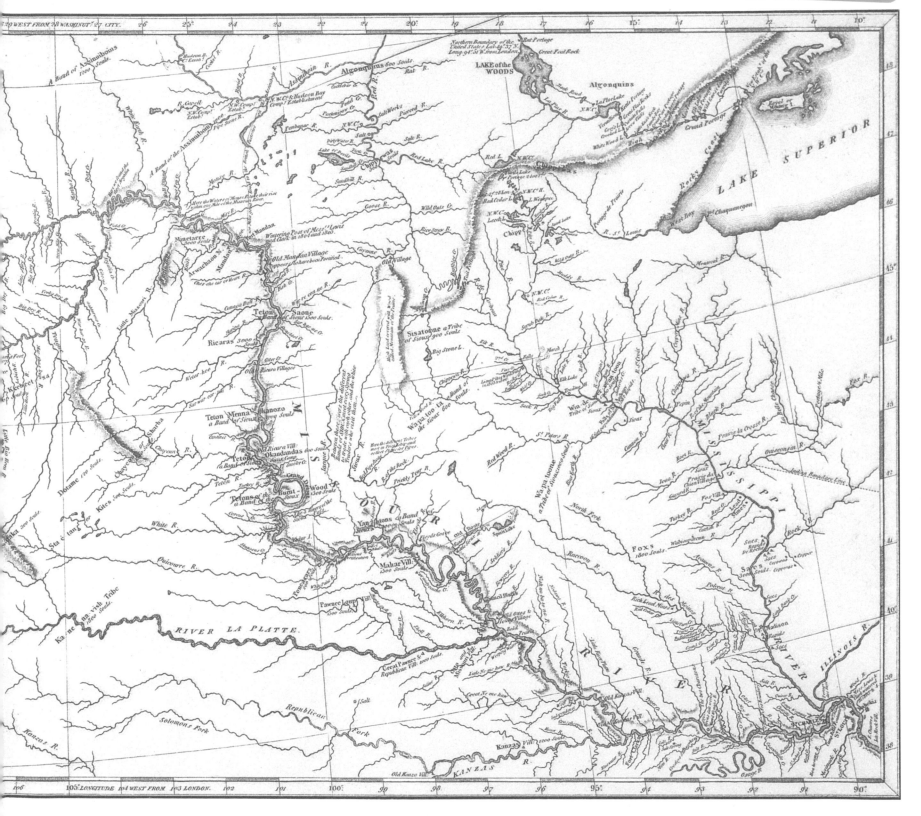

Merry Christmas
to Ed
With My Love—
Elizabeth
2000

A TEHABI BOOK

The Saga of

LEWIS & CLARK

INTO THE UNCHARTED WEST

Thomas Schmidt and Jeremy Schmidt

ACKNOWLEDGMENTS

The authors wish to express their deep appreciation and debt to Gary E. Moulton and the University of Nebraska Press, whose multiple-volume edition of the unabridged Lewis and Clark Journals have so richly endowed this and all thoughtful books written on the subject since the 1980s.

A DK PUBLISHING BOOK

www.dk.com

Alrica Goldstein, *Project Editor*
Dirk Kaufman, *Art Director*
LaVonne Carlson, *Editorial Director*

First Edition
10 9 8 7 6 5 4 3 2 1
Published in the United States by
DK Publishing, Inc.
95 Madison Avenue
New York, New York 10016

Library of Congress Cataloging-in-Publication Data
    Schmidt, Thomas, 1959–
        The saga of Lewis & Clark : into the uncharted West / Thomas Schmidt and Jeremy Schmidt. — 1st American ed.
        —Jacket.
        Includes index.
        ISBN 0–7894–4638–3 (alk. paper)
        1. Lewis and Clark Expedition (1804–1806) Pictorial works.
2. West (U.S.)—Discovery and exploration Pictorial works. 3. Lewis and Clark Expedition.
(1804-1806) Miscellaneia. 4. West (U.S.)-
—Discovery and exploration Miscellanea. I. Schmidt, Jeremy, 1949–
. II. Title. III. Title: Saga of Lewis and Clark.
F592.7.S13 1999
917.804'2—dc21   99–25606
                                 CIP

Printed and bound in Korea through Dai Nippon Printing Company

TEHABI BOOKS

The Saga of Lewis & Clark was conceived and produced by Tehabi Books. Tehabi—symbolizing the spirit of teamwork—derives its name from the Hopi Indian tribe of the southwestern United States. As an award-winning book producer, Tehabi works with national and international publishers, corporations, institutions, and nonprofit groups to identify, develop, and implement comprehensive publishing programs. Tehabi Books is located in Del Mar, California. www.tehabi.com

Chris Capen, *President*
Tom Lewis, *Editorial and Design Director*
Sharon Lewis, *Controller*
Nancy Cash, *Managing Editor*
Andy Lewis, *Senior Art Director*
Sarah Morgans, *Associate Editor*
Tim Connolly, *Sales and Marketing Manager*
Eric Smith, *Marketing Assistant*
Maria Medina, *Administratiave Assistant*
Kevin Giontzeneli, *Production Artist*
Sam Lewis, *Webmaster*
Tiffany Smith, *Executive Assistant*

Curtis Boyer, *Art Production*
Gail Fink, *Editorial Consultant*
Chris Davis, *Map Production*
Mo Latimer, *Editorial Assistant*
Laurie Gibson, *Copy Editor*
Linda Bannan, *Copy Proofer*
Ken DellaPenta, *Indexer*

Contents

Thomas Schmidt writes:

Not long ago, I slid my canoe into the Missouri River at Fort Benton, Montana, and headed down that broad, swiftwater highway into one of the most remote and wild regions that remains on the Great Plains. It was late autumn, and glorious. Deep blue skies overhead, the sun warm on my shoulders. Golden prairie hills slanting down from the rim of the plains to the taut, glassy surface of the river. In the bow sat an old friend. In the satchel at my feet lay two new ones— Meriwether Lewis and William Clark, bound in paper and effectively gagged until we landed at our camp and opened their Journals.

I don't remember when I first met the Captains, but it was in school, many years ago. I certainly didn't think of them as friends. They were just names in a history book. American explorers who, in 1804–06, led an expedition across North America from the Mississippi to the Pacific by way of the Missouri and Columbia rivers. Later, as I roved and worked throughout the Rockies, I often crossed their path, usually in beautiful places. I came to envy their long journey through my favorite part of the world and to admire them as skillful and tenacious wilderness travelers.

MEMBERS OF THE EXPEDITION

> *"Thus my friend, you have a summary view of the plan, the means and the objects of this expedition. If therefore there is anything under those circumstances, in this enterprise, which would induce you to participate with me in it's fatiegues, it's dangers and it's honors, believe me there is no man on earth with whom I should feel equal pleasuure in sharing them as with yourself."* —LEWIS' LETTER TO CLARK, JUNE 19, 1803

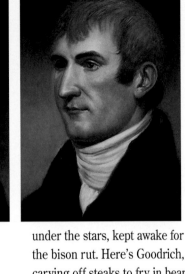

More recently, I had the good fortune to spend a year reading their unabridged Journals and retracing their route from St. Louis to the Pacific. As I made my way up the Missouri, the day-to-day details of their voyage sank in—the sweat, the toil, the sheer joy of seeing new country. I felt drawn to them and gained a deeper respect for what they'd done, what they'd gone through, what they'd brought back. What's more, they began to feel like the best sort of travel companions. Good-natured, energetic, open-minded, generous with their fellows, stoic enough to bear extreme hardship, yet familiar enough to complain about their bowels. They were always accessible, always willing to talk, always ready to hold forth on the landscape that lay before me, or to chat about plants and animals, Indians, or the challenges of river navigation. Add a tot or two of bourbon, a campfire on the Missouri, and it's not hard to see how a thirty-eight-year-old writer in a blue Ford van might begin to feel like one of the boys.

I'm not alone in feeling that personal tie. I have yet to meet a serious student of Lewis and Clark—and they are legion—who regards the Expedition as a purely historical event. The characters are too

CO-CAPTAINS OF THE EXPEDITION

Meriwether Lewis and William Clark were 29 and 33 years old, respectively, when they started up the Missouri. Both were native sons of Virginia, both had served with the army in the Ohio region, and for a short time, Clark had been Lewis' commanding officer. The friendship begun in Ohio became one of America's most famous partnerships. Upon leaving St. Louis, the Expedition roster, part of which is shown here (right), listed 45 men, including the permanent party of 25.

compelling for that, their ancillary adventures too interesting, and the Journals too detailed. Consider Clark, sitting in the flickering yellow light of his campfire, patiently yanking twenty-seven prickly pear thorns from his feet. That's not history, but it sure brings us closer to Clark as a human being. And the Journals are full of that kind of stuff. Here's Lewis, lying under the stars, kept awake for most of one night by the bellow and roar of the bison rut. Here's Goodrich, beaching a four-foot catfish and proudly carving off steaks to fry in bear's oil. There's York, swimming to an island for salad greens; Collins and Hall, swiping whiskey; the entire party, dancing around a bonfire to fiddle music while a crowd of Indians cheers them on.

The Captains tell us so much about day-to-day events that their Journals sometimes read as if they were an enormous bundle of letters written to a good but distant friend. In a very real sense, they were—at least in Lewis' case. The friend was Thomas Jefferson, who had been trying to send an overland expedition to the Pacific since the early 1780s, and whose own interest in such an exploration probably extended back to boyhood. Jefferson had been a close friend of Lewis' father, who died during the Revolutionary War, and the two families had been neighbors for many years. When Jefferson became president in 1801, he brought Lewis, then a twenty-seven-year-old army officer, to the White

"The enterprise &c. is Such as I have long anticipated and am much pleased with, and as my situation in life will admit of my absence the length of time necessary to accomplish such an undertaking I will chearfully join you in an 'official Charrector' as mentioned in your letter, and partake of the dangers, difficulties, and fatigues, and I anticipate the honors & rewards of the result of such an enterprise . . . My friend I do assure you that no man lives with whom I would perfur to undertake Such a Trip &c. as yourself." —CLARK TO LEWIS, JULY 29, 1803

Dear Sir

Washington. US. of America. July 4. 1803.

[handwritten letter of credit from Jefferson to Lewis]

To Capt. Meriwether Lewis.

THE PRESIDENT CALLS

Jefferson wrote Lewis a letter of credit (left) promising reimbursement to "consuls, agents, merchants, & citizens of any nation" who might supply the Expedition with necessities. Below: *"I am at the head of the Missouri. all well, and the Indians so far friendly."* With those hopeful words, Jefferson tested a code matrix, apparently thinking Lewis might need to send secret messages back to Washington. Decoding required a keyword known only by the sender and the intended recipient— in this example, the keyword was "artichoke."

"The river Missouri, & the Indians inhabiting it are not as well known as is rendered desireable by their connection with the Mississippi, & consequently with us. It is however understood that the country on that river is inhabited by numerous tribes, who furnish great supplies of furs & pelty to the trade of another nation carried on in a high latitude, through an infinite number of portages and lakes, shut up by ice through the long season." —JEFFERSON'S SECRET MESSAGE TO CONGRESS, DECEMBER 1802

"The President has been all his life a man of letters, very speculative and a lover of glory, and it would be possible he might attempt to perpetuate the fame of his administration . . . by discovering . . . the way by which the Americans may some day extend their population and their influence up to the coasts of the South Sea." —Spanish Minister to the U.S. Carlos Martinez de Yrujo, writing to his superiors, December 1802

House as his personal secretary, perhaps with the intention of appointing him to lead a western expedition.

Jefferson's chance came in 1802, shortly after Alexander Mackenzie published an account of his 1792–93 journey over the Canadian Rockies to the Pacific. Mackenzie, a prominent Canadian fur trader, saw the transcontinental route as an opportunity for Great Britain to monopolize the lucrative North American fur trade and to strengthen British commercial ties with Asia. Jefferson considered Mackenzie's trip a threat. Though the route itself was impractical, it established a powerful British land claim linking the Pacific Coast with the Crown's inland empire. It was only a matter of time before the British found a more promising route, probably farther south in the disputed Oregon Country (today's British Columbia, Washington, Oregon, and parts of Idaho and Montana). With Spain already holding much of the West Coast, a solid British claim to Oregon would prevent the United States from becoming the nation Jefferson dreamed of—a true continental power stretching from sea to sea. Worse, if the British defeated Napoleon, they could get French Louisiana, which included the west bank of the Mississippi and the entire land mass drained by the Missouri and Arkansas rivers. With Canada, Oregon, and Louisiana under the British crown, King George would control most of North America. Jefferson couldn't let that happen. The best way to prevent it was to establish an American route down the Columbia River system to the Pacific. Various powers, including the United States, had sailed a short distance up the Columbia's estuary. That simple act, in the bizarre calculus of the day, entitled the so-called discovering power to the entire river drainage—as if the tens of thousands of Indians who had been living there for hundreds of generations were as dirt, to be claimed and counterclaimed, bought and sold along with the rest of the land's resources. Spain, Russia, Great Britain, and the United States all claimed to have had gotten there "first" by sea. Jefferson could strengthen the American claim by getting there first by land.

THE JOURNALS
Clark's elkskin field journal, covering the difficult period from September 11 to December 31, 1805, records the Expedition's race against winter over the Lolo Trail and downriver to the sea. Containing 224 pages, 19 maps, and some sketches, it appears to have been written on loose pages and bound some time during the winter at Fort Clatsop.

" all our provisions goods and equipage on Board of the Boat of 22 oars, a large Perogue of 7 oares a Second Perogue of 6 oars, Complete with Sails &c. &c. men Compe. with Powder Cartragies and 100 Balls each, all in health and readiness to Set out. Boats and every thing Complete, with the necessary Stores of provisions & such articles of merchendize as we thought ourselves autherised to precure — tho' not as much as I think necssy for the multitud of Inds. tho which we must pass on our road across the Continent &c. &c."—CLARK, MAY 13, 1804

The most direct route, it seemed, was to ascend the Missouri to its source and make what the best minds of the day assumed to be a short portage over a single dividing ridge to the headwaters of the Columbia. No one knew for sure. There were no dependable maps of the Missouri beyond the Mandan villages (near present-day Bismarck, North Dakota). Everything to the West Coast was terra incognita—an immense blank space with a single, deceptively thin line of conjectural peaks running from north to south.

Jefferson and Lewis began laying their plans in 1802, completely unaware that Napoleon, cash-strapped and eager to hobble the British, would soon offer to sell Louisiana to the United States. Jefferson first got wind of the sale in July 1803. By then, Congress had approved the Expedition, Lewis had gathered much of the equipment and was already headed over the Appalachians. In Pittsburgh, he sat out a long, frustrating delay while the Ohio River dropped and a drunken boatwright tarried over construction of the Expedition's keelboat. Stymied by shoals and low water and already feeling undermanned with a crew of eleven, he dragged the boat downriver, laying over for two weeks in Clarksville, Indiana, to

pick up his friend and former army commander, William Clark. Together, they recruited more men, navigated the rest of the Ohio, ascended the Mississippi to St. Louis, and halted for the winter on the east bank.

The task Jefferson lay before them went far beyond anything previously attempted by European explorers in North America. Not only were they to find the most direct and practical route across lands unknown to European civilization, they were told to map the region, to study it, and to describe in meticulous detail its plants, animals, topography, minerals, and soils. They were to establish formal diplomatic ties with dozens of Indian tribes and to try to woo them from British and Canadian traders into the orbit of an American-based fur trade. Finally, they were to study the tribes and to describe whatever they could—populations, trade patterns, intertribal politics, languages, clothing, dwellings, social customs, food, and whatever else seemed of interest.

Jefferson expected a lot and got most of it. Together, Lewis and Clark traveled 8,000 wilderness miles, mapped a broad path through the Rockies, charted the length of the Missouri and much of the Columbia rivers, got along well with almost every Indian tribe they met, and

PROVISIONS
Clark compiled this partial list of provisions acquired for the journey in mid-May 1804. Among other items, Clark's inventory includes 3,150 pounds of cornmeal, 3,400 pounds of flour, 3,705 pounds of kegged pork, and 600 pounds of "Greese."

SOULARD'S MAP
Antoine Soulard's 1802 map of North America demonstrates the paucity of geographic information available to Lewis and Clark as they made plans for their transcontinental journey. Soulard's sketch of the Missouri River was conjectural but it reflected the widely held—and correct—opinion that the river headed in the Rocky Mountains. But Soulard's representation of the mountain barrier itself woefully underestimated the scale of the Rockies.

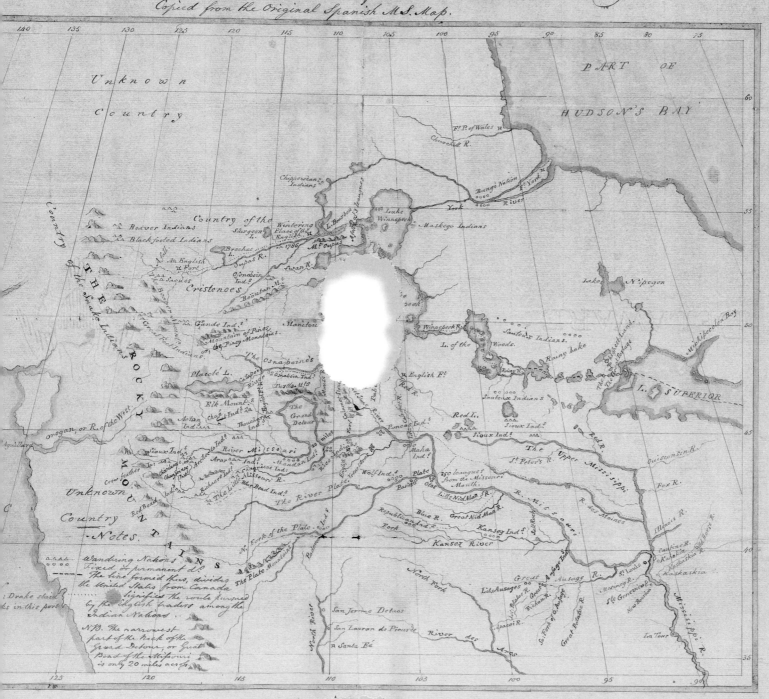

"The sale assures forever the power of the United States, and I have given England a rival who, sooner or later, will humble her pride.—Napoleon Bonaparte, 1803, commenting on The Louisiana Purchase

THE LOUISIANA PURCHASE

As a result of the 1803 Louisiana Purchase, the United States laid claim to a vast, largely unmapped territory. No one knew the full extent of the territory, not even the Native people who occupied it and traveled through it from one end to the other. But clearly it was a huge tract filled with geographic mysteries. For example, when Lewis and Clark reached the Marias River, seen here flowing into the Missouri from the north (left-hand side of photo), they were deep in the heart of the unmapped west, following their instincts and the directions they had collected from Indian informants during the previous winter. Yet no one had mentioned this powerful stream. Which was the true Missouri—the deep, muddy northern branch, or the shallower, wider, clearer southern branch? After days of pondering, the Captains went against the opinions of their men and correctly followed the southern stream.

"Capt. Lewis is brave, prudent, habituated to the woods, & familiar with Indian manners & character. He is not regularly educated, but he possesses a great mass of accurate observation on all the subjects of nature which present themseles here, & will therefore readily select those only in his new route which shall be new."

—THOMAS JEFFERSON, LETTER TO DR. BENJAMIN RUSH, SPRING 1803

MERIWETHER LEWIS
This portrait of Lewis, by Charles B. J. F. de Saint-Mémin, made after the Expedition, shows him wearing what he called *"the most eligant peice of Indian dress I ever saw,"* a short cloak of otter skin trimmed with strips of ermine—a gift from Shoshone chief Cameahwait.

added an astonishing 178 plants and 122 animals to the scientific canon.

Their unparalleled success hinged on their deep friendship and their multiple qualifications. Like their enlisted men, both felt at home in the wilderness, and both were skilled hunters. They were brave, innovative, tough, and decisive. Clark was the cartographer, the better boatman, the more consistent journalist. He had more experience on the frontier and with Indians. He also had the leveler head, the sunnier temperament, the more creative approach to spelling, the longer, happier life.

Lewis had more formal education. Well read, he was a competent practical doctor and had excellent training (thanks largely to Jefferson and his scientific friends) in botany, zoology, geology, and celestial navigation. By most accounts he was the more idealistic of the two, held a more romantic view of the world, was introspective, moody, at times withdrawn, and had bouts of deep melancholia. The best modern minds diagnose him as a manic depressive whose symptoms were aggravated by alcoholism. Eventually, he became suicidal and killed himself in 1809.

I don't doubt it. We need to know it. But I also think we tend to remember Achilles too often for his heel. I prefer to remember Lewis as a quick, inquiring mind, a restless spirit inhabiting a frame physically capable of keeping pace with his tireless curiosity. I like his courage. I like his competence. I like his lively pen, his relentless drive for detail, and his abundant wit that was by turns satiric, ironic, self-effacing, scatological, and bawdy. In short, I like his company. I only wish things could have turned out better for him once he returned to the savagery of American politics.

"The future destinies of the Missouri country are of vast importance to the U.S., it being perhaps the only large tract of country and certainly the first which lying out of the boundaries of the Union will be settled by the people of the U. States."
—Treasury Secretary Albert Gallatin, to Jefferson about the proposed expedition, Spring 1803

"Beginning at the mouth of the Missouri, you will take careful observations of latitude & longitude, at all remarkable points on the river, & especially at the mouths of rivers, at rapids, at islands, & other places & objects distinguished by such natural marks & characters of a durable kind."
—THOMAS JEFFERSON, INSTRUCTIONS TO LEWIS, JUNE 20, 1803

Jeremy Schmidt writes:

I agree. One of the most appealing aspects of the Expedition is how, through the Journals, we get a measure of these men and come away liking them as people. It's no wonder they were good friends. They treated each other well. They were comrades in the best sense. As for what came later, I prefer to picture them in their triumph, on that fast trip down the Missouri in August and September of 1806 having made it to the western ocean and nearly back again, now heading home through the ripe abundance of late summer, riding high on the breast of the current—downstream, downstream.

For it's not the Lewis and Clark of the East who live in our memories. It's Lewis and Clark in the mountains, on the plains, seeing the country at the height of its natural glory. It was an experience that anyone who loves the West can only envy. They saw it before the slaughter of the bison and antelope herds; before it was sliced up by clearcuts, power lines, dams, barbwire fences, and political boundaries. It was not an uninhabited, unknown wilderness. It was the familiar homeland of Indians who were enjoying a historical high point of their own, thanks in large part to the arrival of horses in the early 1700s. Horses gave them mobility and opened trading opportunities. Some tribes, particularly those along the Columbia River, were already supplied with abundant trade goods, on top of their own well-developed material cultures. Most had not yet experienced the bitter loss of their lands to white settlers; and while diseases such as smallpox had made tragic inroads along the Missouri downstream from the Mandan villages, tribes who lived west of there—the Sioux, Shoshone, Arapaho, Blackfeet, Nez Perce, and others—had yet to feel the sting of contact with the white people who called themselves Americans.

The Expedition entered this uncynical landscape with gritty determination but also eager enthusiasm. They loved the place. They had a ball. The work was hard and sometimes dangerous, but they were men of the frontier, and they welcomed the difficulties as inherent parts of the great adventure they knew they were living. For despite all its exploratory achievements and political significance, the journey, was above all else, an adventure. If there hadn't been mountains to struggle over, if the grizzlies hadn't been fierce, if the Sioux had welcomed them with open arms, if they hadn't had to go hungry a few times, if there had been no worries about winter and route-finding and dangerous rapids, it would have been a different and far less interesting trip.

Tom and I have some idea of how it felt. Although we would never compare our experiences with theirs, our passion for the West is largely connected with what remains of the natural scene as they saw it—and that's a considerable piece of country. Together and separately, with friends and our respective families, we've walked and paddled the entire route of the Expedition, and over the last thirty years have spent thousands of nights camped in wild places throughout the Rockies, the Northwest, and the Great Plains. We spent one memorable summer together paddling a canoe across Ontario—up one river system, across a divide, and down another long river to Hudson Bay (our own miniature version of the Voyage of Discovery). On all of our outings, we have had a constant awareness of those who came before us, and we feel enriched for the knowledge of their passing.

It continues to be one of the important gifts of being American that our history is closely tied to our landscape—especially in the West, where

WEST SLOPE FOREST
Opposite left: Dense woodlands, choked with waist-high undergrowth and contrasting starkly with the open plains, awaited the Expedition west of the Continental Divide.
Left: Nez Perce Chief Raven Blanket, photographed by E. S. Curtis.

"I feel myself perfectly prepared, nor do I doubt my health and strength of constitution to bear me through it; I go with the most perfect preconviction in my own mind of returning safe and hope therefore that you will not suffer yourself to indulge any anxiety for my safety."—LEWIS, LETTER TO HIS MOTHER, JULY 1803

"the manly, and soldier-like behaviour; and enterprizing abilities; of both Captain Lewis, and Captain Clark, claim my utmost gratitude: and the humanity shown at all times by them, to those under their command, on this perilous and important Voyage of discovery; I hope will ever fill the breasts of Men who were under their command . . . the President of the United States, did not misplace his judgment, when he appointed them to the command of this party on discovery; which is of so great a magnitude and utility, to the United States and mankind in general." —JOSEPH WHITEHOUSE, IN THE PREFACE OF HIS PUBLISHED DIARY, DECEMBER 1806

things have changed so little, and where the landscape seems to have compelled so many players of history to write it down, to describe what they were seeing in addition to what they were doing. No one ever wrote better material than Lewis and Clark, working together. The Journals tell their story, and the landscape brings it to life. Every time we find ourselves along their route, they are with us, and it's always a pleasure to see them.

Late last summer, I spent an evening on the Continental Divide at Lemhi Pass. This was after twelve days wandering through the tangle of canyons and mountain ranges that make up central Idaho. I was headed home to Wyoming, but I wanted to pause for a while and consider the landscape in the context of the Expedition. I sat in the dry, sun-warmed grass looking west at the turbulence of mountain ridges, and opened a map. Instantly Clark was at my shoulder—Clark the mapmaker, Clark with the passion for understanding how the country was laid out. "There, see?" I told him. "We're sitting on the Divide. This fork flows into the Salmon River. It goes to the Snake and the Columbia. But this here, this canyon, you don't want to go that way. Not at this season. Not in dugout canoes or with horses."

Of course, that's essentially what Clark was told near Lemhi Pass by Cameahwait, the Shoshone brother of Sacagawea. The Shoshones knew the country very well, and drew their own maps with skill and competence. Lewis and Clark didn't need me sitting there with my highway map. But I'd sure hate to be there without them.

THE VOYAGE OF DISCOVERY Hoping to find a single dividing ridge between the Missouri and Columbia drainages, the Expedition instead faced three months of hard travel across numerous ranges. Below, Montana sculptor Bob Scriver depicted the *Explorers of the Marias.*

"June 1st Friday 1804 Set out early, the Same Course S 48° W of Wednesday contd. 4ms passed the Mouth of Little Miry on the Stb & Bear Creek on the Larbd. at 6 Ms this Creek is about 25 yds wide, high rich Land on the Lb Side, S. 45° W to an Island opposit a hill on the S. Sd. 6 Ms."—CLARK, JUNE 1, 1804

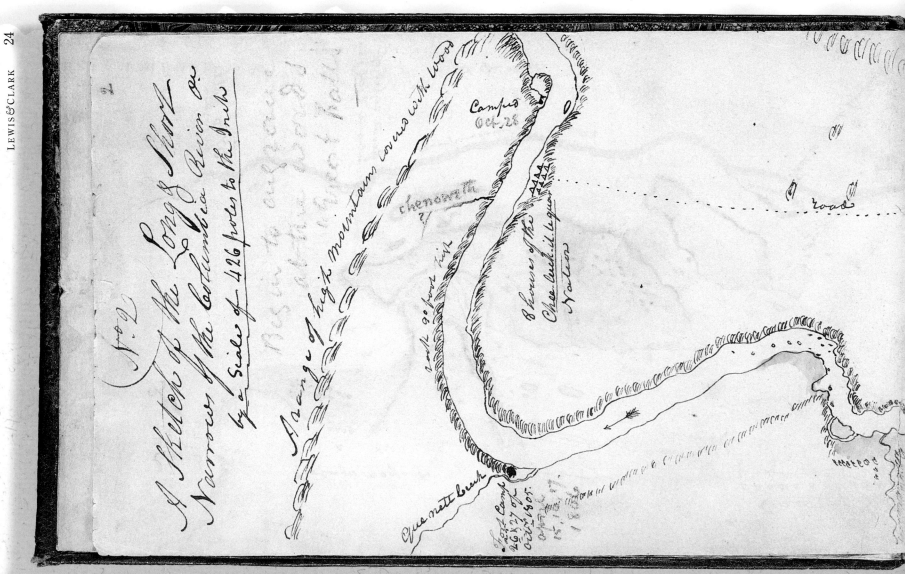

THE JOURNALS.

Clark took chief responsibility for cartography and produced dozens of maps detailing geographic features along their route from St. Louis to the mouth of the Columbia. His exquisite field sketches depicted not only every bend of the rivers but waterfalls, rapids, confluences, landmarks, Expedition campsites, Indian villages, and many other features. The large map above shows the Long and Short Narrows, two stretches of ferocious whitewater on the Columbia River. It also shows a major Indian village just above the Long Narrows and the Expedition's camp at Fort Rock, site of the

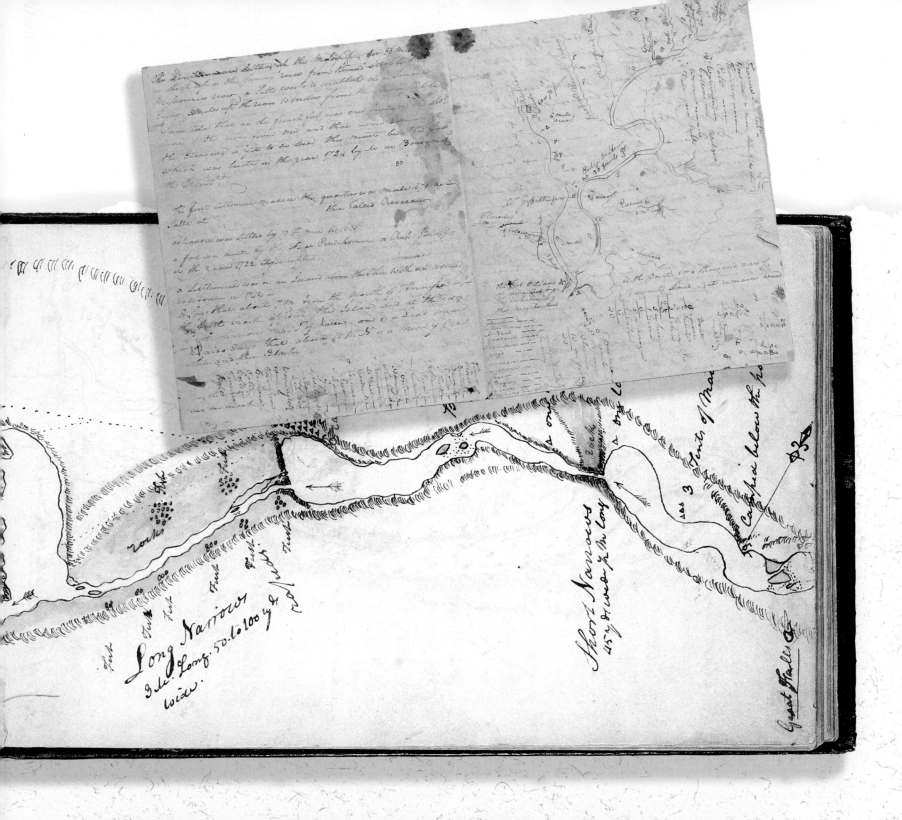

present-day city of The Dalles in south-central Washington. Above Clark's map is his sketch of the Mississippi-Missouri confluence, the starting point for the Expedition. The right branch is the Mississippi; the left branch is the Missouri. Just below the confluence, a triangle on the east bank marks the site of winter quarters, 1803–04. Up the Missouri, a cluster of three triangles marks the site of St. Charles.

ith confidence that we have discovered the most practicable rout which does exist across the continent by means of the navigable branches of the Missouri and Columbia Rivers."

23 Three Forks – July 25–30, 1805
Headwaters of the Missouri

24 Jefferson River – July 30, 1805

25 Lemhi Pass – August 12, 19, 26, 1805
Lewis led main party over, August 26

26 Lemhi River Valley – August 13, 1805
Lewis met Shoshones

27 Salmon River – August 21–31, 1805
*Clark scouted Salmon August 21–26;
main party skirted it August 31*

28 Lost Trail Pass – September 3–4, 1805

29 Bitterroot River Valley – September 6–11, 1805

30 Traveler's Rest – September 9–11, 1805
*Corps started 12-day starvation
trek on the Lolo Trail*

31 Lolo Creek – September 11–13, 1805

32 Lolo Pass – September 13, 1805

33 Lolo Trail – September 11–22, 1805
Traditional Nez Perce route across the Bitterroot

34 Lochsa River – September 14–15, 1805
*Corps detoured from Lolo Trail to Lochsa, climbed
3,000 feet to regain route*

35 Weippe Prairie – September 20–24, 1805
Encountered first Nez Perce villages

36 Canoe Camp – September 25 to October 7, 1805
Built five dugout canoes on the Clearwater River banks

37 Snake River – October 10, 1805

38 Palouse Indians – October 11, 1805
Two Palouse piloted Corps through Snake River rapids

39 Columbia River – October 16–18, 1805

40 Yakimas & Wanapams – October 16–18, 1805
Met these tribes at confluence of Columbia and Snake

41 Walla Wallas – October 18–19, 1805
Met tribe near Wallula Gap

42 Umatillas – October 19, 1805

43 John Day River – October 21, 1805

44 Deschutes River – October 22, 1805

45 Celilo Falls – October 22–23, 1805
Hired local Indians to help portage gear around the falls

46 Tapanash, Wishrams, Wascos – October 22–27, 1805
*Met with various groups living near present-day
The Dalles*

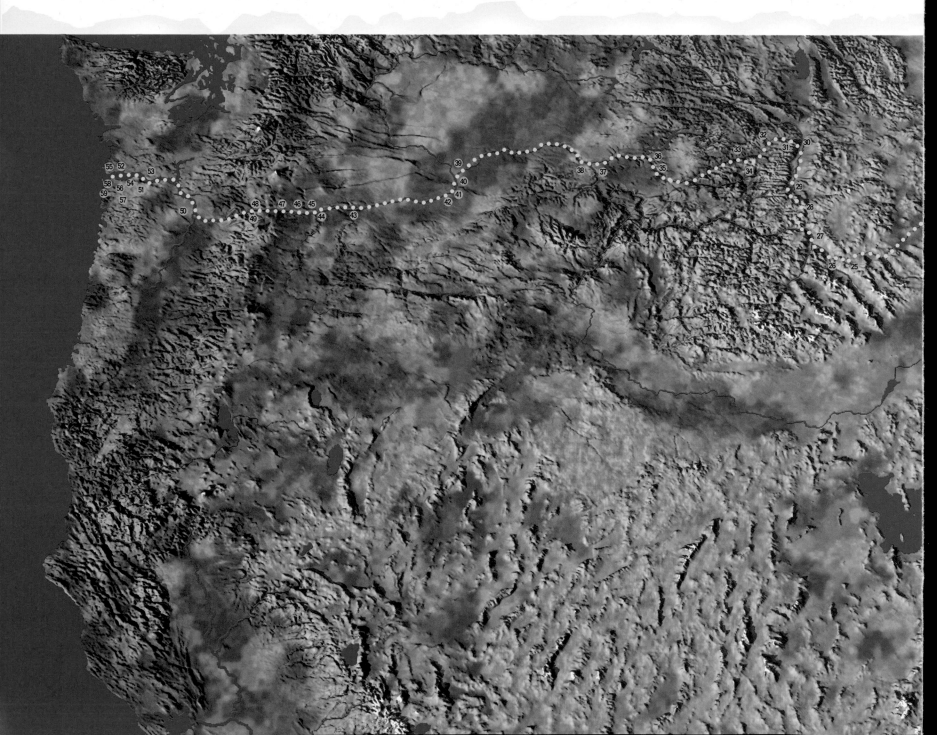

1. **Camp Wood** – December 12, 1803, to May 14, 1804
   Winter Quarters and Expedition jump-off point
2. **St. Louis** – May 14, 1804
   Hub of Missouri River fur trade
3. **St. Charles** – May 16–21, 1804
   Three men court-martialed for misconduct
4. **Osage River** – June 1, 1804
5. **Kansas River** – June 26–29, 1804
   Two men court-martialed for stealing whiskey
6. **Platte River** – July 21, 1804
7. **Council Bluffs** – July 30 to August 4, 1804

8. **Sgt. Floyd Grave** – August 20, 1805
9. **Calumet Bluff** – August 28–31, 1804
   Counciled with Yankton Sioux
10. **Niobrara River** – September 4, 1804
11. **Bad (or Teton) River & Area** – September 24–28, 1804
    Had tense encounter with Texton Sioux
12. **Grand River & Area** – October 8–12, 1804
    Counciled with Arikaras
13. **Mandan & Hidatsa Villages** – October 26, 1804 to April 8, 1805
14. **Fort Mandan** – November 2, 1804 to April 7, 1805
    Winter Quarters

15. **Knife River** – April 8, 1805
16. **Yellowstone River** – April 26, 1805
17. **Musselshell River** – May 20, 1805
18. **Marias River & Area** – June 2–11, 1805
    Unexpected confluence puzzled the Corps
19. **Lower Portage Camp** – June 16–28, 1805
20. **Great Falls** – June 13 to July 13, 1805
    Five major falls forced an 18-mile portage
21. **Upper Portage Camp** – June 18 to July 13, 1805
    Upper base camp for Great Falls portage
22. **Beaverhead River** – August 4–7, 1805

"We are to ascend the Missouri River with a boat as far as it is navigable and then go by land, to the western ocean, if nothing prevents, &c. This party consists of 25 picked Men of the armey & country and I am So happy as to be one of them pick'd Men. . . . We expect to be gone 18 months or two years. We are to Receive a great Reward for this expedition, when we Return." —SGT. JOHN ORDWAY, LETTER TO HIS PARENTS, APRIL 1804

Lewis and Clark's route across western North America begins near St. Louis, follows the Missouri River and several of its tributaries to the Continental Divide in the Rocky Mountains, then descends to the Pacific Coast by way of the Columbia River watershed. The four-thousand-mile voyage west required eighteen months of travel, most of it in boats. The journey home, which included two major deviations from their outbound route, took just six months.

They set off May 14, 1804, in a large, decked keelboat and two smaller, open boats called pirogues. As they towed, rowed, and occasionally sailed against the ferocious currents of the Missouri, the river led them through high, wooded bluffs and eventually onto the Great Plains where they encountered dozens of plant and animal species unknown to science. Along the way, they met and councited with several Indian tribes: the Missouris and Otos at Council Bluffs; the Yankton Sioux near present-day Yankton, South Dakota; the belligerent Teton Sioux at present-day Pierre, South Dakota; the Arikaras near the mouth of the Grand River; and the Mandans and Hidatsas north of present-day Bismarck, North Dakota.

In late autumn, they arrived at the Mandan villages, which lay at the very edge of the territory known to European civilization. They halted there for the season, built Fort Mandan, and passed a cordial winter among their Indian neighbors. In early April, Lewis and Clark sent the keelboat back down the Missouri, laden with specimens, notes, and dispatches for President Jefferson. At the same time, they continued upriver in the two pirogues and in six huge dugout canoes they had carved during the winter. The party now consisted of thirty-two men, a Shoshone woman (Sacagawea), and her infant son.

As they ascended the Missouri into uncharted lands, they survived some shocking encounters with grizzly bears, puzzled over the confluence of the Marias and Missouri rivers, and took a solid month to portage their gear eighteen miles around five major waterfalls at present-day Great Falls, Montana. They abandoned their pirogues below the falls, carved additional canoes above, and pressed onward, following first the Missouri, then the Jefferson and Beaverhead Rivers to a point southwest of present-day Dillon, Montana. It was there that they finally met the Shoshones, bought horses from them, crossed over the Continental Divide at Lemhi Pass, and descended into the Columbia River watershed.

Guided by a Shoshone man, they followed the Lemhi and Salmon rivers north, then climbed over Lost Trail Pass into the Bitterroot Valley, which led them north to the vicinity of present-day Missoula. There they turned west and made their starvation trek along the Lolo Trail to the Clearwater River in Nez Perce territory.

As they recovered from their Lolo ordeal, they built five new canoes, then paddled down the rapids of the Clearwater and Snake rivers to the Columbia, passing dozens and dozens of Indian villages where they bought salmon, dogs, and roots since they were in too much of a hurry to hunt or fish for themselves. Soon, they could make out peaks in the Cascade Range and by early November, they had paddled into the Columbia estuary. Pinned down repeatedly along the north shore of the estuary by storms and huge waves, the Expedition finally reached the Pacific Coast in mid-November—on foot.

They built Fort Clatsop on the south side of the estuary, near present-day Astoria, Oregon, spent a miserable winter there, then doubled back up the Columbia, largely retracing their westbound route as far as the Missoula area. At that point, Lewis and Clark split the command. Lewis took several men nearly due east to Great Falls, then followed the Marias River northwest into the heart of Blackfeet country. There, they skirmished with a small band of Blackfeet, killed two, fled back to the Missouri, piled into the boats, and headed downriver. Clark, meanwhile, returned to Three Forks, struck off to the east, and explored the Yellowstone River. The two separate parties rejoined on the Missouri near present-day Williston, North Dakota, and pulled for home, arriving in St. Louis on September 23, 1806.

THE ROUTE

47 Short and Long Narrows – October 24–25, 1805
Ran hazardous rapids on the Columbia wihout mishap

48 Cascades of the Columbia – October 30 to November 2, 1805
Portaged and ran portions of this 10-mile stretch of rapids; emerged in tidewater

49 Cascade Indians – October 30 to November 2, 1805
Passed Cascade Indian villages and burial vaults

50 Skilloots – November 4, 1805
Skilloots dined with the Corps, swiped Clark's pipe tomahawk

51 Wakiakums – November 7, 1805
Corps first encountered this people on the Columbia River Estuary

52 "Ocian" in View – November 7, 1805
Corps actually saw the Columbia River Estuary

53 Columbia River Estuary – November 7 to December 7, 1805
Spent month in a series of stormbound camps

54 Cathlamets – November 11–15, 1805
Cathlamets paddled in and out of stormbound camp

55 Chinooks – November 15–25, 1805
Had contacts with Chinooks in second stormbound camp

56 Cape Disappointment – mid-November, 1805

57 Fort Clatsop – December 7, 1805 to March 23, 1806
Winter Quarters

58 Tillamook Head – January 7–8, 1806
Clark and 14 others climbed south to see a beached whale; Clark bought blubber from Tillamook Indians

59 Salt Camp – December 28, 1805 to February 21, 1806
Site of beach bivouac where small detachment boiled seawater to make four bushels of salt

It's spring 1804, and William Clark—tall, red-headed, and cheerful—stands on the elevated stern deck of the Expedition's keelboat, watching his men row against the swift brown current of the Missouri River. They sit before him, ten to a side, heaving in rhythmic unison, their backs glistening with sweat, heads bent to the task. Beyond them, at the bow, stand two other men gazing up that vast sheet of turbulent, muddy water, waiting for the next ugly surprise the Missouri is certain to hurl at them.

Underway at last. With Clark on deck, Lewis off rambling among the forested bluffs, and the Expedition's two smaller boats bringing up the rear, the Corps of Discovery is finally, joyfully, underway. They have left behind the gloomy indolence of winter quarters, and, after endless preparations, are now embarked on the grand adventure. Bound for the Pacific through the interior of the continent, they would become the first of their kind to see whatever it was that lay beyond the Mandan villages. The Rockies, certainly, but were those mountains really a gentler barrier than the Appalachians? Would they meet the Welsh Indians? See woolly mammoths? What about that mountain range made of solid salt?

The prospect of the voyage itself was enough to make their blood sing. But it was also mid-May, the sun still a pleasure, the grass soft, the wildflowers and fruit trees in

UNDERWAY

full fragrant blossom, the big hardwoods bursting with a new crop of leaves. Thousands of colorful wood ducks nested along the banks and bobbed among the eddies. Striped chorus frogs sent up their creaking chants from the damp forests, and the morning air glittered with birdsong.

What a welcome change from winter—the long, long winter the Corps had passed on the east bank of the Mississippi, right across from the mouth of the Missouri. There, the waiting, the boredom, the close quarters, the long list of peevish gripes each man carried in his head— all that, and countless other frustrations had taken a toll on everyone. Everyone, that is, except Lewis, who had spent most of the winter across the river in St. Louis, buying more supplies, recruiting more men, and gathering priceless information from the city's fur trade merchants about the Missouri, its tributaries, and its inhabitants. Even Clark had gotten away for a month or so, but the enlisted men had been stuck there with little to do but watch the gray slurry of ice and slush sweep past the muddy banks.

No wonder they'd been so eager to launch the boats and travel the short distance up the Missouri to St. Charles, a French settlement of roughly 450 people that must have seemed like The Big Time to a bunch of guys who'd just spent five straight months marooned in a cluster of forlorn huts. There were shops, taverns, fresh breads and rolls, sweets, sausages, women, and whole crowds of people who had never heard the jokes that had grown so stale in winter quarters. Their pockets jingled with a winter's pay, and the citizens of St. Charles stoked their expectations by inviting them to a dance the first night they were there.

Clark knew his men well by then, so he had put them on notice, threatening to

RIVER CRAFT
Preceeding page: The Expedition headed up the Missouri in one keelboat and two smaller craft called pirogues. This modern rendition by L. Edward Fisher depicts the Expedition traveling through the wooded bluffs of central Missouri on June 4, 1804.

THE EXPEDITION DOG
Lewis' pet Newfoundland, named Seaman or Scannon, served as watchdog, hunter, and companion. A stream in Montana was apparently named for him. Right: High water crowds a line of cottonwoods along the Mississippi River.

Missouri River   Missouri River   Osage River   Mississippi River   Camp Wood   St. Louis

KEEL BOATS

Swiss artist Karl Bodmer, who traveled up the Missouri in 1833–34, painted this scene of a small keelboat moored at a riverside camp. Clark's journal page includes a sketch of the Expedition's 45-foot keelboat, featuring 20 oars. The side view (right) shows how the jointed mast could be lowered and an awning erected over the oarsmen; it also shows the stern deck and its separate awning with a windowed cabin beneath. A waterline sketched along the hull indicates the shallow four-foot draft.

"Those Indians told me Several days ago that they would Come on & hunt and by the time I got to their Camp they would have some Provisions for us, we Camped in a Bend under at the Mo: of a Small creek, Soon after we came too the Indians arrived with 4 Deer as a Present, for which we gave them two qts. of whiskey"—CLARK, MAY 22, 1804

"A great majority of the inhabitants are miserably pour, illiterate and when at home excessively lazy, tho' they are polite hospitable and by no means deficient in point of natural genious, they live in a perfect state of harmony among each other;"—LEWIS, ON THE CITIZENS OF ST. CHARLES, MAY 20, 1804

move the boats to *"a more retired Situation"* if the men disgraced themselves. Perhaps it was too much to ask. Within twenty-four hours, three of them were court-martialed for misconduct, and one got fifty lashes for *"behaveing in an unbecomeing manner at the Ball."* Still, Clark let them have their fun. There were other dances to attend, but no more floggings, and the men, Pvt. Whitehouse said, enjoyed some *"verry agreeable dancing with the french ladies."* All in all, it had been quite a send-off.

LEWIS AND CLARK at ST.CHARLES · MAY 21, 1804 ·

fell, Clark tells us, from a 300-foot cliff, but *"Saved himself by the assistance of his Knife . . . he caught at 20 foot."*

As the days slipped by, the boats passed the last of the white settlements—tiny clusters of houses tucked into the narrow bottomlands beneath the bluffs. The residents were mostly French, but Americans had begun to settle along

Now they were on the river. Three boats. Two Captains. Forty-five men, a couple of horses, and a dog. The men came from the backwoods of the Ohio River Valley, from Army posts, and from French settlements along the Mississippi. Among them were two blacksmiths, a carpenter, several expert boatmen, a tanner, and a slave named York, who had been Clark's companion since boyhood. Twenty-five of them formed what was called "the permanent party," which would man the keelboat for now and make the entire voyage to the Pacific and back. The others manned the pirogues, and would turn back partway along the journey with the maps, notes, and specimens of plants, animals, and minerals the Captains had prepared to that point.

UNDERWAY

In an early illustration of the Expedition leaving St. Charles, Missouri, the keelboat is inaccurately pictured with a front cabin. Right: Budding trees along the river screen a radiant cloud bank in twilight skies.

As the Expedition pushed beyond St. Charles, the river led them beneath high limestone bluffs that rose hundreds of feet above the water. Densely forested, draped with vines and showy wildflowers, alive with birdsong, the bluffs crowded the river and presented Lewis with an irresistible subject for scientific inquiry. He scrambled up the heights—and nearly died. He

the river, too. The Expedition often paused to chat, to get a last look at a cow or a yard full of chickens, and, no doubt, to bask in the admiration of well-wishers. No bumpkins, these locals were well-traveled themselves, accustomed to seeing men off on long voyages into the Missouri country. But the Expedition was going much farther than anyone had gone before, so they deserved an extra jolt of good cheer—and got it. *Bon voyage.* Godspeed . . . hope you keep your hair.

Keeping their hair would be no problem, at least for a while. They had been living among Indians for months. Potawatomis, Sauks, Kickapoos, and others had been frequent visitors to winter quarters, and they were a casual and accepted presence at settlements on the Missouri and Mississippi. Customers to some, relatives to others, friends to many. Getting scalped was not a concern. For now, the big worry was the river itself.

Wild, ferocious, beautiful, and cruel, the Missouri came at them like a colossal firehose, staggering the boats, caving in the forested banks, and sending acres of dirt, sand, stones, and mud—as well as vast snarls of brush, vines, and trees—plunging into the roil and suck of the current. Huge cottonwoods, oaks, and maples swept downriver as masses of lurching flotsam or as individual snags, their roots and branches protruding from the water, the main body of the trunk lurking just beneath the surface, *"between those two Creeks and behind a Small willow Island in the bend is a Prarie in which the Missouries Indians once lived and the Spot where 300 of them fell a Sacrifise to the fury of the Saukees   This nation (Missouries) once the most noumerous nation in this part of the Continent now reduced to about 80 fes. and that fiew under the protection of the Otteaus"*—CLARK, 13 JUNE, 1804

"in passing up on the S. S. opsd. the Isd. the Sturn of the boat Struck a log which was not proceiveable   the Curt. Struck her bow and turn the boat against some drift & Snags . . . with great force; This was a disagreeable and Dangerous Situation, particularly as immense large trees were Drifting down and we lay imediately in their Course,"—CLARK, JUNE 9, 1804

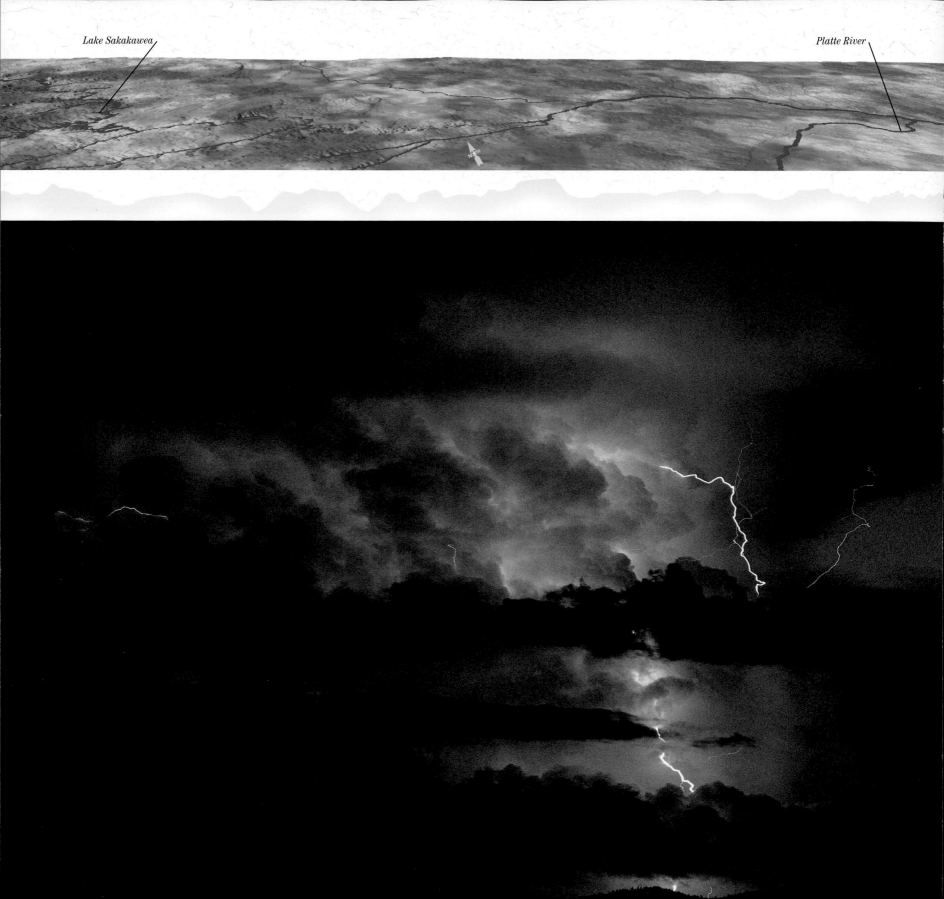

Lake Sakakawea

Platte River

NORTH

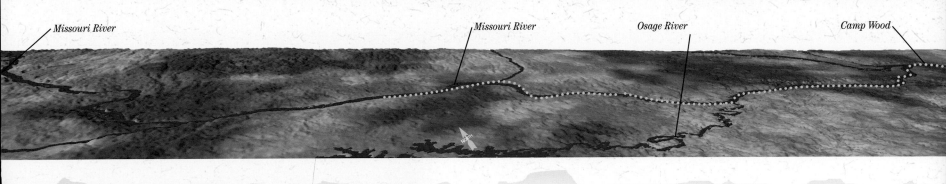

spinning, rolling, ready to take a swipe. Strange currents convulsed the river, and multiple channels—obscured beneath the spring flood—threaded back and forth, crossing one another, joining, dividing, reversing, building up sandbars and islands and just as quickly tearing them down again.

It was chaos, an ever-changing onslaught of brawling brown water, brush, trees, muck, and sand that no modern boater would head into without an outboard motor. Lewis and Clark, of course, had no choice but to bull ahead.

Under the best of circumstances, they could sail, or at least use the sails to give the oarsmen a boost. On those rare days, they might log twenty miles or more. Usually, though, the men rowed, pushed the boats along with setting poles, and hauled them upstream with tow ropes. Towing was the worst, a grueling task that put most of the crew ashore and pitted them in a brutal tug-of-war against the lumbering keelboat, which rode with four full feet of its hull underwater. They strained away at the rope for hours at a time, trudging through the muck, cutting their feet on rocks, dodging snakes, trying to ignore the clouds of mosquitos. Overhanging branches and toppled trees barred their way, and they often had to tow under banks that might collapse at any moment. It was a monumental effort that often bought them just ten miles or so for twelve to fourteen hours of labor.

Throughout each day, the boats crossed and recrossed the river, seeking the slowest water, skirting dangerous sandbars, and angling away from approaching snags or freshly collapsed banks. Sometimes the boatmen chose the wrong route and were forced by shallow water to drop back a mile or so before they could try yet another path through the confusing network of channels.

All of that was routine, but every couple of days they got into serious trouble. They might snag on a sandbar, or a submerged log, unable to move as a huge raft of trees swept directly toward them. Or the boat might pivot on the snag, swing broadside to the current, and start to capsize. Sometimes the tow rope broke, and the boat,

WEATHER REPORT
May 31, 1804, central
Missouri: *"rained the greater part of last night, the wind from the West raised and blew with great force untile 5 oClock p.m. which obliged us to lay by."*
—**CLARK**

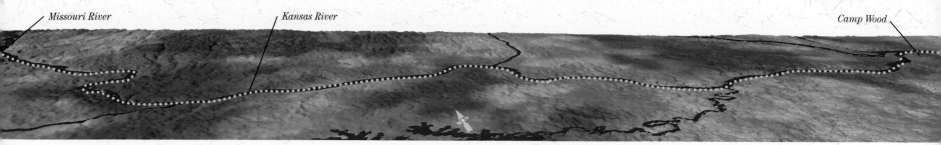

Missouri River   Kansas River   Camp Wood

short-handed, wheeled downstream for a mile or more, striking snags, sandbars, the bank, and overhanging branches before the crew regained control. Powerful thunderstorms whipped the river into great waves, pummeling the boats, driving them sideways onto sandbars and threatening to capsize or swamp them. Masts and oars were broken, cabin windows smashed, and there were narrow misses with snags that could have punched holes in the hull or even sheared off the bow.

Time and again, it was the French boatmen who staved off disaster. They knew the lower Missouri, and they knew what to do during emergencies—swim a rope to shore, pry the boat off a snag, even land in a bad squall and winch the boat over on its side to protect it from high waves. Often part Indian, they came from a long line of boatmen and fur traders who had been working among and marrying into the Missouri River tribes for generations. Their collective knowledge covered not just the Missouri corridor, but stretched hundreds of miles up many of the great river's tributaries. They had names for the creeks, rivers, and other landmarks. They pointed out the sites of abandoned Indian villages, trading posts, and forts and recounted the recent history of various tribes. Much of what they said made it into the Journals and onto Clark's map.

As spring passed and the Expedition continued to nose its way through the forest and bluff country of central Missouri, several parties of fur traders and trappers came floating downriver and paused to swap news. Some had wintered among the Omahas, others among the Pawnees, Osages, Kansas, and Sioux. Most had done quite well for themselves. Their canoes and rafts were loaded with beaver pelts, buffalo robes, and the skins of elk, deer, and bear. Three men were headed home with $900 in fur—a small fortune in those days. Two others had lost everything to prairie fires. The tribes, they said, had already left their winter homes along the rivers and were now far out on the plains, hunting buffalo.

On they went across much of present-day Missouri—lashed by rainstorms, slowed by headwinds, tormented by mosquitos and large ticks, but nearly always in good spirits. Gradually, the land opened up. The abrupt stone bluffs that had lined the river from its mouth fell behind, and the dense riverine forest thinned and receded. Before long, they were traveling through a luscious country of rolling tallgrass prairies interspersed with islands of trees and thickets of plum bushes drooping with fruit.

On most days, Clark remained on the keelboat, jotting down the day's events, taking note of the river's course, and charting each bend, island, and tributary stream. He occasionally got off the boat to stretch his legs and do a little hunting, but it was Lewis who spent most of the time on shore, roving the countryside, studying the land, cataloguing its plants and animals. He must have reveled in the task: out all day, on his own, in new country. On the sandy flats beside the river, he'd have bent over the splay-toed tracks of egrets and great blue herons, and the sharp hoofprints of white-tailed deer. In the shadowy depths of the forest, he'd have stepped around ponds of stagnant water gone emerald green with algae—Edens for snakes, turtles, bullfrogs, and mosquito larva. And out in the tallgrass prairies, he'd have shouldered his way through a head-high jungle of green grass splashed with the vivid red, purple, and yellow blossoms of wildflowers such as blazing star, ironweed, and giant sunflower. Though he saw plenty to keep him occupied, he found little that was new to science—the eastern woodrat, plains horned toad, and the Osage orange. The great rush of previously undescribed species would come later, out on the Great Plains and beyond.

While Lewis botanized, the party's hunters also roamed the land. They worked in advance of the boats on horseback, shooting deer and black bear all the way across western Missouri. They often made their own camps and stayed out for

FIELD AND GAME
After reaching western Missouri, the riverine forest opened up around lush prairies. Clark reported seeing hundreds of white-tailed deer hopping and skipping along the points of the river. **Left:** Prairie grasses mix with pink lupine on the shortgrass plains of Montana.

"I concld [concluded] to hunt on a Willow Isd [island] Situated close under the Shore, in Crossing from an Island, I got mired, and was obliged to Craul out, a disegreeable Situation & a Diverting one of any one who Could have Seen me after I got out, all Covered with mud, I went my Camp & [s]Craped off the Mud and washed my Clothes, and fired off my gun which was answered by George Drewyer who was in persute of me & came up at Dark we feasted of meet & water"

—CLARK, JUNE 24, 1804

days at a stretch, packing meat down to the river and going on. In early June, two of the best hunters returned to the boats *"much worsted,"* Clark wrote, *"they being absent Seven Days depending on their gun, the greater part of the time rain, they were obliged to raft or Swim many Creeks."* Game was so thick that the hunters had little trouble supplying the men with all they could eat and more. They made jerky with the surplus, and to their suppers of venison or bear, the men sometimes added greens, parched corn, or meal. But mostly, the diet was a cardiologist's nightmare—meat, meat, and more meat. Probably on the order of nine pounds a man every day.

In the evening, a military precision marked their camps. When the boats landed, guards were posted on the bank and at the perimeter and were relieved throughout the night. The rest of the men pitched the tents, laid out their bedding, gathered firewood, divided into separate messes, and cooked supper. They reserved a portion of the meal for the following day, so no travel time would be wasted on cooking. Often, the Captains issued a dram of whiskey or brandy, and the men would sing and dance to fiddle music late into the night. As gales of laughter rose beside the river, Lewis and Clark sat apart from the men, scribbling away at their portable desks by candlelight. When it was time to turn in, each man had a mosquito *bier* to keep the worst of the bugs at bay. Even so, droves of large ticks crawled in with them.

By mid-June, the Expedition had pressed beyond present Columbia, where the Missouri jogs north for about twenty miles or so and then bends off to the west. The boatmen told the Captains they had now entered the worst part of the river. There were more sandbars, islands, and narrows that funneled and accelerated the current and left them with no option but to

A LAND RICH WITH GAME Whitetailed deer (right) formed the principal staple of the Expedition's diet all of the way across Missouri, supplemented by black bear and occasionally wild greens such as watercress. Beavers (above) lived in riverbank dens and along tributary streams. In the deciduous forests along the river, racoons (opposite) were common.

head straight into the worst of it. One day, they almost capsized the boat. On the next, they struck and pivoted on a snag, hit a sandbar, and were then nearly *"Swallowed up by the roleing Sands,"* Clark wrote. The current got so strong that they could make no headway even with all of the men rowing with the help of a stout, favorable wind. They had to tow *"under a bank Constantly falling."*

After several days of fighting this difficult and dangerous water, the Captains called a halt in order to make a new tow rope from a thick cable Lewis had bought in Pittsburgh. They also needed twenty more oars, which they carved from ash trees taken in the rich riverine forests that lined the banks. While the men worked, Clark noted that most of them were sick. Several had dysentery. Two-thirds were afflicted with boils, skin ulcers, or cysts—as many as eight or ten *"tumors"* on some men. With the germ theory of disease still half a century in the future, Clark could only speculate about the cause. He blamed it on the water, which held, he said, half a common wine glass of mud per pint. Actually, the principal cause was not what they drank, but what they ate. Their high-protein meat diet was nearly devoid of fruits and

"The Plains of this countrey are covered with a Leek Green Grass, well calculated for the sweetest and most norushing hay — interspersed with Cops [copses] of trees, Spreding ther lofty branchs over Pools Springs or Brooks of fine water. Groops of Shrubs covered with the most delicious froot is to be seen in every direction, and nature appears to have exerted herself to butify the Senery by the variety of flours raiseing Delicately and highly flavered raised aboved the Grass which Strikes & profumes the Sensation, and amuses the mind throws it into Conjecterng the cause of So magnificent a Senerey in a Country thus Situated far removed from the Sivilised world to be enjoyed by nothing but the Buffalo Elk Deer & Bear in which it abounds & Savage Indians." —CLARK, JULY 4, 1804

vegetables, and the jerky they ate was probably contaminated with bacteria. Add to that infected mosquito bites, tick heads left in the skin, cuts and scrapes, and, finally, the fact that they rarely bathed or washed clothes. It's a wonder they didn't get sicker.

Fortunately, the rising heat of summer promised a more balanced diet. Wild fruit, laced with antiscorbutics, ripened along the banks and on the prairies. Plums, grapes, cherries, raspberries, gooseberries, and apples hung heavily from vine and branch, swelling with juice and sugars. The men took a lively interest in how the fruit was coming along. When the cherries ripened, Pvt. Whitehouse wrote, the men *"pulled a Great Quantity"* and *"put them in the Barrel of whiskey."* Songbirds flitted among the berry patches. Black bears gorged on mulberries. Deer browsed among the hawthorns, feeding in astonishing numbers. *"Deer to be Seen in every direction,"* Clark noted on June 30. *"Thier tracks ar as plenty as Hogs about a farm."*

At the Kansas River, the Captains laid up for a few days to *"recruit the party."* As usual, what the Expedition considered a rest stop seems awfully busy to modern eyes. They cleared trees at the point between the rivers, then built across it a defensive breastwork of shrubs and logs six feet high (an unusual precaution they apparently never repeated during the journey). They unloaded one of the pirogues, turned it over, and repaired its hull. They cleaned the keelboat, and set out all manner of goods to dry—gunpowder, blankets, clothes, bags of food, tents, packs . . . . The place must have looked like a yard sale. They also cleaned their rifles, repaired the tow rope, jerked more meat, hunted, fished, dressed deer skins, and flogged two of their comrades for stealing whiskey (an irreplaceable comfort) from the common supply.

If *that* was rest, then think of what a towering chore it must have been to wrestle those boats upriver. We of the soft feet and remote-control era can scarcely imagine it. To them, though, extreme physical labor went with the territory. So did danger. After re-packing, they pulled away from the mouth of the Kansas and promptly grounded the stern of the keelboat on a sandbar. The bow swung with frightening speed toward a snag that Clark said

would have smashed off her bow and sunk her in deep water. It missed by six inches.

North by northwest, now, they pressed on while the full sweltering force of a Midwestern summer bore down upon them. Hot. Muggy. Inescapable. The whole world felt like a sauna, and the sand was so hot it scalded their bare feet and sent them scurrying back to the boats for moccasins. For several days running, Clark noted that the men had become *"verry feeble,"* or were *"verry much over powered with the heat."* He marveled at the sweat running off them in streams. Soon, they began complaining of intense headaches, and one collapsed from heat stroke. Lewis bled him and gave him saltpeter, a diuretic. It was the standard, useless, remedy of the day. What the man needed was more water and electrolytes—Gatorade.

But all was not misery. Far from it. On Independence Day, after making a very respectable fifteen miles, the men fired off the keelboat's swivel gun and knocked back an extra gill of whiskey. There were signs of elk and bison, curious Indian mounds to investigate, and the land had opened up even more. The trees had thinned, and the hills along the river had retreated into the distance, leaving a wide expanse of relatively flat bottomland covered with sprawling prairies.

Not far below the mouth of the Platte River, Clark followed some fresh elk tracks across the bottomland and up the wooded gulches and ravines that cut into the hills. *"After assending and passing thro a narrow Strip of wood Land Came Suddenly into an open and boundless Prarie, I Say bound less because I could not See the extent of the plain in any Derection . . . This prospect was So Sudden & entertaining that I forgot the object of my prosute."*

It was July 19th, a glorious midsummer's day, and Clark, a woodland creature, had emerged onto the eastern margin of the Great Plains and was seeing for the first time in his life prairies on an oceanic scale. Knee-high grass stretched off across the endless billowing hills to the vanishing point and beyond—all the way to the Rockies, wild and free, full of bison, pronghorn, and wolves, badlands, buttes, horse-mounted nomads, and riverside villagers—most of whom would welcome them as friends.

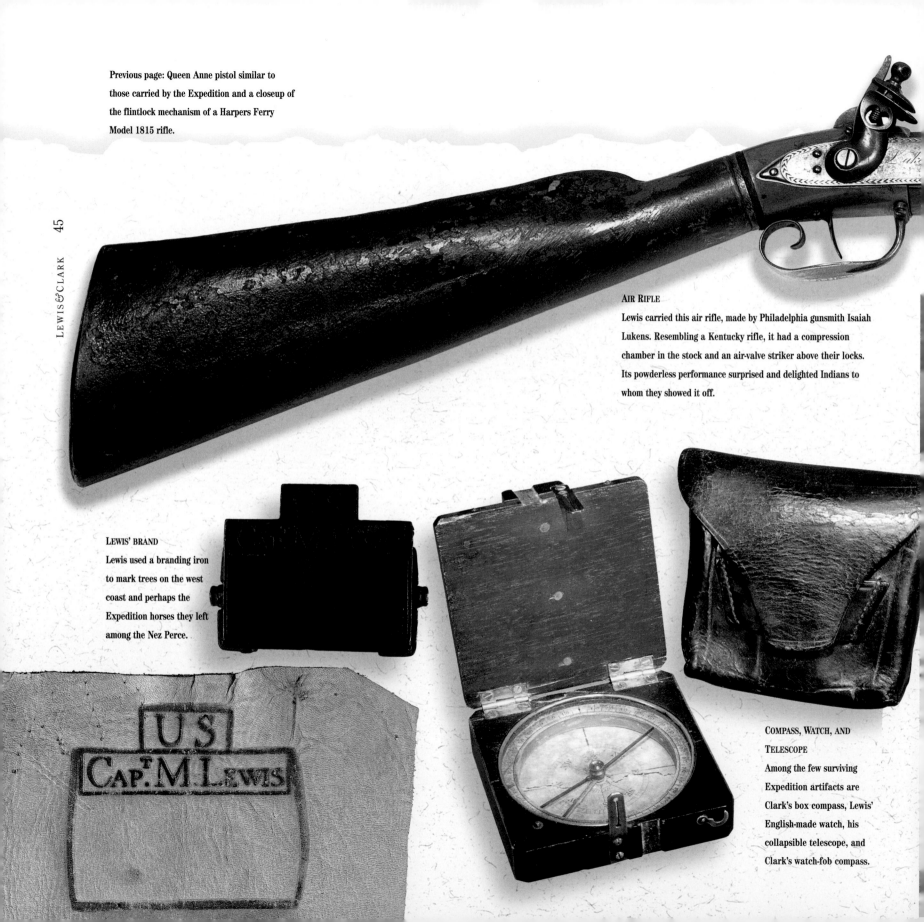

Previous page: Queen Anne pistol similar to those carried by the Expedition and a closeup of the flintlock mechanism of a Harpers Ferry Model 1815 rifle.

AIR RIFLE

Lewis carried this air rifle, made by Philadelphia gunsmith Isaiah Lukens. Resembling a Kentucky rifle, it had a compression chamber in the stock and an air-valve striker above their locks. Its powderless performance surprised and delighted Indians to whom they showed it off.

LEWIS' BRAND

Lewis used a branding iron to mark trees on the west coast and perhaps the Expedition horses they left among the Nez Perce.

COMPASS, WATCH, AND TELESCOPE

Among the few surviving Expedition artifacts are Clark's box compass, Lewis' English-made watch, his collapsible telescope, and Clark's watch-fob compass.

"the water of this river . . . throws out a greater preposn. of Swet than I could Suppose Could pass thro: the humane body Those men that do not work at all will wet a Shirt in a Few minits & those who work, the Swet will run off in Streams" —CLARK, JULY 6, 1804

Lewis and Clark outfitted the members of their Expedition with the finest equipment they could lay their hands on. Armed with a letter of credit from President Jefferson and well informed by the best minds of his time, Lewis gathered weapons, boats, provisions, clothing, scientific instruments, medicines, reference books, maps, presents for the Indians, tools, camping gear, and many other items. He acquired a great deal of it in the East, but added much more while the Corps of Discovery wintered near St. Louis in 1803–04. Given their near total lack of knowledge about what lay to the west of the Mandan villages in present-day North Dakota, it is a testament to the Captains' careful planning that during the entire course of the voyage, the Expedition ran short of just three important items: whiskey, tobacco, and Indian trade goods.

The men headed up the Missouri armed with rifles, muskets, pistols, one small cannon, and a couple of blunderbusses. The rifles included fifteen prototypes of the Harper's Ferry Model 1803, a .54 caliber muzzle-loading flintlock that was to become the army's standard issue rifle. In addition to those rifles, Lewis and Clark, and probably some of the men, also carried their own civilian "Pennsylvania" or "Kentucky" long rifles. Some carried Model 1795 muskets, which were .69 caliber smoothbore flintlocks that could be loaded with either a leaden ball or a handful of birdshot. The cannon, or swivel gun, was mounted on the bow of the keelboat and could be aimed in any direction. It fired a one-pound ball or its equivalent in smaller projectiles (musket balls, nails, pebbles in a pinch). Gunpowder was stored in wooden kegs and in sealed lead containers which, once empty, could be melted down into bullets.

The men were also issued knives, tomahawks, shirts, blankets, tobacco, and mosquito netting. Oiled linen doubled as sails for the boats by day and shelters for the men at night. They cooked in kettles over an open fire most nights, but also brought along a small galley stove. Provisions included pork packed in brine, flour, biscuit, honey, ground corn, dried beans and peas, salt, sugar, coffee, whiskey, and lard.

The Captains knew they would need to build things along the way—winter quarters and canoes, for example. They would also need to repair or replace damaged equipment and worn-out clothing. So they packed axes, saws, augers, mallets, and other carpentry tools, as well as sewing kits and a portable blacksmithy (which proved crucial to survival during their winter among the Mandans).

They also paid close attention to the packing of twenty-one bales of trade goods that would be given to Indian leaders as presents and used to barter for food, horses, and guide services. The trade goods included colorful glass beads, uniform coats, hats, knives, mirrors, fish hooks, scissors, ribbon and cloth, blankets, paint, and many other manufactured items coveted by the tribes.

In addition to all that gear, the Captains brought along folding telescopes, compasses, sextants, chronometers, and various surveying instruments to help them navigate, to chart the courses of rivers, and to measure distances and elevations. Most important for us, they made sure they had plenty of paper and ink on hand to record what they saw, felt, and thought during every step of the journey.

EQUIPPED AND PROVISIONED

A HISTORICAL TREASURE

By far, the most important artifacts of the Expedition are the journals kept by Lewis, Clark, and several of the enlisted men. Here, one of Clark's journals, known to historians as the "elkskin-bound journal" opens to his entry for October 15, 1805, when the Corps was approaching the confluence of the Snake and Columbia Rivers. On the opposite page, Clark has drawn a diagram showing Indian groups of the Columbia River Basin.

WEATHER FRONTS

Following page: Thunderheads form over the Great Plains.

The Great Plains, where the sky stretched out bigger than life over a rolling prairie rippling in the wind, drew them onward. The plains surrounded them, astonished them, and pleased them.

Work on the river was easier, but only a little. In late summer, water levels were lower. Sandbars emerged. Floating debris became less of a concern. But still, the current was strong and a good day meant eighteen or nineteen miles of constant effort. The men were either in the water, up on the banks, crashing through the underbrush, or on the boats poling and rowing. Mosquitoes were terrible, the size of house flies. For protection, they smeared themselves with bear grease, then sweated like hogs in the hot sun. Sores and dysentery and all sorts of minor ailments troubled them. Violent storms swept down, black-bellied, roaring with thunder and packing wind gusts that filled the air with sand and threatened to capsize the pirogues.

If they had complained, it would be understandable. If they had come to view the river and its never-ending valley as an adversary, no one would fault them. But on the contrary, they loved what they were doing. Despite hard work, discomfort, and danger, they were having a great time. Clark, in a typically mixed description of a

ONTO THE PLAINS

day, wrote, *"Several men with verry bad Boils. Everything in prime order men in high Spirits. a fair Still evening Great no. Musquitors this evening."*

After all, they could have had boils and mosquitoes back in Ohio. They could have been working hard at any number of dreary tasks. Instead, they were a hand-picked crew of strong young men embarked on the great adventure of their time, traveling through a new country whose beauty and richness took their breath away—that is, when they got a chance to pause and look around. Most of the time, the enlisted men labored in the river trough, which was cut several hundred feet beneath the open prairie. Their view was of muddy water, timbered bottoms, and rumpled grassy hills. When not fighting the current, camp chores kept them busy. The hunters had a better deal; they got to climb up and roam in the big open. It seems that they rotated the hunting duties to some degree, and when they laid over, everyone had an opportunity to do a little exploring. Lewis and Clark also hunted, but their purpose was broader. They had the enviable task of going wherever their curiosity led.

Except for the French boatmen who had been there before, the men had never seen such space. They were woodsmen, most of them recruited from the Ohio River Valley where pioneer farmers were hard at work hacking out clearings beneath hardwood giants. If you lived there, you rarely had a long view. Even the highest hills were covered with trees, and if you managed to find an opening on the edge of a cliff or some other vantage point, you gazed out over an eternity of treetops.

How different it was on the prairies. Like the frontiersmen said, when you get out there, you can see the wind coming out of next week, and four guys working together, if they squint, might see all the way into next month.

Two centuries later, we can share some of those feelings. Despite the dams that have turned most of the Missouri into flood-control reservoirs, isolated stretches of the river remain essentially as they were. In those places, the Missouri still hurries through bottomlands thick with cottonwoods. You can walk on patches of native prairie along the valley rim just as the Captains did. You can get a sense of how the country looked, and smelled, and to some degree how it felt. But there is no way to recreate the feeling of being completely in the open, with no roads or fences or rails slicing up that glorious continuity. When Lewis climbed to a high point and narrowed his eyes at the distant horizon, the country was a seamless whole. He must have thought about other exploration possibilities. It was his job to think about them. With a good horse and a different mission, he could have ridden a thousand miles in any direction without having to get down to open a single gate. We can scarcely imagine the sense of freedom and potential a landscape like that could engender.

Yet they felt no need to roam far. The river was a dazzling line to follow, leading them deep into the

A VAST LANDSCAPE

Far Right: The Great Plains in late summer: golden, dry, windswept, and lonesome. Lewis and Clark emerged onto the Great Plains, one of the world's largest grasslands, during July 1804. They would remain on the plains for another 13 months, including their winter sojourn among the Mandans in present-day North Dakota.

Right: Deerskin-hide painting of Plains Indians, c. 1900.

"This being my birth day I order'd a Saddle of fat Vennison, an Elk fleece & a Bevertail to be cooked and a Desert of Cheries, Plumbs, Raspberries Currents and grapes of a Supr. quallity. . . . Musquetors verry troublesom, the Praries Contain Cheres, Apple, Grapes, Currents, Rasp burry, Gooseberris Hastlenuts and a great Variety of Plants & flours . . . What a field for a Botents [botanist] and a natirless [naturalist]" —CLARK, AUG 1, 1804

country they most wanted to see. It seems that every time Lewis or Clark went out, they came across something new and wonderful. Often, it was an animal previously unknown to science. On July 30, a badger: *"his Shape & Size is like that of a Beaver, his head mouth &c. is like a Dogs with Short Ears, his Tail and Hair like that of a Ground Hog, and longer . . . his legs are short and when he moves Just sufficent to raise his body above the Ground He is of the Bear Species. We have his skin stuffed."*

They noted anything that caught their interest, including a bull snake, which didn't bellow as they had been told, but *"it hisses remarkably loud."* There were porcupines, beaver, wild turkeys, egrets, red foxes, an astonishing abundance of elk, and a new species of deer, the black-tailed or mule deer. At first they thought the small wolfish predators that yipped and howled and cunningly avoided capture were some new kind of fox; but on closer inspection, they began calling them prairie wolves. We know them today as the wily and musical coyote.

Plants new to science included Indian tobacco, aromatic aster, buffalo berry, hoary sagebrush, and purple coneflower. Lewis and Clark did not leave us a comprehensive bird list but described many, including several new species: sharptailed grouse, poorwill, and *"a remarkable bird of the Spicies of Corvus, long tail of a Greenish Purple, Varigated a Beck like a Crow white round its neck comeing to a point on its back, its belley white feet like a Hawk abt. the size of a large Pigeon"* It was a magpie. In the spring they sent a live one, along with a live prairie dog, all the way back to Jefferson.

Health was an ongoing concern that didn't stop with bug bites, heat exhaustion, pustules, and venereal disease. Lewis nearly ended his trip when he did some mineral prospecting that involved tasting the dirt and breathing

NEW CREATURES
The Missouri River (left) bends among the rumpled prairie hills that overlook the river and its bottomlands throughout much of the Great Plains. As the Expedition emerged onto the vast grasslands, new animals kept turning up: mule deer, prairie dogs, coyotes (below), pronghorn (antelope), and white-tailed jackrabbits. The badger (above left) was new to Lewis, but not to science. It had been described as early as 1778, from Canadian specimens.

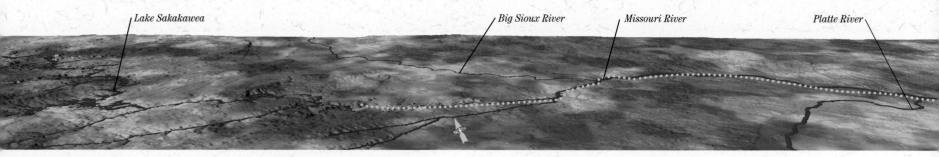

its vapors. The sample included toxic compounds, perhaps arsenic; in frontier slang, he like to died. Sgt. Charles Floyd, unfortunately, did. He died of a sudden illness that might have been a ruptured appendix. It proved to be the Expedition's only fatality, a remarkable fact considering the many near misses they survived.

One who came close was George Shannon. The youngest member of the Corps, and not the most skilled outdoorsman, he failed to return from a hunting trip. Worried that he'd had an accident, search parties went out but found no sign of him. At length his tracks turned up on the riverbank, pointing upstream ahead of them. Evidently, he thought the boats had passed him by and he was hurrying to catch up. John Colter went ahead to bring him in but couldn't catch him. Poor guy. Shannon must have been worried and dismayed and in a terrible lather. Although he had his rifle, he wasted his few bullets and was forced to live off berries for the most part. He killed a rabbit with a stick loaded into the rifle in place of a bullet but that was the limit of his imaginative foraging. After chasing the party for sixteen days, he gave up, and waited by the riverbank in hopes that a trading boat would pass. Imagine his surprise to see not traders but his smiling, waving friends heave into view.

South of what is present-day Sioux City, Lewis was mystified by a huge raft of white sailing down the river toward them. It turned out to be millions of feathers riding on the flood. Shortly, they arrived at its source—an island covered with white pelicans. Evidently the river had risen enough to lift moulted feathers from the island in a single mass. Lewis shot one of the birds. With typical curiosity he filled the beak with water and wrote that it held five gallons. Never mind the questionable significance of a twelve-pound bird's ability to hold forty pounds of water; it was just another noteworthy

PRONGHORN ANTELOPE
Pronghorn, the fleetest of plains mammals, astonished Lewis and Clark. So fast were the herds of pronghorn that Lewis even had trouble distinguishing the animals' basic colors as they streaked across the prairie.

""we Stoped to Dine under Some high Trees near the high land on the L. S. in a fiew minits Cought three verry large Catfish (3) one nearly white, Those fish are in great plenty on the Sides of the river and verry fat, a quart of Oile Came out of the Surpolous fat of one of those fish"—CLARK, JULY 29, 1804

natural history fact in a land filled with them, recorded by a man of boundless curiosity.

On August 23, they ate their first buffalo. Joseph Field shot it and came running excitedly to tell them. Twelve men hustled off to bring in the meat. They roasted the choice parts that evening. Knowing that buffalo would soon be a major part of their diet, they must have been pleased to find it as good as the French boatmen had told them it would be.

On September 7, Clark and Lewis together walked into *"a Village of an annamale the french call the Prarie Dog."* These were the first they'd seen. The rodents sat up like picket pins, whistled in alarm, and dove for cover. The Captains called for help in catching one, and we can imagine the high spirits that followed, men digging into the burrows, running to block escape tunnels, hauling barrels of water. They dug six feet deep without reaching the nest. Probing with a pole, they realized they weren't half way. They poured in barrel after barrel of water, and finally *"Killed one & Cought one a live."*

GROUSE

As the Expedition moved farther out onto the plains, Clark reported *"Grouse, Larks & the Prarie bird is Common."* They were also fascinated by a small, burrowing animal that lived in large communities on the grasslands—*"an annamale,"* Clark wrote, *"the french Call the Prarie Dog."*

Lewis tells us about a delightful day he spent rambling above the river. Packing a lunch, he left before dawn with two hunters. In the lowlands they sampled their way through a wild plum orchard. On a higher bench they walked into a huge prairie dog town, where Lewis marveled at the way the little creatures had mowed the grass to the perfection of a bowling green. He noted the large numbers of coyotes, hawks, and skunks in the area—*"wolves of the small kind, halks and some pole-cats"*—and reckoned they were feeding on the rodents. Beyond the dog town, they climbed the river breaks to the open plains where Lewis described a tremendous view of the river and a line of grassy hills to the west: *"this scenery already rich pleasing and beatiful, was still farther hightened by immence herds of Buffaloe, deer Elk and Antelopes which we saw in every direction feeding on the hills and plains."* He estimated that he could see three thousand buffalo in one view. But what he really wanted was a pronghorn. Clark had shot a male three days before, and Lewis wanted to collect a female.

Not so easy. When he had first seen pronghorn (he called them goats, a name that, along with antelope, is still commonly used in the west), he commented that they moved so fast he couldn't determine their color. Now, he tried to stalk a group of them. He might as well have tried to sneak up on falcons. The animals, ever alert, kept their distance with almost casual indifference. When they stopped, it was on a knob from which they could see in all directions but one, and from that direction came the wind. There was no way to approach unseen or unsmelled, but Lewis tried. He was still two hundred paces out when they caught his scent, and vanished. He hurried to the knob, but by the time he got there, his quarry was flying over the hills three miles away. *"it appeared reather the rappid flight of birds than the motion of quadrupeds. I think I can safely venture the asscertion that the speed of this anamal is equal if not superior to that of the finest blooded courser."*

In fact, far superior. Lewis would have enjoyed knowing that the pronghorn is the fastest land animal on the continent, capable of sprinting more than sixty miles per hour. It would certainly not have surprised him to know that the eyes of pronghorn are equal to those of eagles; or that pronghorn were at that time as numerous as buffalo. Reading his journal, we can only regret that he didn't know the frontiersman's trick of hiding in a depression while wiggling a white flag on a stick. Pronghorn are incautiously curious, and will approach closely to investigate strange things. Pulling that trick would have delighted Lewis. No doubt he'd have written a detailed and lively account.

"The Wind blew hard West and raised the Sands off the bar in Such Clouds that we Could Scercely See this Sand being fine and verry light Stuck to every thing it touched, and in the Plain for a half a mile every Spire of Grass was covered with the Sand or Dust"

—CLARK, NEAR VERMILLION, SOUTH DAKOTA, AUGUST 23, 1804

A month later he would see Arikara Indians killing pronghorn during the October migration, when great herds crossed the Missouri on their way to wintering grounds in the Black Hills. While in the river, they were easy prey. Men shot them from the banks while boys swam among them with clubs. Clark would count fifty-eight carcasses from that one incident.

In addition to animals, they found all sorts of curiosities, from the supernatural to the prehistoric. Near present-day Vermillion, South Dakota, Indians warned them away from a *"mountain of evel Spirits,"* a malevolent place guarded by fierce eighteen-inch-high demon warriors with big heads and deadly aim. Of course the Captains had to investigate. They found the hill standing singular and isolated in the middle of the plains, and climbed it. Instead of demons, they saw flocks of brown martens on its lee side, gorging on the clouds of insects that sheltered there from the wind.

Fifty miles farther, they came to a place where the bluffs rose so regular and straight that Clark decided he was seeing ancient fortifications gone to partial ruin. He surveyed and sketched them and wrote a detailed military analysis of their defensive characteristics. In fact, they were natural sand ridges. Later, they searched in vain for an active volcano—probably a burning coal vein—described by a trader in St. Charles. And on a ridge in Gregory County, South Dakota, they puzzled over *"a back bone with the most of the entire laying Connected for 45 feet those bones are petrified, Some teeth & ribs also Connected."* Judging from its shape, they decided it was a giant fish, and they weren't far wrong. The bones were from a pleisosaur, an aquatic dinosaur.

Northward. Westward. The river valley led them slowly into the Dakotas. On September 18, they made seven miles. The next day, twenty-six and a quarter. On the 20th, thirty miles. As the country became drier, wildlife became even more abundant. Some weeks before, Clark was impressed to see herds of a few hundred buffalo. Now the explorers were seeing them by the thousands.

Sometimes their observations are a puzzle to us. Among new species noted by Lewis was the white-tailed jackrabbit. He chased one, measured its leaps at twenty-one feet, and wrote a long descriptive entry about its appearance and habits. This is fine and interesting enough, but it seems odd that Lewis would go on at such length about a common long-eared

rodent while neither man had much to say about wolves. *"A great number of wolves about this evening,"* Clark wrote in a typical entry, following that remark with no elaboration. He might as well have been reporting on biting insects: *"Great no. Musquitors this evening."* Sure, there's not much reason to go on about mosquitoes, but wolves in great numbers? Our eyes widen at the thought. Of course, wolves lived all over the country back then, and Clark probably viewed them with the common frontier attitude that wolves were varmints and pests.

Another predator would soon impress them a whole lot more—a creature with a towering reputation known to plains people as the white bear, or the grizzly. They had heard about the great bear. They knew that the Indians feared and respected it. They listened to stories of its legendary ferocity, but they had no real concept of its true and frightening power. Armed with the best rifles of their time, they weren't concerned for their safety and were rather eager to meet one. It appears that during the fall of 1804, the only member of the Expedition who actually saw a grizzly was Cruzatte, and his encounter only whetted their curiosity. Out hunting alone on October 20, Cruzatte came upon a grizzly, wounded it, and was so *"alarmed by the formidable appearance of the bear he left his*

ENCOUNTERS

The Corps killed their first bison (left) in August 1804 near present-day Sioux City. Clark shot their first coyote (above) on September 18, 1804 near present-day Chamberlain, South Dakota. The Expedition first crossed paths with a grizzly bear (below) in late October 1804, when Cruzatte wounded one near present-day Bismarck, North Dakota, and then fled as the great bear charged.

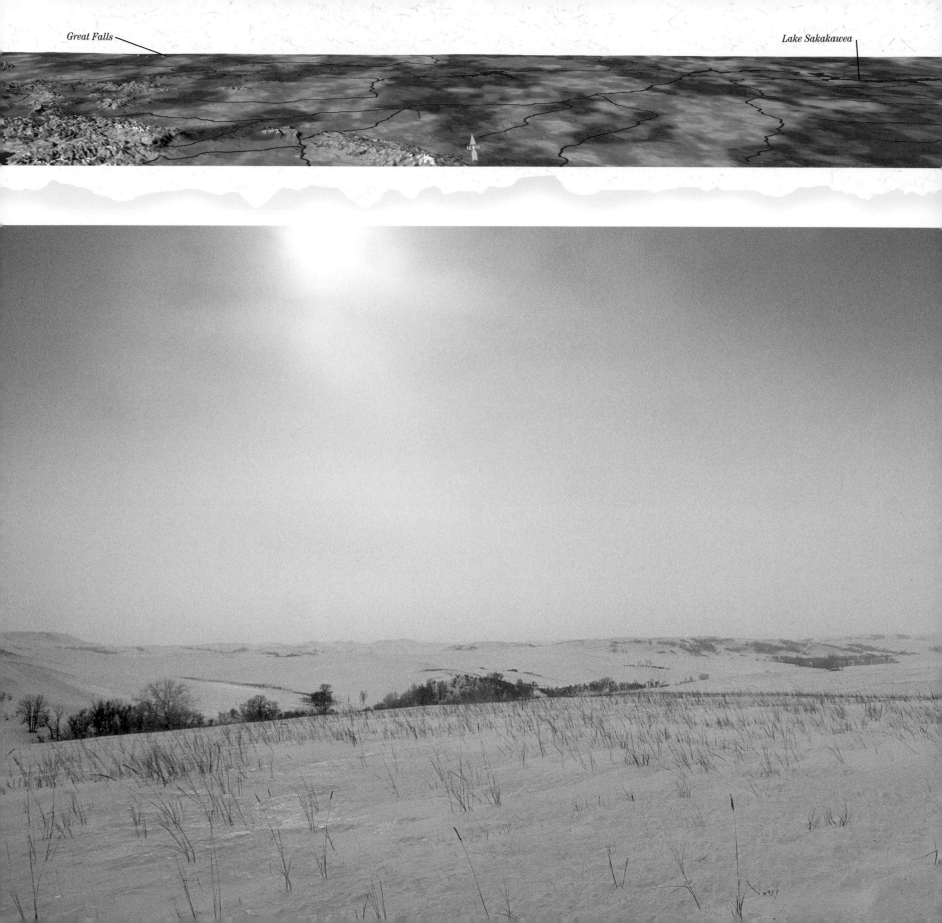

Great Falls

Lake Sakakawea

NORTH

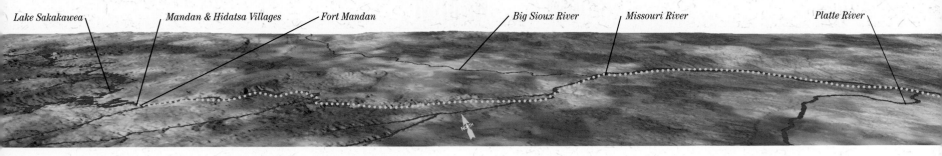

tomahawk and gun," Lewis wrote. If his description seems understated, remember that he hadn't yet experienced for himself the awesome rage of a wounded grizzly. But we can imagine how it appeared to poor Cruzatte, blind in one eye and nearsighted in the other, suddenly confronted by that blurred, bellowing apparition.

Later, Clark went to look at the tracks, and reported them to be *"double the Sise of the largest track I ever Saw."* From that observation, offered in hushed respectful tones, the bear's reputation would only grow. The Expedition would spend much of the next year in grizzly country. Charged at close range, stalked on the open plains, chased over high banks into the river, they would all get their chance to run from the bear that feared nothing.

Now, as October waned, they were pushing against both the river and the tides of autumn. Cold winds and leaden skies warned of the approaching winter. Migrating waterfowl streamed past, headed the other way. Long honking vees of Canada geese, snow geese, and brant flew overhead, even at night. Flurries of ducks settled and rose like leaves in the wind. They saw terns, swans, gulls, and *"an emence number of Plover of Different kind Collecting and takeing their flight Southerly."* Like the birds overhead, buffalo and pronghorn were also on the move, raising dust on the plains, darkening the banks, and swimming across the river—always with wolves and coyotes at their heels.

These were all good signs. If the land continued to offer such abundance, they would have little trouble supplying themselves with food during the winter. As for shelter and other comforts, the Mandan villages lay ahead. If the Mandans proved amenable to having them as neighbors, it would be a good place to dig in and wait for spring.

MEADOWLARK

Below: John J. Audubon's portrait of a Western Meadowlark.

Left: If the Corps did not reach the Mandan villages before winter, they would have to face the icy, inhospitable plains on their own.

"They are a handsome stout well-made set of Indians & have good open Countenances, and are of a light brown colour, and have long black hair, which they do wear without cutting; and they all use paint in order to compleat their dress."—PVT. WHITEHOUSE, AUGUST 2, 1804, DESCRIBING THE OTOS AND MISSOURIS

Had their journey been no more than the exploration of a new and richly endowed landscape, Lewis and Clark would have had a big adventure. But this was more. They weren't here just to see the country. They were here to begin the process by which the United States would establish proprietorship over the new territory that had just doubled the nation's size. That meant treating with the people who already lived there—native people who naturally felt that this was their land, as it had been for some time, thank you. They had their own trading systems and political alliances, and the simple statement that they were now the subjects of a new distant white chief did not by itself change a thing. Yet that was basically what Lewis and Clark were trying to do—to bring the Indian tribes into a mutually beneficial partnership and lay the foundation of a trading empire.

For this extremely complicated diplomatic mission, they were not well equipped. Although Lewis had put thoughtful effort into choosing gifts and merchandise samples for distribution among the tribes, the Captains had only a rudimentary understanding of the people they would meet and the dynamics of prairie politics. This was no fault of theirs. They had tried to learn. They had diligently asked questions of everyone who might have something to offer, but nonetheless they suffered from a lack of background information—what the State Department would now call briefing materials. In addition to that handicap,

AMONG THE PRAIRIE TRIBES

their mission held an inherent contradiction. Getting to the West Coast and back meant they had to keep moving, but effective diplomacy required the kind of understanding that would come only by spending a lot of time with the people concerned. By necessity, they were less diplomats than tourists moving quickly through a series of foreign countries whose customs and relationships they understood only to a superficial degree.

For most of the summer, they had few contacts with Indians. Everyone was out on the plains hunting buffalo, and the river corridor was, for the most part, deserted. Not until August 3 did they organize their first council with some members of the Oto and Missouri tribes. At the meeting, Lewis delivered a long speech on behalf of the Great Chief in the East. He spoke about the benefits of trade, encouraged them to make peace with their neighbors, and presented them with some token gifts—medals, certificates, tobacco. The men marched and fired their rifles. The Captains brought out some technological wonders including a magnifying glass and an air rifle. The chiefs were polite and made positive comments of their own concerning friendship and trade.

INDIAN ENCOUNTERS

The Expedition encountered various nomadic and village-based Indians throughout the summer and fall of 1804: the Otos and Missouris, the Yankton Sioux, Teton Sioux, Arikara, Mandan, and the Hidatsa. Opposite page: The decorated buffalo-hide shield (top left) reflects the reverence felt among plains people for the central staple of their physical and spiritual life. A somewhat fanciful 1829 rendition (middle) pictures a Sioux warrior charging across the plains. The horse and travois (bottom right) were the two essential elements of prairie transport.

The Captains scored that meeting a success. But a second encounter on August 18 was less friendly. These Oto chiefs, among whom was influential Little Thief, weren't impressed by the speech, or the face paint and beads they were given, and even less by the certificates that declared them to be allies and friends of the United States. What they really wanted were the practical things that would make their lives easier, such as metal tools and cloth; they also wanted rifles and ammunition that would improve their military standing among neighboring tribes. Told by Lewis and Clark that such items would be coming later, they asked for whiskey to tide them over, but did not get that either. Although Little Thief said he was willing to travel to Washington, D.C., to meet his new white father, the council ended with sour feelings on both sides.

Next it was the Sioux. Lewis and Clark had been warned about them, and anticipated trouble. The first of the nomadic plains tribes the expedition would encounter, they had a reputation for what the white traders considered river piracy.

HIDATSA

In 1833–34, Karl Bodmer painted this portrait of Pehriska-Ruhpa, a Hidatsa warrior and leader of the Dog Band. He wears leather leggings, a red woven cape, and an elaborate headdress of magpie and turkey feathers.

By exacting tribute from traders, and sometimes refusing to allow boats to go any farther, the Sioux maintained a choke hold on the flow of goods beyond their territory. They could get away with it. They were strong and capable fighters.

Yet they had their own rivalries, which helped the Captains in their first Sioux encounter.

In late August, they met members of the Yankton branch of Sioux, who desired protection from their neighbors, the Teton Sioux, and were eager to talk. The riverside council was held with all the pomp and ceremony that both sides could muster. Undoubtedly, it was something to see: everyone in fancy dress appropriate to their culture, acting solemn and proper for the most part, but erupting in enthusiastic celebration for a firelight dance.

For the Captains, it was a roaring success. All the right words had been spoken. The Yankton seemed to accept that although the Expedition had few presents to give, they were establishing ties for the future. They even agreed to send a delegation to Washington. To reinforce the atmosphere of cooperation, the Captains made what was probably a big mistake. They assigned Pierre Dorian to remain with the Yanktons, to work for peace, and to recruit other chiefs for the trip east. Because he spoke Sioux, Dorian was the best man for the job, but it left them without the interpreter they would need a month later when they met the Teton Sioux near modern-day Pierre, South Dakota.

That one was a different and disquieting experience. The meeting spanned four days, and although there were some good moments, there were also some very bad ones. With no common language, neither side understood the other. Each made assumptions based on ignorance. On the first day, the speechmaking and talk degenerated into a tense standoff with rifles cocked, bows strung, swivel guns loaded, a group of warriors gripping the bow rope of a pirogue, and Clark standing before them on the bank with his sword drawn and his blood running hot. That potentially explosive situation—it could have been the end of the Expedition—was defused but not resolved. With the complicated manners common to diplomacy, the parties tried other approaches. The boats moved a few miles

INDIAN LIFE

Lewis and Clark urged various Indian leaders to travel to Washington, D.C., to visit President Jefferson. An Osage chief, Le Soldat du Chene (top), made the trip in 1805. The engraving of an Omaha woman (left) was used to illustrate an early account of the Expedition's journey. The Captains were so impressed with the Plains Indian tipi that they acquired one during the winter of 1804–05 for their own use the following year. Hunters in wolfskin disguise (right) approach a herd of bison in this 1845 painting by the frontier artist George Catlin.

"The Souix is a Stout bold looking people, (the young men hand Som) & well made, the greater part of them make use of Bows & arrows Some fiew fusees I observe among them not with Standing they live by the Bow & arrow . . . the Warriers are Verry much deckerated with Paint porcupin quils & feathers large leagins & mockersons, all with buffalow roabs of Different Colours. the Squars wore Peticoats & and a white Buffalow roabes with the black hair turned back over their necks & Sholders." —CLARK, AUGUST 30, DESCRIBING THE YANKTON SIOUX

AMONG THE TRIBES

On August 29,1804, Sgt. Pryor returned from a visit to a Yankton Sioux village. Clark gives us his description: *"The Sceouex Camps are handson of a Conic form Covered with Buffalow Roabs Painted different Colours and all Compact & hand Somly arranged, covered all round an orpen part in the Center for the fire, with Buffalow roabs each Lodg has a place for Cooking detached, the lodges contain 10 to 15 persons—a fat dog was presented as a mark of their Great respect for the party of which they partook hartily and thought it good & well flavored."*

upstream and camped beside a large village where, instead of being challenged, the Captains were carried like heroes from lodge to lodge on ceremonial buffalo robes borne by squads of young men. There was more speechmaking that evening, accompanied by smoking, eating, and in general taking the measure of each other. The Sioux women danced to the beat of tambourines. They were followed by the men who sang out their war deeds, and so it went

until late at night, in apparent friendliness.

Yet things remained tense. Several incidents very nearly erupted into violence. The Tetons vastly outnumbered the whites, and it was clear that at least some tried to stop the Expedition and take whatever they could seize. Equally clear is that they could have done it. That the Captains got past without a shot being fired demonstrates that they handled themselves well. They were also very lucky.

Back in January, Thomas Jefferson had written these words to Lewis: *"On that nation [the Teton Sioux] we wish most particularly to make a friendly impression, because of their immense power, and because we learn they are very desirous of being on the most friendly terms with us."* A year later during the Dakota winter, William Clark, still smarting from the experience, wrote in his journal: *"These are the vilest miscreants of the savage race Unless these people are reduced to order, by coercive measures, I am ready to pronounce that the citizens of the United States can never enjoy but partially the advantages which the Missouri presents."* Wishful thinking had run smack into harsh reality; it was a pattern that would be repeated many tragic times over the next century in the American West.

Upstream from the Sioux camps, the expedition met the

PEACE PIPE

Right: As Lewis and Clark made their way up the Missouri during the summer and fall of 1804, they met in formal council with several Indian tribes. John Clymer's 1979 painting, *Peace Pipe*, portrays the all-important offering of the pipe.

"as Soon as I landed 3 of their young ment Seased the Cable of the Perogue, one Soldiar Huged the mast . . . the 2d Chief was exceedingly insolent both in words and justures to me declareing I Should no go off, Saying he had not recived presents Suffient from us — I attempted to passify him but it had a contrary effect for his insults became So personal and his intentions evident to do me injurey, I Drew my Sword and ordered all hands under arms at this motion Capt. Louis ordered all in the boat under arms, the fiew men that was with me haveing previously taken up their guns with a full deturmination to defend me if possible." —CLARK, SEPTEMBER 25, 1805, AMONG THE TETON SIOUX

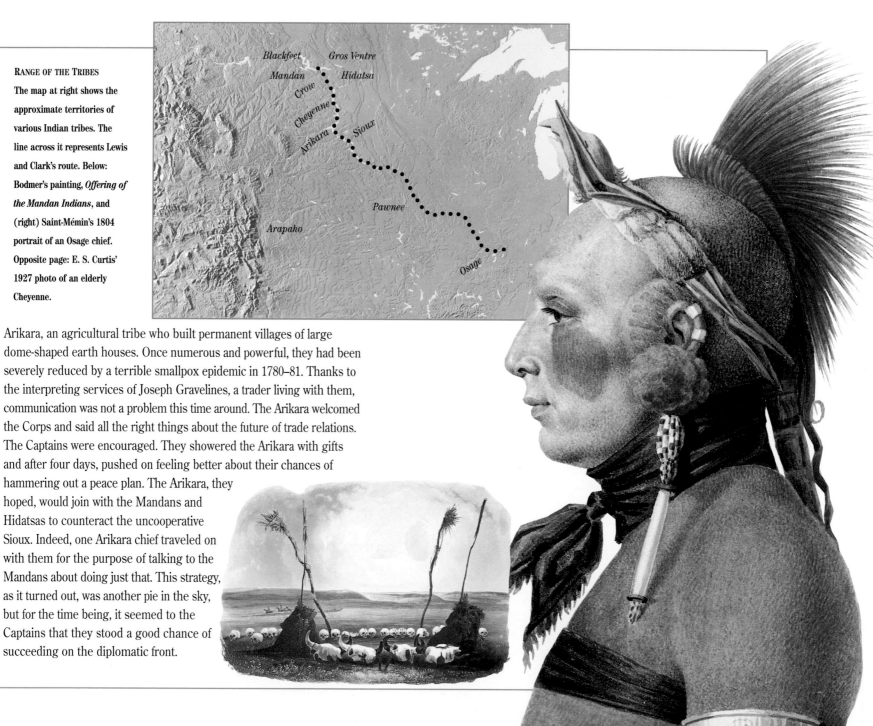

"a curious Cuistom with the Souix as well as the reckeres is to give handsom Squars to those whome they wish to Show Some acknowlegements to—The Seauix we got Clare of without taking their Squars, they followed us with Squars 13th two days. The Rickores we put off dureing the time we were at the Towns but 2 Handsom young Squars were Sent by a man to follow us, they Came up this evening and peresisted in their Civilities."—CLARK, OCTOBER 12, 1804, AMONG THE ARIKARA

RANGE OF THE TRIBES
The map at right shows the approximate territories of various Indian tribes. The line across it represents Lewis and Clark's route. Below: Bodmer's painting, *Offering of the Mandan Indians*, and (right) Saint-Mémin's 1804 portrait of an Osage chief. Opposite page: E. S. Curtis' 1927 photo of an elderly Cheyenne.

Blackfeet
Gros Ventre
Mandan
Hidatsa
Crow
Cheyenne
Arikara
Sioux
Pawnee
Arapaho
Osage

Arikara, an agricultural tribe who built permanent villages of large dome-shaped earth houses. Once numerous and powerful, they had been severely reduced by a terrible smallpox epidemic in 1780–81. Thanks to the interpreting services of Joseph Gravelines, a trader living with them, communication was not a problem this time around. The Arikara welcomed the Corps and said all the right things about the future of trade relations. The Captains were encouraged. They showered the Arikara with gifts and after four days, pushed on feeling better about their chances of hammering out a peace plan. The Arikara, they hoped, would join with the Mandans and Hidatsas to counteract the uncooperative Sioux. Indeed, one Arikara chief traveled on with them for the purpose of talking to the Mandans about doing just that. This strategy, as it turned out, was another pie in the sky, but for the time being, it seemed to the Captains that they stood a good chance of succeeding on the diplomatic front.

"The river being very low and the season so far advanced that it frequently shuts up with ice in this climate we determined to spend the Winter in this neighborhood." Lewis, October 31, 1804

The neighborhood Lewis referred to was north of present-day Bismarck, North Dakota, at the mouth of the Knife River. Within a few miles of each other stood five earth-lodge villages—two Mandan and three Hidatsa—with a population of around 4,000 people. Both tribes hunted buffalo from horseback but also raised crops and lived in permanent settlements. This concentration of people had turned the Knife River villages into a trading center visited by tribes from across the northern plains and white traders from St. Louis and Canada. It was a good choice for winter quarters and the best place in the region for gathering information.

MANDAN CHIEF
Bodmer's engraving of the
Mandan chief Mato-Tope.

The Hidatsas were initially wary of the Expedition, but the Mandans opened their arms in welcome. Aided by a French Canadian trader named René Jessaume who had lived with the Mandans for some fifteen years, the Captains spent a few days talking, smoking, and making speeches, and then went looking for suitable winter quarters. The first priority was a good supply of trees for firewood and shelter. This they found on the east side of the river across from one

A MANDAN WINTER

Mandan village and about six miles downstream from the other. Fort Mandan, as they called their winter home, was a triangular stockade eighteen feet high, enclosing huts for sleeping, cooking, and storage.

November passed, the nights grew long and the cold deepened: minus thirty degrees, minus forty, even lower. This was cold beyond the experience of men from milder climates—the insistent, penetrating cold of the interior plains. Subzero air flowed down from the Arctic and settled in for days at a time, defying the feeble sun, creating a dense ice fog that covered trees, bushes, animals, and men with layers of rime. The men packed their clothes with fur, but still suffered from mild frostbite. Too late, they thought to pull their keelboat onto shore, and found it firmly gripped by ice; it took three weeks of intense labor to work it free.

The cold gave them big appetites requiring tons of meat. How they would have managed without their Indian friends is hard to imagine. Early in December, just as the first cold wave struck, the Mandans alerted them to buffalo in the area, loaned them horses, and took them out on a hunt. They made numerous joint hunting trips, roaming far, and sometimes staying out for several days.

Both Lewis and Clark had important indoor work to do. They spent long hours interviewing

"we Camped on the L. Side a short distanc below the 1st mandan village on the L. S. many men women & Children flocked down to See us — Capt Lewis walked to the Village with the Chief and interpeters, my Rheumitism increasing prevented me from going also, and we had Deturmined that both would not leave the boat at the Same time untill we Knew the Desposition of the Nativs,"

—CLARK, OCTOBER 26, 1804, AMONG THE MANDANS

"this village is Situated on an eminance of about 50 feet above the Water in a handson Plain it Containes houses in a kind of Picket work. the houses are round and Verry large Containing Several families as also their horses which is tied on one Side of the enterance"

—CLARK, OCTOBER 27, AMONG THE MANDANS

"*the ice came dow in great quantites the river rose 13 inches the last 24 hours I observed extrodanary dexterity of the Indians in jumping from one Cake of ice to another, for the purpose of Catching the buffalow as they float down . . . The Plains are on fire in view of the fort on both Sides of the River, it is Said to be common for the Indians to burn the Plains near their villages every Spring for the benifit of ther horse, and to induce the Buffalow to come near to them.*" —CLARK, MARCH 30, 1805

"the huts were in two rows, containing four rooms each, and joined at one end forming an angle. When rasied about 7 feet high a floor of puncheons or split plank were laid, and covered with grass and clay; which made a warm loft. The upper part projected a foot over and the roofs were made shed-fashion, rising from the inner side, and making the outter wall about 18 feet high. The part not inclosed by the huts we intended to picket. In the angle formed by the two rows of huts we built two rooms, for holding our provisions and stores." —SGT. GASS, NOVEMBER 3, 1804

RITUALS

Neither the Mandans nor the Hidatsas organized major ceremonies during the cold winter months, so Lewis and Clark missed the spectacular Okipa ritual, a creation drama staged every summer. The Curtis photo (left) shows a dancer with body paint and headdress of buffalo fur and willow branches. Catlin's painting (below) depicts a summer dance. The Corps did witness, and at least several of the men participated in, a buffalo-calling ritual, which involved the transmission of spiritual force through sexual intercourse.

Young men offered their wives to old, accomplished hunters and warriors in the hope of acquiring a share of their elders' power. Certain strangers, such as the men of the Corps of Discovery, were also viewed as sources of great power and were therefore in demand. Clark said, *"we Sent a man to this Medisan Dance last night, they gave him 4 Girls all this is to cause the buffalow to Come near So that They may kill thim"*

SYMBOLS OF COURAGE

Crow's Heart (below, right) wears a necklace of grizzly bear claws, symbols of strength, courage, and accomplishment.

anyone they could find about the country to the west. The Mandans were not great travelers, but the Hidatsas ranged as far as the Rockies and cheerfully described the rivers, mountain ranges, wildlife, and people who lived there. White traders who came down from Canada were also happy to talk. Then, as now, geography was a natural topic among residents of the mountains and plains, and many were keen observers. Gradually, the Captains developed a fairly detailed picture of the landscape and its people that proved essential to the Expedition's success.

One meeting was fateful. Toussaint Charbonneau, a trader living with the Hidatsas, came looking for work as an interpreter. With him was his wife—a young Shoshone woman, fifteen years old and six months pregnant, kidnapped four years earlier by Hidatsas on a raiding trip to the Missouri headwaters. Her name was Sacagawea. Recognizing how important she could be when they reached the mountains, the Captains readily added them both to the roster.

As winter wore on, it became clear that the Expedition needed more food than they could get by hunting. Again, the Mandans stood ready, this time with corn for sale. To pay for it, the Expedition blacksmiths set up a forge and pounded out iron tools and battle-axes. In addition, both Captains engaged in doctoring tribe members' various ailments. On one memorable evening, Lewis delivered Sacagawea's baby, Jean Baptiste, later nicknamed Pompy. The Expedition had its own health concerns, including syphilis,

MANDAN RAIN DANCE
Earth lodges were clustered in large, walled villages and the roofs could be used as both stage and grandstand for ceremonial gatherings, as depicted in Catlin's painting, *Rain-making Mandan.*

MANDAN EARTH LODGES
Though the Corps of Discovery built its own fort across the Missouri from a large Mandan village, the men spent considerable time inside large dome-shaped earth lodges such as those pictured on these pages. Bodmer depicts one spacious interior, with a fire in the center, a smoke hole in the roof, room for an extended family and a couple of prized horses. The family slept on raised platforms along the perimeter of the lodge.

the most pervasive consequence of that extremely sociable winter.

For despite the hard work of surviving and the military routine of the fort, there was plenty of time for visiting. Earth lodges were warm shelters heated by central fires vented through openings in the domed roofs. There were soft robes to lie on, good food, and good company. When filled with men and women feasting and talking and dancing around a fire stirred up to provide light—drums and tambourines setting the beat while Cruzatte fiddled—the earth lodges became lively social centers.

All winter, the Captains worked on their report to Jefferson. They had much to relate on the topics of geography, biology, ethnography, commerce, prairie politics, and the many other matters that commanded their attention. A good portion of their writing was an assessment of trading and settlement potential. In a summary of seventy-two western tribes, they went so far as to estimate the dollar value of trade with each group, along with the items that would comprise that trade. In the end, the report they sent downriver with the keelboat ran 45,000 words in length and was accompanied by four wooden boxes and a large trunk loaded with specimens and artifacts. The shipment also included three cages containing live animals: a prairie dog, four magpies, and a grouse. Only the prairie dog and one magpie survived the journey to Washington, but the optimism came through loud and clear. It must have pleased Jefferson to read, among Lewis' closing words: *"I can foresee no material or probable obstruction to our progress, and entertain therefore the most sanguine hopes of complete success."*

PIPE

Smoking the pipe was a common goodwill gesture among the tribes Lewis and Clark encountered. They acquired this Mandan ceremonial pipe c. 1804–06.

PRARIE FASHION

Beautifully decorated leather clothing and finery for horses were prized possessions on the Northern Plains. These fringed leggings (c. 1835), with their bold blue and white vertical pattern, were made from tanned hides decorated with trade beads. Also made from leather, the saddle blanket (c. 1835) is embellished with trade cloth, pony beads, and tiny metal cones.

SEEKING SPIRITS

In E. S. Curtis' 1908 photograph, *Offering the Buffalo Skull,* a Mandan man lifts a bison skull toward the sky. This illustrates part of a ritual in which a warrior, after fasting, would carry a bison skull and medicine bundle to a high point before dawn. Standing on the skull, facing sunrise, he would look for indications of the outcomes of prospective war expeditions.

HIDE PAINTING

This hide painting demonstrates that Lewis and Clark were not the only ones documenting events on the Great Plains. In the spring of 1805, they sent Jefferson a bundle of their own written materials along with this Native account of a battle pitting the Sioux and Arikaras against the Mandans and Hidatsas. Jefferson hung the painting in his Monticello home.

Following page: Bodmer's 1834–35 painting of the Missouri River in midwinter shows Mandans crossing the ice with Fort Clark and an adjacent Mandan village on the point in the background.

"We saw immence herds of buffaloe Elk deer & Antelopes. Capt Clark killed a buffaloe and 4 deer in the course of his walk today; and the party with me killed 3 deer, 2 beaver and 4 buffaloe calves. the latter we found very delicious. I think it equal to any veal I ever tasted."—Lewis, April 21, 1805

Lewis and Clark rarely had a good thing to say about Toussaint Charbonneau, the French trapper who signed on to the Expedition with his wife, Sacagawea, during the winter of 1804–05. They describe him as a temperamental, overbearing wife-beater whose outrageous demands for special treatment nearly cost him his place on the voyage and whose incompetence as a boatman nearly lost the Expedition one of its pirogues. Still, Charbonneau endeared himself to the entire party as a cook, especially when he turned his hand to making six-foot buffalo sausages called *boudin blanc,* or "white pudding."

Here, Lewis describes the process in a journal passage written May 9, 1805, while the Expedition camped near present-day Fort Peck, Montana. It reveals not only Charbonneau's rustic culinary flare but also captures some of the jovial, good-hearted atmosphere that must have pervaded the Expedition's camps when the going was relatively easy. Best of all, it shows Lewis in top form as an ebullient fireside companion, brimming with mischief and puckish wit, satiric barbs, and elegant scatologic references. It's not hard to imagine him reading it aloud by firelight as Clark rolls off a stump, barely able to contain his laughter.

TWO DIPS AND A FLIRT

"from the cow I killed we saved the necessary materials for making what our wrighthand cook Charbono calls the boudin blanc, *and immediately set him about preparing them for supper; this white pudding we all esteem one of the greatest delacies of the forrest, it may not be amiss therefore to give it a place. About 6 feet of the lower extremity of the large gut of the Buffaloe is the first mosel that the cook makes love to, this he holds fast at one end with the right hand, while with the forefinger and thumb of the left he gently compresses it, and discharges what he says is not good to eat, but of which in the squel we get a moderate portion; the mustle lying underneath the shoulder blade next to the back, and fillets are next saught, these are needed up very fine with a good portion of kidney suit [suet]; to this composition is then added a just proportion of pepper and salt and a small quantity of flour; thus far advanced, our skilfull opporater C——o seizes his recepticle, which has never once touched the water, for that would intirely distroy the regular order of the whole procedure; you will not forget that the side you now see is that covered with a good coat of fat provided the anamal be in good order; the operator sceizes the recepticle I say, and tying it fast at one end turns it inwards and begins now with repeated evolutions of the hand and arm, and a brisk motion of the finger and thumb to put in what he says is* bon pour manger; *thus by stuffing and compressing he soon distends the recepticle to the utmost limmits of it's power of expansion, and in the course of it's longitudinal progress it drives from the other end of the recepticle a much larger portion of the [blank] than was prevously discharged by the finger and thumb of the left hand in a former part of the operation; thus when the sides of the recepticle are skilfully exchanged the outer for the iner, and all is compleatly filled with something good to eat, it is tyed at the other end, but not any cut off, for that would make the pattern too scant; it is then baptised in the missouri with two dips and a flirt, and bobbed into the kettle; from whence after it be well boiled it is taken and fryed with bears oil untill it becomes brown, when it is ready to esswage the pangs of a keen appetite or such as travelers in the wilderness are seldom at a loss for."*

"*I also saw several parsels of buffaloe's hair hanging on the rose bushes, which had been bleached by exposure to the weather and became perfectly white. it every appearance of the wool of the sheep, and tho' much finer and more silkey and soft. I am confident that an excellent cloth may be made of the wool of the Buffaloe.*" —LEWIS, APRIL 18, 1804

"Set out verry early wind hard a head from the N.W. proceeded on passed all the villages the inhabitents of which flocked down in great numbers to view us, I took my leave of the great Chief of the Mandans who gave me a par of excellent mockersons, one Canoe filed with water every thing in her got wet."

—CLARK, APRIL 8, 1805

April 7, 1805. Spring has broken over the Great Plains, and Captain Lewis is striding along the east bank of the Missouri River, rifle in hand, shot pouch slung across his shoulder, moccasins scuffing up the tender shoots of new grass. In the warm, clear air of early evening, the promising scent of damp soil rises from the earth. Radiant wildflowers bob in the angled sunlight, and long shadows stretch across the land, revealing every fold and undulation among the smooth, grassy hills that line the river.

From the top of a knoll, Lewis can still see the keelboat gliding downstream in the distance with its cargo of letters, maps, reports, and specimens for President Jefferson. Upstream, the rest of the boats—six new dugout canoes and two pirogues—work against the glassy current, poised at last to enter the Great Unknown.

What joy. What pleasure. What pride Lewis must have felt to look down upon *"this little fleet."* The boats, he said, while *"not quite so rispectable as those of Columbus or Capt. Cook were still viewed by us with as much pleasure as those deservedly famed adventurers ever beheld theirs."*

And indeed, the boats were every bit as important to the Expedition as the Santa Maria was to Columbus, or the Resolution to Cook. As Lewis put it: *"We were now about to penetrate a country at least two thousand miles*

OFF THE MAP

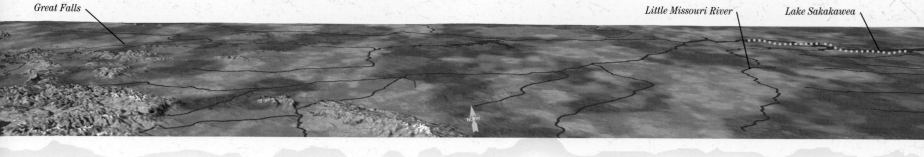

in width, on which the foot of civilized man had never trodden . . . these little vessells contained every article by which we were to expect to subsist or defend ourselves."

They were about to drop off the edge of the map and enter lands entirely unknown to European civilization. The Spanish, out for treasure and blood, had marched north from Mexico as far as the Platte River by the 1590s. The French, out to extend the fur trade, had explored west across Canada during the seventeenth century, had contacted the Mandans in 1738, and had even reached the Black Hills of South Dakota by 1743. And the British, of course, had found their own impractical route over the Canadian Rockies in 1793.

That left what is now the great northwest quadrant of the United States unexplored. It appeared on the best maps of the day as a giant blank space. The prospect of filling that void with cold, hard fact delighted Lewis as well as the rest of the party. He said the men were in *"excellent health and sperits, zealously attatched to the enterprise, and anxious to proceed."*

Though they set off for uncharted land, they did not go in complete ignorance. During their long winter of merriment and comradery with the Mandans, the Captains had learned about what lay ahead from dozens of Indians representing many different tribes. So they knew to look for certain landmarks—places we know as the Yellowstone River, Great Falls, Gates of the Mountains, Three Forks, and the Bitterroot Range. They knew they would need to buy horses to portage over the mountain barrier, and they knew who to buy the horses from: the Shoshones. They also knew how to talk to them, thanks to Sacagawea.

But if much of their information was good, some of it was just plain wrong. They were supposed to get around Great

SACAGAWEA

Sacagawea, below, was a teenage Lemhi Shoshone who had been abducted by the Hidatsas and sold at the Mandan villages to Toussaint Charbonneau, a French Canadian trader. Both of them, along with their infant son, accompanied Lewis and Clark to the Pacific Coast and back.

Opposite: Sunset over the Upper Jefferson River, which flows through Sacagawea's homeland. Previous spread: In the spring of 1805, the Expedition pressed on into a country of deeply eroded badlands, wooded coulees, and scabrous cliffs—a beautiful but severe landscape.

Falls, for example, with a half-mile portage across a fine and open plain. The trip over the mountains? A half day, max—and on the other side they'd find a river that would lead them west across flat, easily traveled terrain.

Lewis and Clark may have misunderstood what they were told. Or, the Indians might have been doing exactly what European cartographers had been doing for generations when asked about the region—offering their best guess. The Captains were not naive enough to believe everything they heard. The only way to know for sure was to go there and see it for themselves.

At first, the land looked much the same as it had for hundreds of miles the previous summer and fall. The Missouri led them through a broad, flat-bottomed trough lined on either side with bare, dome-shaped hills that rose to the plains as a rumpled embankment. Before long, though, the river made a wide bend to the west and entered a more rugged and angular landscape of buttes, knobs, gulches and coulees, exposed soil, and crumbling rock.

Paddling, rowing, sailing, towing, the Corps of Discovery made excellent progress against a much gentler Missouri River than they had faced the previous spring. Eighteen, nineteen, even twenty-three miles a day was not unusual. Still, strong winds could stop them cold, and the cumbersome dugouts—more than thirty feet long and roughly three feet wide—did take some getting used to. They were tippier than the pirogues and much more vulnerable to crosswinds, choppy water, and high waves. The men swamped one the first day out, drenching thirty pounds of gunpowder and half a bag of biscuit. It wouldn't be the last time.

Lake Sakakawea Mandan & Hidatsa Villages Fort Mandan Missouri River Platte River

NORTH

Grouse are about Short and eye. Cock Cock which on the and hood Mountains to the Mountain the Columbia the Great falls they go in large or singularly hide hide remarkably close when pursued short flights &c

the feathers about its head pointed and stiff Some hairs the base of the beak. feathers fine and Stiff about the ears. This is a faint likeness of the of the Plains or Heath the first of those fowls we met with was Missouri below in the neighbour of the Rocky and from which papu between and Rapids Gauges and make

The large Black & White Pheasant is peculiar to that portion of the Rocky Mountains watered by the Columbia River. at least we did not see them untill we reached the waters of that river, nor since we have left those Mountains. they are about the size of a well grown hen. the contour of the bird is much that of the redish brown Pheasant common to our country. the tail is proportionably as long and is composed of 18 feathers of equal length, of a uniform dark brown tiped with black...the feathers of the ... a dark brown black and white. the black

"the man I had sent up the river this morning returned . . . he saw several of the bighorned anamals in the couse of his walk; but they were so shy that he could not get a shoot at them; he found a large horn of one of these anamals which he brought with him." —LEWIS, APRIL 26, 1805

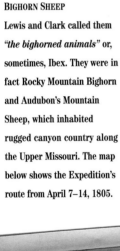

There were more boats this spring, but fewer men. The Captains had paid off most of the French boatmen the previous autumn and had sent several enlisted men back to St. Louis with the keelboat. Now they were down to the "permanent party" of twenty-five who would complete the voyage to the Pacific. Though military order still marked the daily routine, these men had been on the trail now for eleven months—sharing all the pleasures, dangers, discomforts, strains, and surprises of foreign travel. They knew one another, liked each other, counted on each other, and worked very, very well together. Flogging was a thing of the past, and the stiff formality that had surfaced at times between the Captains and the men seemed to have faded away. Though there was never any question about who was in charge, both Captains reveal in the Journals a growing sense of familiarity and fondness for their men. There was mutual respect, a shared sense of good cheer, of give and take, friendship—even brotherhood—that would serve them well as they faced extreme hardships in the months ahead.

For now, though, the travel was easy and the awakening land beautiful. Buds broke open among the thin line of cottonwoods and elms that grew beside the river. Snow geese and whooping cranes flapped by, and twittering flocks of cedar waxwings fluttered overhead. Hidatsa hunting parties headed downriver toward the villages, their dogs and horses laden with meat. Other Hidatsas camped along the banks, waiting for the big antelope migration to begin—much as today's duck hunters watch for the skies to darken over the Mississippi flyway.

BIGHORN SHEEP
Lewis and Clark called them *"the bighorned animals"* or, sometimes, Ibex. They were in fact Rocky Mountain Bighorn and Audubon's Mountain Sheep, which inhabited rugged canyon country along the Upper Missouri. The map below shows the Expedition's route from April 7–14, 1805.

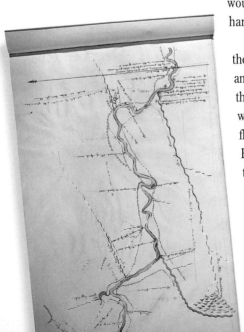

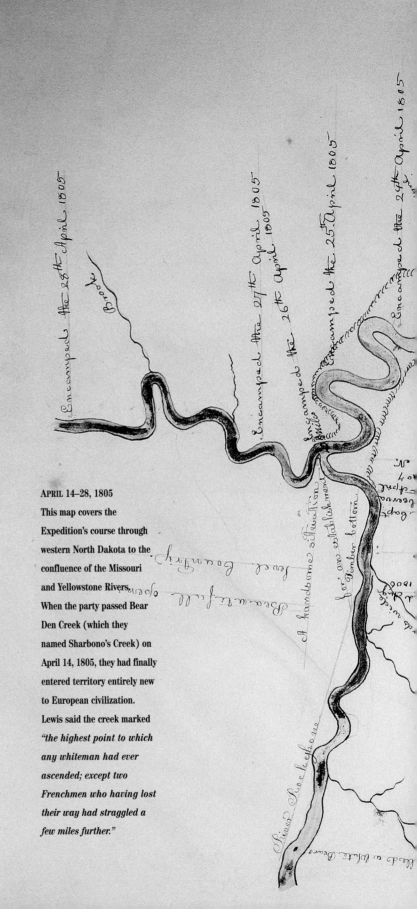

APRIL 14–28, 1805
This map covers the Expedition's course through western North Dakota to the confluence of the Missouri and Yellowstone Rivers. When the party passed Bear Den Creek (which they named Sharbono's Creek) on April 14, 1805, they had finally entered territory entirely new to European civilization. Lewis said the creek marked *"the highest point to which any whiteman had ever ascended; except two Frenchmen who having lost their way had straggled a few miles further."*

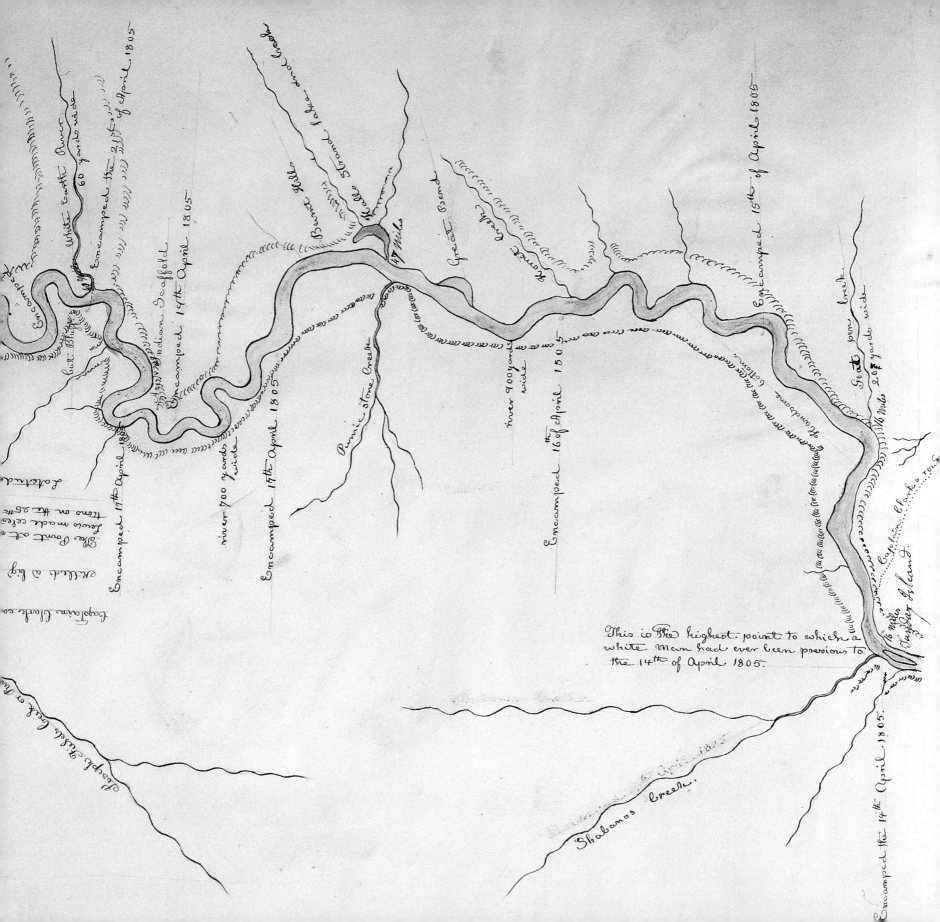

This is the highest point to which a white Man had ever been previous to the 14th of April 1805.

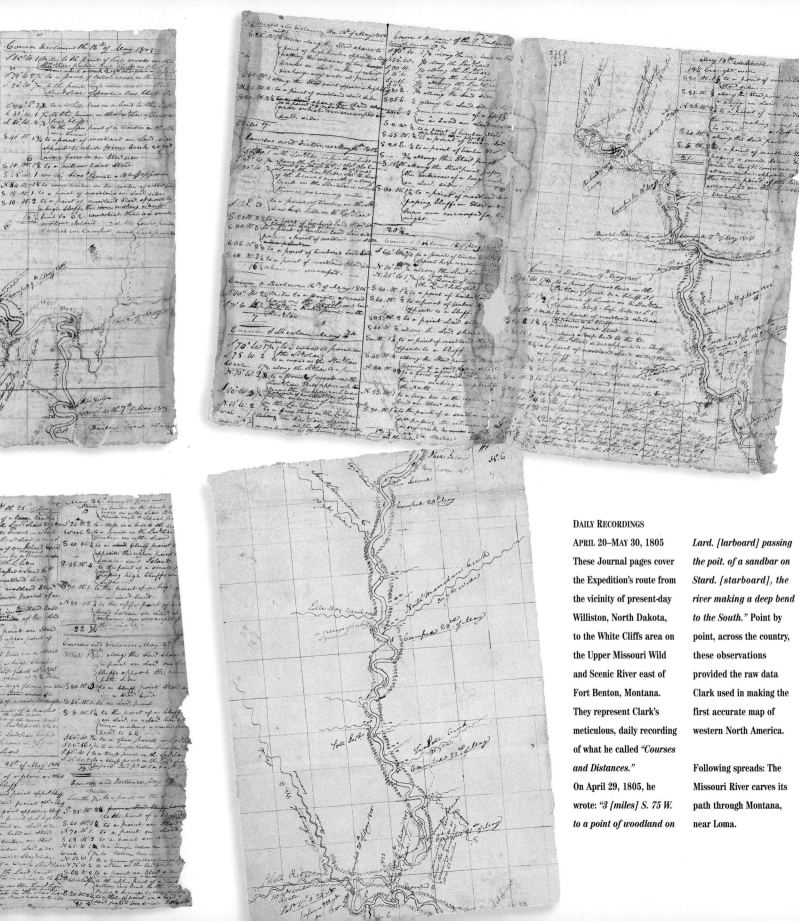

DAILY RECORDINGS
APRIL 20–MAY 30, 1805
These Journal pages cover the Expedition's route from the vicinity of present-day Williston, North Dakota, to the White Cliffs area on the Upper Missouri Wild and Scenic River east of Fort Benton, Montana. They represent Clark's meticulous, daily recording of what he called *"Courses and Distances."*
On April 29, 1805, he wrote: *"3 [miles] S. 75 W. to a point of woodland on*

Lard. [larboard] passing the poit. of a sandbar on Stard. [starboard], the river making a deep bend to the South." Point by point, across the country, these observations provided the raw data Clark used in making the first accurate map of western North America.

Following spreads: The Missouri River carves its path through Montana, near Loma.

Great Falls

Missouri River

Yellowstone River

Little Missouri River

Lake Sakakawea

NORTH

At camp, the men still pegged out tents, but the Captains slept in a large bison-hide tipi, which they shared with Drouillard, Charbonneau, Sacagawea, and her infant son, Jean-Baptiste. Everyone wore more leather clothing now, and they spent many an evening or wind-bound day sewing new moccasins, leggings, and buckskin shirts. Though game was scarce at first, meals were better this season, thanks to Sacagawea, who gathered wild vegetables such as Jerusalem artichokes, breadroot, and wild onions.

As the boats pressed upriver, Lewis and Clark took turns roaming the banks, cataloging the plants and animals and investigating with pen and palate various curiosities such as a burning bluff of coal, roasted beaver tail, and springs of *"extreemly unpleasant"* mineral water that purged their innards. Then, near the mouth of the Little Missouri River in northwestern North Dakota, they began to see grizzly bear tracks. They were enormous, bigger than a man's head even if you didn't count the claws, and they crisscrossed among the gnawed carcasses of drowned bison that had washed up along the banks.

"The Indians give a very formidable account of the strengh and ferocity of this anamal," Lewis wrote, *"which they never dare to attack but in parties of six eight or ten persons; and are even then frequently defeated with the loss of one or more of their party."* Indeed, two Hidatsa had been killed the previous winter. But, Lewis added, the Indians were poorly armed with bows, arrows, and indifferent muskets. Surely Americans armed with fine Pennsylvania long rifles had little to fear. *"The men as well as ourselves are anxious to meet with some of these bear."*

How times have changed. Today, most Rocky Mountain hunters dread close encounters

WHITE CLIFFS AREA

The Missouri glides past a section of the White Cliffs (left), a long series of sandstone formations that sometimes rise hundreds of feet from the water as sheer cliffs, eroded bluffs, towers, and arches. The landscape impressed Lewis, who wrote on April 31, *"As we passed on it seemed as if those seens of visionary inchantment would never have and end."*

"this anamall is said more frequently to attack a man on meeting with him, than to flee from him. When the Indians are about to go in quest of the white bear, previous to their departure, they paint themselves and perform all those supersticious rights commonly observed when they are about to make war uppon a neighbouring nation." —LEWIS, APRIL 13, 1805, ON THE GRIZZLY BEAR

with grizzly bears, despite carrying high-powered rifles capable of firing five rounds or more in quick succession. In 1805, an adept hunter could reload just twice a minute, and his rifle was not much good beyond a hundred yards or so—even for deer, much less griz. Lewis and the others would get their chance with the "white bear" soon enough. For now all they could do was place a hand next to each new set of monstrous paw prints and marvel.

During late April, they pushed across the rest of present-day North Dakota—past the White Earth and Little Muddy rivers to the mouth of the Yellowstone and beyond. As they crossed into eastern Montana, the Missouri cut through a broken high-plains landscape, meandering beneath dry bluffs, buttes, and shortgrass hills that stood two hundred to three hundred feet above the water. Bitter weather slowed them occasionally—it snowed in early May—but for the most part they sped along, often sailing under favorable winds and logging more than twenty miles a day.

The country, Clark wrote, was beautiful beyond description. The deer, elk, and bison were fat and so plentiful the men could afford to be choosy about their meat. They watched huge herds of migrating antelope swim the river, emerge exhausted, and fall easy prey to the wolf packs that waited for them along the banks. They saw bighorn sheep (probably Audubon's mountain sheep, now extinct) scampering among the steep bluffs and badlands hills, shot several, and wrote the first scientific descriptions of that animal.

Here, too, sixteen days after seeing his first track, Lewis finally got to test his mettle against a grizzly bear. He and another man were out ahead of the boats, ambling along the bank, when they came upon a pair of grizzlies and shot them. One bear fled, but the other charged, and

BEAR HUNT

By the time the Expedition reached Great Falls, the men had learned to respect the power of the grizzly bear. Right: Catlin painted dramatic prairie scenes, including this hunting incident involving Plains Indians and grizzly bears. The bear had a fearsome reputation and some tribes regarded a grizzly hunt as a feat equivalent to a raid on an enemy camp. Below: Radiant sunlight strikes the toothy ramparts of the White Cliffs area, east of Fort Benton, Montana.

"we had no means of weighing this monster; Capt Clark thought he would weigh 500 lbs. for my own part I think the estimate was too small by 100 lbs. he measured 8 Feet 7 1/2 Inches from the nose to the extremety of the hind feet . . . & 3 F. 11 I. around the neck . . . the heart particularly was as large as that of a large Ox. his maw was also ten times the size of a black bear and was filled with flesh and fish . . . this animal also feeds on roots and almost every species of wild fruit." —LEWIS, MAY 5, 1805, DESCRIBING A GRIZZLY BEAR

"the Perogue was under sail when a sudon squawl of wind struck her . . . and instantly upset the perogue and would have turned her completely topsaturva, had it not have been from the resistance mad my the oarning [awning] against the water . . . such was their [the crew's] confusion and consternation at this moment, that they suffered the perogue to lye on her side for half a minute before they took the sail in. The perogue then wrighted but had filled within an inch of the gunwals; Charbono still crying to his god for mercy, had not yet recollected the rudder, nor could the repeated orders of the Bowsman, Cruzat, bring him to his recollection untill he threatened to shoot him instantly if he did not take hold of the rudder and do his duty. the waves by this time were running very high, but the fortitude resolution and good conduct of Cruzat saved her." —LEWIS, MAY 14, 1805

the men ran off, scrambling to reload. They ran for seventy yards, checking over their shoulders as they busily poured a measure of powder into their rifle barrels, dropped in a ball, rammed home the wadding, primed the firepan, cocked back the flint, turned, aimed, and pulled the trigger. The bear, a small male, dropped dead.

"It is asstonishing to see the wounds they will bear before they can be put to death," Lewis wrote later that night. *"But in the hands of skillfull riflemen they are by no means as formidable or dangerous as they have been represented."*

Lewis' bravado faded six days later, though, when Clark and Drouillard (the party's best hunter) brought down a colossal griz near present-day Wolf Point. That bear stood nearly nine feet tall, weighed five hundred to six hundred pounds, and died hard. *"We Shot ten Balls into him,"* Clark wrote, five of which passed through its lungs. Still, the bear swam halfway across the river to a sandbar and roared for twenty minutes before it died. It was so heavy that most of the party had to lend a hand to haul the carcass onto the bank.

That got everyone's attention. When another grizzly swam ahead of the boats the following day, no one bothered to go after it. *"I find,"* Lewis wrote, *"that the curiossity of our party is pretty well satisfyed with rispect to this anamal."*

Pretty well, but not quite. Farther upriver, six of the party's best hunters saw another huge bear dozing on a beach and managed to creep within forty paces of it. According to plan, four of the men quietly leveled their rifles, fired simultaneously, and hit the bear, which jumped to its feet and charged. According to plan, the two reserve hunters calmly aimed and fired. But the bear kept coming. So much for plans. Everyone scattered. Two shoved off in a canoe. The others ducked into the brush, frantically reloaded, and fired again. It made no difference. The bear tore in after them, ran two off a twenty-foot cliff into the river—and then dove in after them. Finally, one of the remaining hunters shot it through the head.

"These bear being so hard to die reather intimedates us all," Lewis wrote. *"I must confess that I do not like the gentlemen and had reather fight two Indians than one bear."*

But the Expedition was given no such choice. The surly gentlemen with four-inch claws would harass them all the way to the base of the Rocky Mountains—stalking them, chasing them, swatting at their heels, driving them from kills, lurking about their camps at night, raiding their provisions. At Great Falls the bears would become such a menace that Lewis would order the men to sleep with their rifles and to go about in pairs—never alone, even on the most basic physical errand.

By late May, they were roasting buffalo tongues among the tightly folded hills, eroded bluffs, and steep, gravelly headlands of the Missouri River Breaks in central Montana. From the tops of the bluffs, the Captains began to see mountains rising from the plains: the Bear's Paw and Little Rockies to the north, the Judith Range to the south, and in the distant southwest, the Highwood Mountains near Great Falls.

They were getting closer, but they still had a long way to go, and the river was getting much more difficult. The current had quickened, and shoals of sharp rocks extended far out into the channel like wing dams, forcing the boat crews to tow in frigid water up to their armpits. If they weren't wet and cold, their feet ached from tramping barefoot across beds of sharp gravel. To add to their frustration, the elkskin tow ropes kept breaking, and men fell headlong into the mucky banks.

But there were compensating pleasures. The Captains still had enough whiskey, rum, and brandy to dole out a restorative jolt from time to time. And Charbonneau—that hapless boatman but valuable chef—fried sausages six feet long that he made from chopped meat, kidney fat, and the lower

GREAT FALLS GRIZZLIES The Expedition continued its series of confrontations with grizzly bears during the portage around Great Falls. The bears were particularly numerous around the Upper Portage Camp, which lay close to a cluster of islands the party named the White Bear Islands.

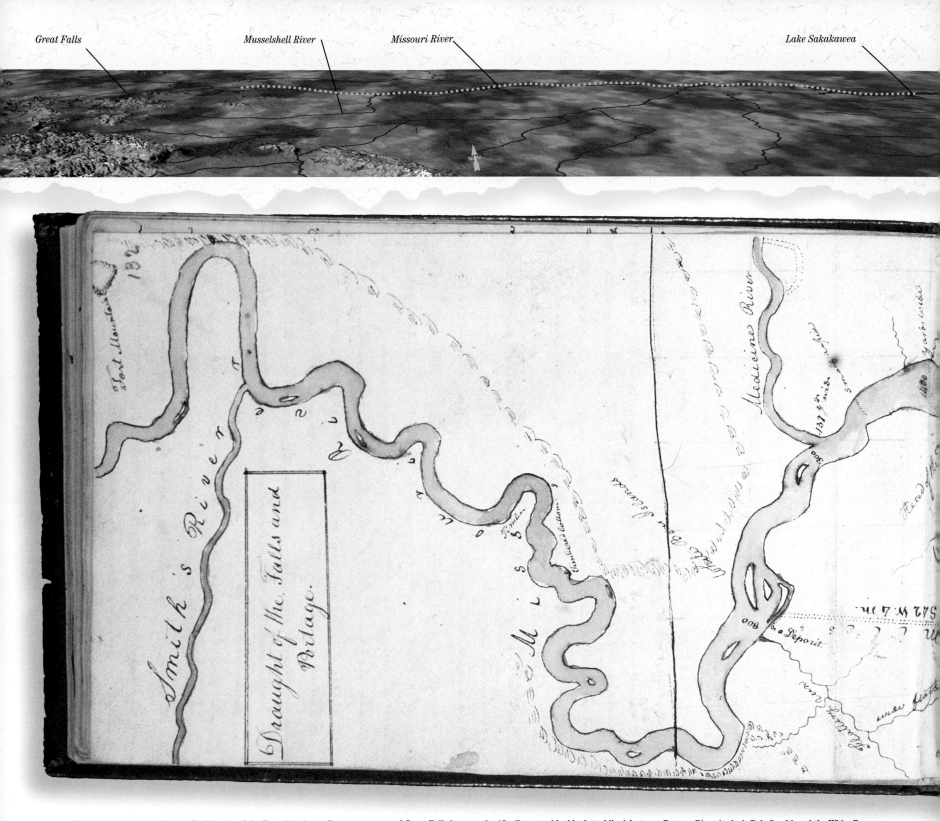

Great Falls   Musselshell River   Missouri River   Lake Sakakawea

NORTH

GREAT FALLS PORTAGE ROUTE Clark's map of the Expedition's grueling portage around Great Falls lays out the 18-mile route (double dotted line) between Portage River (today's Belt Creek) and the White Bear Islands. The party stored equipment and provision in caches (marked Deposits) at either end of the route. Today's Sacagawea Spring (which Lewis called "Sulpher Spring") lies opposite the mouth of what he called Portage River. Today, upriver and along the south bank, Giant Springs is marked "Large Fountain," and today's Sun River flows in from the top of the map as "Medicine River."

"[Great Falls] formes the grandest sight I ever beheld . . . the irregular and somewhat projecting rocks below receives the water in it's passage down and breaks it into a perfect white foam which assumes a thousand forms in a moment sometimes flying up in jets of sparkling foam to the hight of fifteen or twenty feet and are scarcely formed before large roling bodies of the same beaten and foaming water is thrown over and conceals them. in short the rocks seem to be most happily fixed to present a sheet of the whitest beaten froath for 200 yards in length and about 80 feet perpendicular."—LEWIS, JUNE 13, 1804

intestine of the bison. *"This white pudding,"* Lewis said, *"we all esteem one of the greatest delacies of the forrest."*

And if the river was difficult, at least it was beautiful. By May 31, they had moved out of the arid, desiccated portion of the Missouri Breaks that Clark had called *"The Deserts of America,"* and were now camping among the fulsome prairie hills and creamy sandstone formations of the White Cliffs area northeast of present-day Fort Benton. Lewis was impressed. *"The water in the course of time [. . .] has trickled down the soft sand clifts and woarn it into a thousand grotesque figures which with the help of a little immagination and an oblique view at a distance, are made to represent eligant ranges of lofty freestone buildings [. . .] As we passed on it seemed as if those seens of visionary inchantment would never have and end."*

A few days later, the boat crews towed through a set of yellowish badland bluffs, rounded a bend, and were confronted by a nasty surprise— the mouth of a major river. Today, we know they were at the Marias River, which flows into the Missouri from the north. But to Lewis and Clark, who had no map and whose Indian sources were of no help, the confluence presented them with an excruciating dilemma. Which of these two powerful streams was the Missouri and which the tributary? To make the wrong choice now, Lewis said, *"would not only loose us the whole of this season but would probably so dishearten the party that it might defeat the expedition altogether."*

High stakes indeed.

JUNE 13, 1805

Lewis, hiking overland, heard *"a roaring too tremendious to be mistaken for any cause short of the great falls of the Missouri"* **(right). Clark's map (below) of what he called** *"Handsom Falls,"* **today's Rainbow Falls, also takes in Crooked Falls, which still bears the name Clark gave it. Both falls are upriver of Great Falls.**

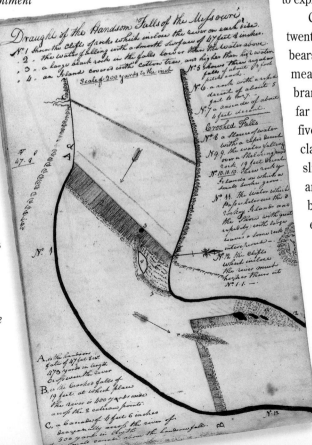

They measured the river widths, probed the beds, timed the currents, climbed the bluffs, scanned the diverging river courses, consulted the men, and *"busily employed"* their *"cogitating faculties."* All to no conclusive end. The north fork was deeper and looked just like the Missouri they'd known since St. Louis: whitish brown, turbid, roiling, with a muddy bed. The south fork was much wider and faster, but its waters were *"perfectly transparent,"* Lewis wrote, and its bed stony. Not at all like the Missouri.

Even so, he and Clark suspected that the south fork was the true Missouri. Its clarity made sense for a river that should soon lead them into the mountains, where clear water was the rule. And the Indians had told them that the Missouri ran clear at Great Falls, which could not be too far ahead. Still, the Captains decided to explore both forks before making a decision.

Clark's party hiked up the south fork, got within twenty-five miles of Great Falls, and ran into five grizzly bears before returning to the confluence. Lewis, meanwhile, trudged nearly eighty miles up the other branch before deciding that it probably trended too far north to be the Missouri. His was a miserable, five-day excursion, the weather rainy and cold, the clay-like gumbo mud along the tops of the bluffs as slick as a toboggan run. He slipped, at one point, and skittered to the brink of a ninety-foot drop before saving himself by jamming his spear-like espontoon into the muck.

The bottomland offered a safer route, but also had its drawbacks.

"Continued our rout down the river," Lewis wrote, *"Sometimes in the mud and water of the bottom lands, at others in the river to our breasts and when the water became so deep that we could not wade we cut footsteps in the face of the steep bluffs with our knives and proceeded."*

Back at the confluence, he and Clark announced their decision to follow the south fork. It was a guess, a good and defensible guess, but they still had their doubts—especially after every other member of the Expedition, including the most respected boatman, told them they were making a mistake. So. They decided to send Lewis ahead of the boats on foot. If he didn't find the Great Falls of the Missouri soon, they would know they had taken the wrong fork and could more quickly correct their error.

Lewis and his small advance party hiked for two days across the plains north of the river canyon before they began to hear *"the agreeable sound of a fall of water."* Soon, they saw *"spray arrise above the plain like a collumn of smoke."* Within an hour or so, they had clambered down into the rock-lined gorge *"to gaze on this sublimely grand specticle"*: a thundering cascade of explosive whitewater that plunged over cliffs at least eighty feet high and three hundred yards wide.

GREAT FALLS

While finding Great Falls (left) confirmed that the Corps was on the Missouri as they wanted to be, it also marked the start of a long and arduous portage.

What a satisfying moment of affirmation it must have been for Lewis to stand in the mist and concussive presence of that waterfall. Whatever anxiety he may have felt about wasting precious time on the wrong river—whatever tension, doubt, or worry—was now obliterated, flushed downriver with the foam. Elated, he and his men settled in for a feast of buffalo humps, tongues, marrow bones, and fried cutthroat trout (new to science) drudged in cornmeal, pepper, and salt.

The next morning he sent a man back to Clark with the good news, then set off along the north rim to scout a portage route. He thought he'd be back for lunch, that a jaunt of a few miles would lead to a fine launching point amid calm waters. No such luck. He returned long after dark with sobering news. The Expedition faced not just one *"sublimely grand object"* but five—all of them major waterfalls, each separated by impassable rapids. The men would have to haul their boats and tons of gear and provisions across at least sixteen miles of sun-wracked plain bristling with prickly pear cactus.

Within a couple of days, Lewis had rejoined Clark on the south bank of the Missouri a few miles below the first falls. There, they established a "saw a vast number of buffaloe feeding in every direction arround us in the plains, others coming down in large herds to water at the river; the fragments of many carcases of these poor anamals daily pass down the river, thus mangled I pesume in decending those immence cataracts above us. as the buffaloe generally go in large herds to water and the passages to the river about the falls are narrow and steep the hinder part of the herd press those in front out of their debth and the water instally takes

base camp on a pleasant ramp of grass overlooking the Missouri and began to prepare for the overland ordeal. By now they had decided to make the portage across the flatter plains south of the river. Clark took off with a small party to survey and mark the best route (it would stretch for eighteen miles) while Lewis remained in camp to supervise preparations.

A great deal of work had to be done. The men emptied the boats, hid both pirogues, and drew most of the dugouts upriver a mile or so to Belt Creek—a scrubby little side canyon of crumbling rock where the actual portage would begin. They unpacked and sorted through the heaps of cargo, drying all manner of goods and equipment in the sun, stashing some of it in a large cache pit and repacking the rest into bundles they could carry up to Belt Creek. They cobbled together four sets of *"truck wheels"* that would fit under the canoes and would allow the men to load the dugouts and roll them across the plain

BELT CREEK

The Missouri River, which courses past the mouth of Belt Creek (opposite), marked the start of the 18-mile portage around Great Falls.

SACAGAWEA SPRING

Lewis collected water from this sulphurous spring (below) near Great Falls to help treat Sacagawea for a life-threatening illness that modern scholars believe was pelvic inflammatory disease brought on by gonorrheal infection.

like wagons. They also broke open the metal parts for an iron-frame boat, which Lewis intended to assemble at the far end of the portage. Covered with animal skins, the boat was capable of carrying eight thousand pounds and was supposed to replace one of the pirogues.

In addition to overseeing all this, Lewis had a medical crisis on his hands. Sacagawea had arrived in camp near death. Palsied and in great pain, she had a nearly imperceptible pulse, a high fever, and was at times deranged. Lewis thought she suffered from *"an obstruction of the mensis"* brought on by a cold. Modern scholars say it was pelvic inflammatory disease brought on by gonorrheal infection. In any case, her illness alarmed the Captains for a couple of reasons. First, their hearts went out to her. She was a young mother with an infant in arms, a steady travel companion, a good friend. Second, as expedition commanders, they recognized that she was, as Lewis put it, their *"only dependence for a friendly negociation with the Snake Indians on whom we depend for horses"* to get over the Rockies. Lewis treated her with sulphur water from a nearby spring (which you can still walk to below the falls), poultices of Peruvian bark, and opium. Luckily for the Expedition, she recovered within a few days.

By June 21, Clark's surveying crew was back in camp and all made ready for the first trip across the portage route. They packed a load of baggage to the stony plains above Belt Creek, wrestled up one of the canoe wagons, and piled it high. The next morning, they took their places at the tow ropes and along the gunwales, braced their moccasined feet, and leaned into the work. The solid cottonwood wheels turned, momentum built, and the men staggered forward as the sun rose behind them.

Empty, one of those thick, slab-sided dugouts probably weighed something like a thousand pounds. Heaped with gear, Lewis said, the burden was *"as much as they can possibly move with."* Clark wrote that *"the men has to haul with all their Strength wate & art, maney times every man all catching the grass & knobes & Stones with their hands to give them more force in drawing on the Canoes & Loads."* They stopped frequently to rest and at every halt, Lewis said, *"these poor fellows tumble down and are so much fortiegued that many of them are asleep in an instant . . . some are limping . . . others faint and unable to stand for a few minutes."*

them over the cataracts where they are instantly crushed to death without the possibility of escaping. in this manner I have seen ten or a douzen disappear in a few minutes. their mangled carcases ly along the shores below the falls in considerable quantities and afford find amusement for the bear wolves and birds of prey; this may be one reason and I think not a bad one either that the bear are so tenatious of their right of soil in this neighbourhood." —LEWIS, JUNE 17, 1805

"I begin to be extremely impatient to be off as the season is now waisting a pace nearly three months have now elapsed since we left Fort Mandan and not yet reached the Rocky Mountains I am therefore fully preswaded that we shall not reach Fort Mandan again this season if we even return from the ocean to the Snake Indians." —LEWIS, JUNE 30, 1805

The plains were hot, water scarce, and the hardened soil underfoot pockmarked with sharp bison tracks nearly as painful as the prickly pear thorns that pierced their feet. The wagon body kept breaking down, then gave out entirely with just a half mile to go. As darkness fell, the men hoisted what they could onto their backs and stumbled down to the river as darkness fell. Then, to top off everything, they were greeted by a group of wolves who had eaten nearly all the meat Clark had cached there for the men.

What an incredible thrash! Hungry, dead tired, sore, their feet cut by cactus thorns, the men got a few hours of sleep, then hiked back to do it all over again. Clark went with them and would remain for six days at the lower portage camp, supervising the loading of baggage and caching of surplus gear while the portage crew shuttled between the two camps. Lewis and a few others stayed above, where they put together the iron-frame boat, received the baggage, and revived the portage crews with rounds of stiff drinks and suet dumplings. Despite all the grim labor, the portage crew often had enough energy left at the end of the day to mend moccasins, haze grizzly bears out of camp, and dance to Cruzatte's fiddle.

They made the round-trip four times, moving all of the gear and boats across the portage in just eleven days. That's an amazing pace. A brilliant pace when you consider that the typical brigade of French *voyageurs* (as tough a breed as ever lived) took ten full days to lug their packs across the Grand Portage west of Lake Superior. One-way distance? A mere nine miles—and they didn't even have to portage their canoes because they had boats waiting for them.

It usually took the Expedition's men one day to reach the upper camp and one day to return and stage for the next push. On the second and third trips, they hoisted sails and got a boost from the incessant prairie winds. They were doing so well that they might have completed their task in just eight days if the skies hadn't opened up during their final trip. Violent thunderstorms morphed the soil into slick gumbo mud, filled the ravines and gullies with deep rushing water, and stranded them in the open. While they waited to proceed, a hailstorm hammered them bloody—knocked men down and might have killed some, Clark said, if they hadn't found

shelter under the boats. The same day, Clark himself nearly died in a flash flood that swept through a gully where he had taken shelter along with York, Sacagawea, her baby, and Charbonneau.

That last, miserable trip took four days and ended on July 2. By then Lewis had serious doubts about his iron-frame boat. After covering the frame with the skins of twenty-eight elk and four bison, he could find nothing to seal the seams. He'd expected to use pine pitch, but there were no pine trees near Great Falls. Nonetheless, he spent seven precious days finishing the boat and experimenting with charcoal and beeswax before finally giving up on July 9. The next day, Clark started building two more dugouts, which were launched on the evening of July 14—twelve full days after the portage ended.

Twelve full days. That's what the failure of the iron-frame boat and its remedy had cost the Expedition. If instead the Captains had assigned a small party of men to build canoes as soon as the group had landed at Great Falls on June 17, they might have been underway again by July 3. The rivers would have been higher, their ascent of the Jefferson and Beaverhead easier. They would have met up with the Shoshones earlier and, most importantly, they would have missed the early snowstorm that made their trip across the Lolo Trail such misery.

But that's just armchair quarterbacking—a rosy backward glance from a rear-echelon pogue in the Hindsight Division. If they'd shoved off twelve days earlier, they also might have run into the Blackfeet—a well-armed party of Blackfeet who would not have been pleased to hear Lewis' plans for a trading system that would supply all of their enemies with American rifles. Like the old trapper says: things coulda got right ugly.

As it stood, things were bad enough. Their epic portage had robbed them of a solid month of prime, midsummer travel days, with the vast ramparts of the Rocky Mountains dead ahead.

COTTONWOODS

Trees along the Missouri thinned the farther west the Expedition traveled. After portaging Great Falls, they were fortunate to find a grove of cottonwoods with trees barely large enough to make two canoes of what they considered to be suitable dimensions. One was 25 feet long, the other 33; both about 3 feet wide.

On August 10, 1805, Meriwether Lewis was hiking toward Lemhi Pass with a troubled mind. The journey had gotten hard. Almost desperate. The crew was bone tired, showing signs of low morale. After a month of extreme labor in the swift but diminishing waters of the Missouri, the Jefferson, and finally the Beaverhead rivers, they were near the limits of navigation. Hauling the dugouts over rocky shallows, they struggled to make five or six miles a day. Too slow. Too hard. It was time to ditch the boats and go overland. But they couldn't do that without horses, and horses had to be bought from the Shoshones. Where were the Shoshones? If they couldn't find them, if they failed to cross the mountains before winter, the whole endeavor could come apart. It was already mid-August. Nights were getting cold. In frustration, Lewis had left the river party and hurried ahead on foot.

It had been miserable work, coming upstream from Great Falls in the stifling mid-summer heat—up through the deep canyon called Gates of the Mountains, to a long stretch where the river ran fast and

"OVER THOSE TREMENDIOUS MOUNTAINS"

"We entered much the most remarkable clifts that we have yet seen. . . . the river appears to have forced it's way through this immence body of solid rock for the distance of 5 3/4 miles. . . . nor is ther in the 1st 3 miles of this distance a spot except one of a few yards in extent on which a man could rest the soal of his foot."—LEWIS, GATES OF THE MOUNTAINS, JULY 19, 1805

shallow through numerous braided channels, and the men spent much of their time in the water, pulling and poling against the current. Lewis heaved a pole himself, and complained about three pests—mosquitoes, gnats, and prickly pear. He likened them to the plagues of Egypt. Buffalo were behind them now; they hunted elk, antelope, deer, and occasional waterfowl. Usually they had enough to eat, but some days the hunters shot nothing.

From the time they entered the mountains, near modern-day Helena, they had kept their eyes peeled for the Shoshones. Trying to improve their chances of making contact, Clark and several hunters hiked ahead of the canoe party. They walked on Indian roads and came across empty campsites, punctured their feet with cactus spines, tore their moccasins open on sharp rocks, and wore themselves out searching. They covered twenty to thirty miles a day, sometimes more, but found no one.

At length, they entered country familiar to Sacagawea, who told them that Three Forks was not far upstream. It was at Three Forks, a summer campground for the Shoshones, that she had been abducted by the Hidatsas four years earlier. Perhaps they would find her people there? No. When the Expedition hauled in at the forks on July 27, the valley was deserted, and the men were in rough shape. Lewis had already decided on laying over for a couple of days when

BITTERROOTS

Although the Expedition crossed difficult and rugged mountains, they detoured around the highest and most forbidding, such as Trapper Peak (preceding page), which rises to the west of Conner in Montana's Bitterroot Valley. Below: Approximate territories of western Indian tribes, c.1805.

Opposite: View of Gates of the Mountains.

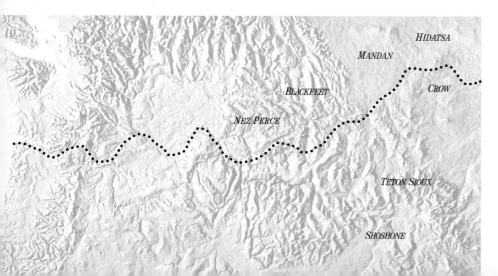

HIDATSA

MANDAN

BLACKFEET

CROW

NEZ PERCE

TETON SIOUX

SHOSHONE

Snake River   Lemhi Pass   Horse Prairie   Beaverhead River   Jefferson River   Three Forks

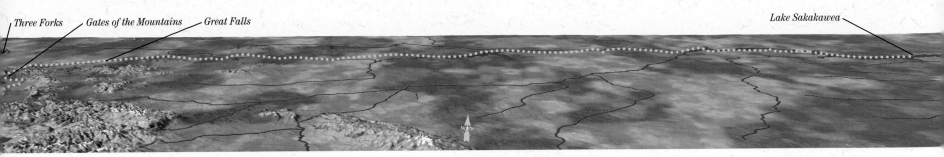

Three Forks — Gates of the Mountains — Great Falls   Lake Sakakawea —

NORTH

Clark and the walking party strode wearily into camp. With bulldog determination, they had trekked a full day up each of the three branches of the Missouri. Clark had ruined his feet, and now sick and running a fever, he rejoined the river party agreeing that everyone needed a rest.

But two days only. On the third day, feeling the press of time, they were off again.

They named that fork the Jefferson and worked their way toward its headwaters. Forward progress meant wading in the cold water, dragging the boats over the shoals, slipping on the rocks, and sometimes having to double-team on the drag lines. When the Jefferson forked, they correctly chose the middle stream, the Beaverhead; but first, Clark attempted the Big Hole, which seemed to head more directly into the mountains. It turned them back decisively, swamping two canoes and overturning another. They lost gear in that accident, and one of the men who slipped beneath the heavy craft in shallow water was almost crushed. The canoes were becoming as much a burden as a means of transport. But they couldn't abandon them, not yet, not without horses to carry the baggage. And still, no sign of the Shoshones.

On August 8, having made less than twenty-five miles in four days, Lewis decided to strike out on foot to reach the source of the Beaverhead. From there he would go over the mountains to the Columbia, wherever he found it, and down that river until he found Indians. Drouillard, Shields, and McNeal would come with him. Even if the trip took a month, he was determined to return with horses.

Three days later, the four men were trekking toward Lemhi Pass through Montana's most perfect hay meadow, Horse Prairie. In early August, the grasses were lush and the men's moccasins were soaked from crossing the soggy ground. They could see for miles in all directions. To the north, the Pioneer Range spread its graceful bulk. Ahead, rumpled tan hills climbed to the timber-fringed saddle of Lemhi Pass.

THREE FORKS

The view of Three Forks 200 years after the Expedition shows a landscape much as Lewis saw it in late July, 1805, when he stood where this photo was taken. The Gallatin River flows from left to right in the foreground, curving around the prominent, flat-topped promontory. Just beyond the rock, the Madison and Jefferson Rivers join to form the official headwaters of the Missouri River. At this point, they had a decision to make and correctly chose to follow the westernmost branch, which they named for President Jefferson. Following pages: John Clymer's painting illustrates the Expedition making its way up the Jefferson, with Clark in the lead.

"we begin to feel considerable anxiety with rispect to tthe Snake Indianns. if we do not find them or some other nation who have horses I fear the successfull issue of our voyage will be very doubtfull or at all events much more difficult in it's accomplishment. we are now several hundred miles within the bosom of this wild and mountainous country, where game may rationally be expected shortly to become scarce and subsistence precarious without any information with rispect to the country not knowing how far these mountains continue, or wher to direct our course to pass them to advantage or intersept a navigable branch of the

Columbia, or even were we on such an one the probablility is that we should not find any timber within these mountains large enough for canoes if we judge from the portion of them through which we have passed. however I still hope for the best, and intend taking a tramp myself in a few days to find these yellow gentlemen if possible. my two principal consolations are that from our present position it is impossible that the S.W. fork can head with the waters of any other river but the Columbia, and that if any Indians can subsist in the form of a nation in these mountains with the means they have of acquiring food we can also subsist." —LEWIS, JULY 27, 1805

Then, suddenly, there was a rider up ahead. A man on horseback two miles away, standing, peering at them. It was an elegant horse, Lewis noted. His heart must have leaped. Here was his chance. But he blew it. He and his companions apparently lacked a coordinated plan for what to do if they actually met a Shoshone. They knew the Indians would be wary of strangers. Lewis could have asked Charbonneau and Sacagawea to come with him; Sacagawea not only spoke the language, but she was carrying a baby. Her presence would have signaled peaceful intentions. War parties and desperadoes don't come walking along with women and infants, yelling in the native tongue, "Howdy! Let's talk!" Why hadn't he brought her along?

He doesn't explain, and we can only speculate. She had nearly died of an illness back at Great Falls. Maybe she was still weak. He didn't know where this foot journey would take him over *"Those Tremendious Mountains"* and was perhaps not willing to expose her to that uncertainty. But then why didn't he at least learn a few useful phrases from her? For whatever reason, he did not, and now he and his three well-armed, buckskin-clad companions were an unsettling (but intriguing) sight. As they edged cautiously forward, so did the Shoshone. Lewis laid his blanket on the ground, held up trinkets, adopted the posture of someone who welcomes contact. But at the critical moment when Lewis stopped a few hundred yards from the Indian, Shields, out on the flank, kept moving. The rider, feeling threatened, whipped his horse, leaped a creek, and disappeared in the shrubby willows. Lewis must have felt desolate. There went his ride. Worse, if that man raised the alarm, other Indians in the area might either vacate the region or a party of warriors mounted on those handsome horses might just sweep down and whack off some heads, no questions asked. End of Expedition. Certainly no horses.

Onward they trudged. They spent the night along Trail Creek, and on the next day, August 11, climbed the steep grassy hillside to Lemhi Pass. Approaching the

HORSES

Approaching the Continental Divide, the Expedition's most urgent need was for horses to help them over the mountains. They planned to meet the Shoshone Indians and barter for enough horses to carry men and baggage to a tributary of the Columbia, where they could build canoes and paddle on to the Pacific. Below: A Shoshone warrior.

summit, Lewis must have been a raging torrent of mixed emotions. He suspected that this was the Continental Divide. He didn't know what he'd see on the other side, but he hoped to see country like what he'd just come through—the open, generous landscape of Montana, where mountains were decently spaced, and rivers had room to flow free of constricting canyons and impassable cascades. He knew that if he came back this way, he could float all the way to St. Louis, down the Beaverhead, the Jefferson, and the Missouri with only one significant impediment, Great Falls. He could do it in a fine Virginia rowboat.

Going east would be easy. But as he would soon learn, the same rowboat going west would be a mess of splinters within a few miles.

* * *

You can drive to Lemhi Pass today on a narrow gravel road that closely follows the route Lewis walked. It's lovely country. In August, the irrigated hayfields of Horse Prairie are green and turning golden. Hillsides are parched a light tan. Dark strips of conifers shelter in the hollows, while willows and aspens stretch out along streambanks. A hundred vertical feet or so below the pass, a spring described by Lewis as the *"most distant fountain of waters of the mighty Missouri"* emits a sweet, clear flow. The map names it Sacagawea Spring. Shrine-like, it hides in a grove of spruce and fir.

HORSE PRAIRIE

The sprawling western landscape of Horse Prairie, Red Butte, Montana.

The pass is a benign saddle, just a gentle curve in the long ridge. You can stroll easily in either direction. If the wind isn't blowing too hard, it's a welcoming spot that has not changed much since Lewis stepped onto it— the same grass, the same flowers. But he was probably not looking at the ground. There was only one thing on his mind. It's likely that his eyes narrowed, his face pinched a bit. Shading his face with one hand (he'd have been looking into the sun), he peered ahead. Maybe his heart fell.

He was standing on what was then the western boundary of the United States, looking at the start of one of the most tangled, contrary landscapes on the continent: central Idaho, where rivers tie themselves in knots, and the only difference between up and down is whether or not you've just stumbled. There's nowhere flat to speak of. There are no easy

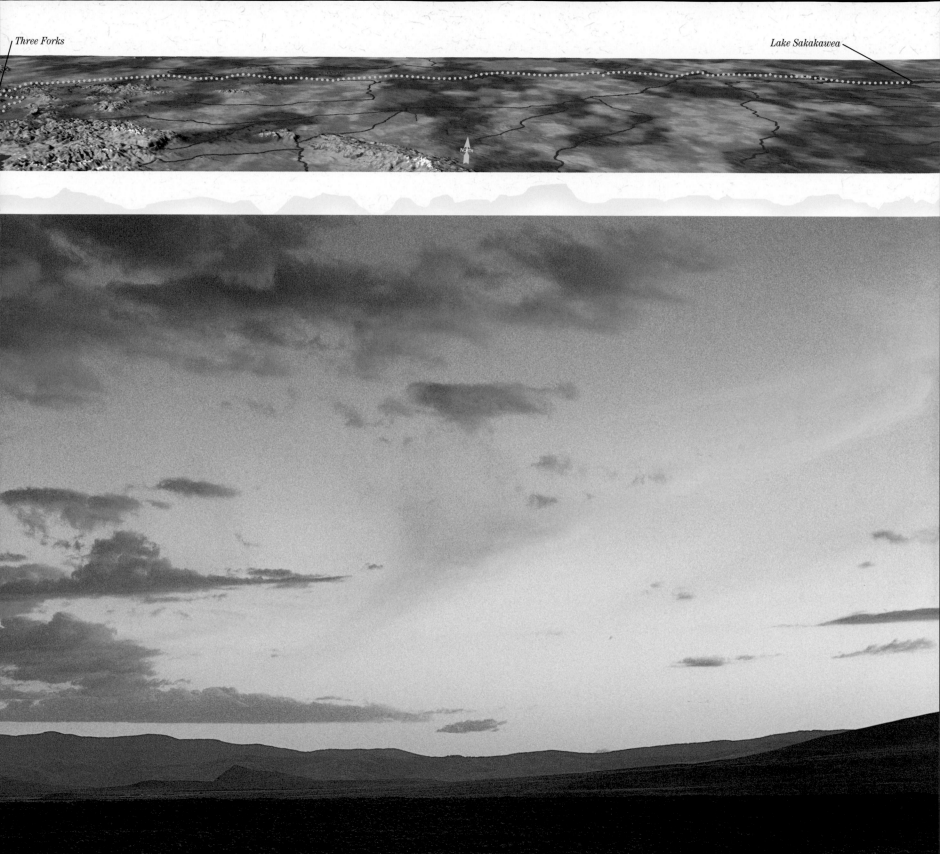

NORTH

"with my glass I discovered from his dress that he was of a diffrent nation from any that we had yet seen, and was satisfyed of his being a Sosone . . . I got nearer than about 100 paces when he suddonly turned his hose about, gave him the whip leaped the creek and disapeared in the willow brush in an instant and with him vanished all my hopes of obtaining horses for the preasent." —LEWIS, AUGUST 11, 1805

routes, and there was no straightforward path for Lewis to discover. The only things that move easily across that country are birds, and even they deal with air made turbulent by the difficulty of forcing its way over God's own geologic train wreck. Whatever Lewis thought he was looking at, he wasn't seeing the half of it.

Specifically, he was gazing down slopes steeper than the ones he'd come up, into a valley whose bottom he could not see, and up the other side to an ocean of mountain ridges fading into the distance. You can only wonder what went through his mind and that of his friends. They must have talked about it, speculating on what lay unseen in the valleys and canyons below those far summits. It was late in the day. They were peering into purpling shadows.

One good thing happened. The next afternoon, having reached the Lemhi River Valley, Lewis met an elderly Shoshone woman. He came upon her suddenly, before she could flee, and convinced her by gesture and gifts that he meant no harm. That was a good thing, because it wasn't long before the war party he had worried about came thundering into view. Alerted by a man who had seen them earlier in the day, they were ready to do swift battle. Lucky for Lewis and his friends, they stood in the protective influence of an old woman who spoke to the warriors and showed them the beads and other gifts these white fellows had given her. If the irony—and the value of a woman—didn't strike Lewis then, it must have three days later when the chief of this group, Cameahwait, friendly but cautious, turned out to be Sacagawea's brother.

But that moment of revelation was yet to come. For now, Cameahwait

SALMON RIVER MOUNTAINS The view westward from Lemhi Pass (left) has changed little in the 200 years since Lewis arrived here. In August 1804 it marked not only the Continental Divide, but also the western boundary of the newly acquired Louisiana Territory; as such, it was also the western frontier of the United States. Beyond the pass, Agency Creek flows down to the Lemhi River, and from there to the Salmon River. In the distance, the Salmon River Mountains hint at the ruggedness of the country that lay ahead of the Expedition as it moved across what is now Idaho.

Below: In this Curtis photograph, a Plains Indian on horseback surveys gentler country in Montana.

"the Prickly Pear is now in full blume and forms one of the beauties and one of the greatest pests of the plains." —LEWIS, JULY 15, 1805

Summer 1804 on the Lower Missouri: Lewis is ahead of the boats, walking across lush prairie. He spies an unfamiliar plant and stoops to look closer. Carefully, he pulls it out of the ground, shakes the dirt from its roots, and tucks it gently into his field notebook. That evening, while the men are busy with camp chores, he carefully sketches and describes the plant. We see him in candlelight, bent over his portable writing desk. It's an engaging image of a keen naturalist afforded the opportunity to wander through a new landscape and blessed with sufficient time to record what he sees.

But imagine him again, this time on the Upper Missouri short of Three Forks. It's hot. The work is hard, the going tough. Lewis is not riding high and dry while the men labor. He's lending a hand, getting fully involved. No one is eating well. They're working like dogs, and they're worried about finding the Shoshones and buying horses. These matters could easily distract Lewis from his responsibilities as a naturalist, yet he continues to observe and record details of the country, from sunflowers in bloom to blue flax to bighorn sheep on cliffs above the river. On July 17, he runs through a list of trees and shrubs, saying of the yellow currant, *"the leaf is petiolate of a pale green and resembles in it's form that of the red currant common to our gardens.   the perianth of the fructification is one leaved, five cleft, abreviated and tubular . . .,"* and so on, in fond detail. During these hard weeks, his notes go beyond the difficulties of travel to include many plant and animal descriptions along with observations on the landscape, the weather, and even an occasional personal note.

Clark, meanwhile, walked long sections of the trip to Three Forks on raw, bloody, cactus-riddled feet. He and a few companions covered many miles each day. He had to have been exhausted. He wrote about it: *"The Misquetors verry troublesom my man York nearly tired out, the bottoms of my feet blistered."* Yet all the while, he doggedly maintained his mapping work,

HEAD-FLATTENING

Clark's sketch shows the infant head-flattening technique commonly practiced among the Chinookan-speaking tribes of the Lower Columbia. *"This is done in order to give a greater width to the forehead, which they much admire,"* **Lewis wrote. The cosmetic privilege marked superior status; slaves were not permitted to flatten their heads.**

tracking directions with a compass and estimating distance with his practiced eye.

It was that way the whole trip. Whether thrashing through willows; scrambling across dry, rocky slopes; following the bends of a river; or toiling through dense forests in the Rockies, Clark logged geographic statistics with astonishing accuracy, and drew beautiful maps of what he saw. From our modern perspective, armed with odometers, optical rangefinders, global positioning units, accurate maps, and road signs to tell us how far we have traveled, it's hard to understand how he could do it so well. What follows is a typical sample of his meticulous data, covering the first half of July 13, 1805:

"S. 10° E.   1 1/2   to a point of low trees on the Lard. side passing a willow island on Lard. side

S. 36° E.   1 to a point of wood on the Stard. side

South 1 to a clift of rocks in a bend on Lard. side

S. 45° W. 1 1/2   to some trees in a bend, passing a timbered islad on the Stard. side.

South 1 1/4 to a point of low timber on the Stard. side"

Work like that requires constant attention. Of course, it was a collaboration. Just as Clark made journal entries on all subjects, Lewis also

KEEN OBSERVERS

"I killed an otter which sunk to the bottom on being shot . . . the water was about 8 feet deep yet so clear that I could see it at the bottom; I swam in and obtained it by diving."
—LEWIS, JULY 22, 1805

helped with the mapping. Together or singly, they had to be on the job every hour of every day.

It appears that both men carried field notebooks at least part of the time. These might have been little more than a few loose sheets on which they scribbled sketches and observations during the course of a day. Clark's elkskin journal, for example, started out as unbound sheets of letter paper, and was sewn into a book at some point along the way; it covers the period of September 11 to December 31, 1805. It also appears that they carried, as part of their luggage, leather-bound journal books sealed inside tin boxes. The Captains would pull them out when opportunities arose—during layovers, in the evening, in winter quarters, and so forth—and transcribe into them expanded versions of their field notes, adding summaries and other observations in the process. Sometimes they wrote directly into the bound books. They also copied from each other, creating duplicate records, probably to safeguard the information.

How they kept their notes is not fully known, although judging from the Journals themselves, it's clear that they followed no consistent procedure through the whole journey (which comes as no surprise to anyone who has tried to keep a journal on a long trip). Routine is the first casualty of travel. Many factors would have made it difficult. There were days of hunger, exhaustion, illness, and terrible weather. Some nights the party did not reach a campsite until 10 P.M. Even their social schedule would have interfered. During their meetings with Indians, staying up late smoking, talking, and dancing would have left little time to catch up on writing. Yet somehow they always managed to cover the necessary ground. There isn't a day of the Expedition that wasn't described in some detail. To history's great benefit, Lewis and Clark observed and wrote and sketched their hearts out, page after page, week after week, for all of the twenty-eight months from St. Louis to the coast and back.

The result is both a priceless historic document and a great read. The journals provide us with a unique and detailed view of the land through which they traveled; an attentive chronicle of the people they encountered; and the dramatic, sometimes comic, always interesting narrative of the Expedition's progress.

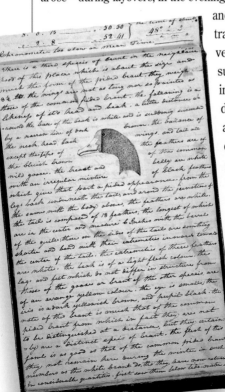

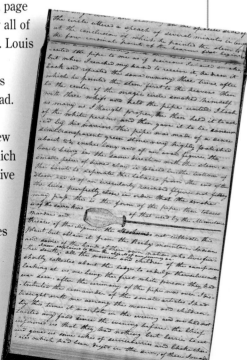

OBSERVATIONS IN A NEW LAND Lewis and Clark illuminated their journals with sketches of various animals, plants, and Native technology; (left) the head of a brant, *Anser albifrons*; (above) a sprig of Oregon grape, *Berberis nervosa*; and (right) a journal page with Lewis' sketch of a Shoshone pipe.

"Capt Lewis informed me he found those people on the Columbia River . . . The Great Chief ofthis nation proved to be the brother of the Woman with us and is a man of Influence Sence & easey & reserved manners, appears to possess a great deel of Cincerity." —CLARK, AUGUST 17, 1805

and his warriors were relieved that these were white men and not raiding Blackfeet. They dismounted and welcomed Lewis with open arms to the point that he grew *"heartily tired of the national hug."* They went back to the Shoshone camp together, where they smoked and talked through sign language. What Lewis learned was not encouraging. Game was scarce here. Cameahwait could offer only some berry cakes to eat. And worse, although this was indeed the Pacific drainage, Cameahwait said this river, the Lemhi, flowed into another, the Salmon, which entered an impassable canyon. If they wanted to go west, they would have to make a long trip north to a trail used by the Nez Perce Indians to get across the mountains. It would be a rough and hungry trip.

Lewis understandably did not want to accept that, and anyway, the first priority was to get the Shoshones to help with portaging. They had hundreds of horses, but they were reluctant to follow him back across the Divide. They had good reasons for not trusting strangers and feared a trap. Lewis persisted. He challenged their manhood and held out the lure of dazzling trade goods if they would come meet his party at the forks of the Beaverhead. They agreed, with great hesitation, and two days later, arrived at the forks. Clark came in a day later, and now they talked in earnest through Charbonneau and Sacagawea. It seems that the young Shoshone woman didn't realize who Cameahwait was at first; they had been talking a little while when awareness struck. She stood suddenly, went to him, threw her blanket over his shoulders, and wept.

What luck. Thousands of miles downriver they had met a teenage mother, and brought her along primarily because they wanted the services of her French husband. They

NAMESAKES
The sprawling western landscape constantly turned up new plants and animals. Among the species that carry the Captains' names are Clark's Nutcracker (above) and the Lewis Monkeyflower (below). Following spread: Looking placid and navigable here, the Salmon River soon becomes a difficult white-water river that Clark quickly recognized as far too hazardous to attempt.

had made several wrong turns (that is, if they had known of the Nez Perce route from Great Falls, they might have stayed far to the north), and there were other paths they could have taken, but they took this one and ran smack into Sacagawea's brother, who just happened to be the chief of his band. It's hard to say how things could have turned out better for them; it seems like sweet unbidden providence.

The next days were spent wrangling the portage. Cameahwait left, promising to return with enough horses for the Corps. Clark and eleven men went with him, intending to check out the river and begin building canoes if it looked floatable. Lewis and the remaining crew prepared the loads for horseback, built pack saddles, dug a cache for the surplus gear, and tried to keep themselves fed. It appeared that food was going to be a problem. There was little game here. The Shoshones were hungry and eager to head east to the plains where they would hunt buffalo. There was disagreement among the tribe about whether to help the Expedition. Cameahwait himself was torn, but in the end he honored his promise. The portage was accomplished, and Lewis began buying horses.

LEMHI PASS

Below, sagebrush slopes and timbered mountain ridges near Lemhi Pass are characteristic features of central Idaho's rugged terrain. Right, Clark's elkskin-bound journal with his observations of weather, sun, and moon.

Meanwhile, Clark had seen enough of the Salmon River Canyon. Five days of hard trekking had taken him to a point where he could see that travel on the river was impossible. When he rejoined Lewis, he and the men who had gone with him were hungry and starting to express concern. If this was any indication of what was to come, they were in for a hard go of it.

But what choice did they have? Cameahwait laid it out clearly. There was no way through the central mountains. It was either the Nez Perce trail, or the bleak lava plains of southern Idaho—or retreat.

Their decision to proceed was pure courage. Already depleted by the struggle from Great Falls, worn down by a dwindling food supply, they were fearful of entering unknownterritory so late in the year.

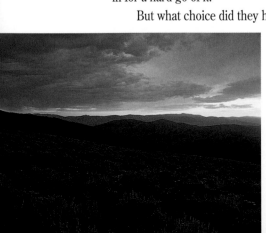

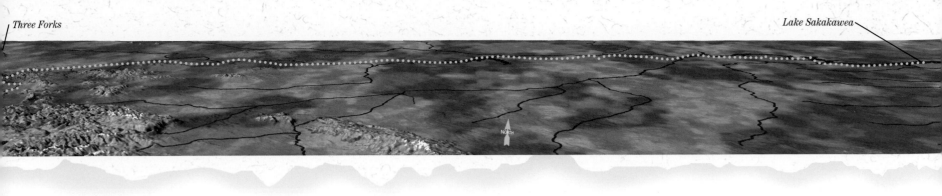

Sunday 30th Septr 1805   Forks

a fine morning our me securing
a little cool, all at work doing something
exept 2 which are very sick, great number
of small Duck passing up and down the
river this morning.

Took equal altitudes with Sextent at Camp
Apposite the junction of   River
                          and   River
                   Sunday 30th Septr 1805

A.M.	H.	M.	S.	P.M.	H.	M.	S.
	8	49	32.5		4	5	23.5
	"	51	17.5		4	7	9.
	"	53	8.5		4	8	58.5

altitude produced from this observation
is 42° – 50 – 45.

Observed time and distance of Sun and Moon
nearest Limbs ☉ West. with Sextent

	Time			Distance		
P.M.	H.	M.	S.			
	4	21	44	91°	57	00
	"	22	53	91	57	90
	"	23	52	91	58	0
	"	24	37	91	58	15
	"	25	35	91	58	15
	"	26	42	91	58	30
	"	27	39	91	58	45
	"	28	17	91	59	15
	"	29	43	91	59	45
	"	31	10	92	0	0
	"	32	15	92	0	15
	"	33	8	92	0	45
	"	34	23	92	1	15
	"	35	30	92	1	30
	"	36	20	92	1	45

"he informed us [that his relations] were numerous and resided in the plain below the mountains on the columbia river, from whence he said the water was good and capable of being navigated to the sea; that some of his relations were at the sea last fall and saw an old whiteman who resided there by himself and who had given them some handkerchiefs such as he saw in our possession.—he said it would require five sleeps wich is six days travel, to reach his relations."

—LEWIS, SEPTEMBER 10, 1805, ON MEETING A NEZ PERCE AT TRAVELER'S REST

At the end of August, it could snow any day. Even at river level, the nights were frosty. But they had horses now, and Lewis had convinced Old Toby, a Shoshone man, to guide them, and on that thin strand of confidence they hung their fortune. They must have understood what they were risking. Although lacking experience in high mountains, they were exceedingly competent outdoorsmen. They knew horses. They knew the bush. And they knew their abilities enough to assess the considerable danger of what they were about to attempt.

On the first leg, Old Toby led them across high, stony ridges to the North Fork of the Salmon. From there, having to cut their way through dense thickets in places, they bushwhacked *"over emence hils and Some of the worst roade that ever horses passed,"* and somewhere near Lost Trail Pass (their exact route is disputed by researchers), crossed into the Bitterroot Valley.

They were getting a taste of what lay ahead. Much of the way, they followed a trail (they called it a "road" in those pre-vehicular times), but nothing as clear as the graded paths used by horsemen these days. It was more like a game trail, unimproved and littered with blowdowns. Several horses fell on the steep slopes; one was crippled from a fall. And where horses can fall, so can men. The Corps was not riding here. They were walking in soft moccasins, which on rocky slopes are about as slippery as wool socks. Hacking their way through thick brush, climbing over deadfalls, scrambling across steep gravel, enduring snow, sleet, and rain was tough enough without also feeling the pinch of hunger. Earlier in the journey Lewis had written that to eat plentifully, the party needed one bison every day, or an elk and a deer, or four deer. That wasn't possible here, and they weren't the only ones going hungry.

Along the East Fork of the Bitterroot River, at Ross' Hole, they met a band of Salish, or Flathead, Indians coming the other way, bound for the buffalo plains—400 people, 500 horses, 33 lodges, and nothing to eat but berries. The Corps managed to buy additional horses and exchanged seven of their poorer ones. But there was no feasting. When they parted company, it must have worried them to see all these Indians, on short rations, anxiously hurrying toward the plains while their own group continued west. They made better time below Ross' Hole, covering the seventy-six miles to Traveler's Rest, south of present-day Missoula, in four days. The country was lush, yet the hunters brought in only a few deer, a few grouse, and some berries. To make up the deficit, they ate the last of their flour and nearly all their cornmeal. Hunger was staring them in the face. So was the toughest traveling of the entire journey.

If it seems that after eighteen months on the trail, the Expedition should have been hardened enough to endure anything the mountains could throw at them, recall what they had done in just the past four months, starting with the Great Falls portage, where the effort was so severe that men fell asleep on rest breaks; the month of dragging cumbersome hollowed-out logs up the swift and rocky rivers, tormented by mosquitoes and heat; then two hard weeks converting the Expedition to horseback

THROUGH THE MOUNTAINS
Steep evergreen forests and cool autumn weather greeted the Corps as they began their arduous trek over the Bitterroot Range guided by a Shoshone man they called Old Toby. The journal page (left) shows a fish weir, or trap, used by Shoshones living on the Salmon River.

Following page: Packer Meadows, Glade Creek, Montana.

"The Mountains which we passed to day much worst than yesterday the last excessively bad & Thickly Strowed with falling timber & Pine Spruc fur Hackmatak & Tamerack, Steep & Stoney our men and horses much fatigued" — CLARK, SEPTEMBER 14, 1805

and hiking over the Divide; Clark's exhausting reconnaissance of the Salmon River, when no one in his party got enough to eat; and most recently, the 170-mile mountain trek to Traveler's Rest. Keep in mind that having horses to carry your load doesn't mean things get easy. You still have to walk the long hours through rough country. You have to load and unload the animals, make and break camp, hunt for food, haul it back, and cut it up and roast it over a fire—maybe in the rain—and maybe still feeling hungry, you lie down on the cold ground to sleep. In the morning, you catch the horses and start all over again, and it doesn't matter that you've been doing it every day for months, that your competence has grown so that even as a young man you have the experience of a veteran. Eventually the strongest body starts to wear down and needs a good, long recuperation.

But there was no time. They departed Traveler's Rest on September 11 and enjoyed half a day of fairly easy travel. It was on the second day that the country revealed its true character. Clark was already showing signs of fatigue when he wrote, *"The road through this hilley Countrey is verry bad passing over hills & thro' Steep hollows, over falling timber &c. &c.   continued on & passed Some most in tolerable road on the Sides of the Steep Stoney mountains, which might be avoided by keeping up the Creek which is thickly covered with under groth & falling timber."*

If it wasn't steep and rocky, it was a deadfall-choked streambed. They had an awful

PACKER MEADOWS

A pleasant opening in the dense evergreen forest surrounding Lolo Pass presented the Expedition with a rare stretch of easy travel at the end of a hard day. After topping the pass, Clark wrote, *"the road was verry fine, leavel open & firm Some mountains in view to the S E & S W. Covered with Snow."* They followed the meadow for a couple of miles and camped where the mountains closed in on either side.

Snake River   Salmon River   Lolo Pass   Traveler's Rest   Three Forks

NORTH

time. Horses fell down the timbered slopes; they ran out of food and couldn't kill enough game, so they killed colts. They scrounged for small meat: grouse, crayfish, even a coyote that someone shot. Near the end of the crossing, in an entry about food, Lewis writes *"Fields also killed a crow,"* and leaves the sentence unfinished. You can't help but wonder if they contemplated eating it. Or if they actually did. You have to be really hungry to eat a crow.

It snowed on the 16th of September. The very thought brings a shiver. September snow comes down wet, and because the ground isn't yet frozen it turns to slush as it piles up. You step in it and create a puddle. The trees drip like leaky rain gutters. Everything gets slippery. You can't stand on logs or slanted rocks without putting a hand down to steady yourself. Trails turn muddy beneath a slick layer of snow. It's hard enough in lug-soled boots. In moccasins, it would be hell. *"I have been wet and as cold in every part as I ever was in my life,"* Clark managed to scribble in his journal that night. He had seen four deer, but his rifle misfired seven times. They killed a colt for dinner. They slept on soggy ground in soggy blankets *"in a thickly timbered bottom which was Scercely large enough for us to lie leavil, men all wet cold and hungary."*

It was no better the next day, which ended with a miserable camp at what Expedition member Joseph Whitehouse called a *"Sinque hole full of water."* Having seen no game, they killed another colt to eat. Damp to the skin, muddy and hungry, and seemingly lost in the cold gray forest, they had reached a mental and physical low point. The Journals spare us emotional details, but the party's weariness is clearly evident. The Captains decided that Clark should take a few men with light loads and push ahead in hopes of finding food to send back.

That day turned out to be the darkness before dawn. Clark *did* manage to send food back. They *were* near the end of that awful trail, and on September 22, the main party dragged themselves to Weippe

WET SNOW

The mountains were rugged, the trails nearly nonexistent, and the men hungry. But it was the wet, sloppy snow that fell on the Lolo Trail on September 16, 1805, that made the Corps truly miserable.

Prairie, and the Nez Perce villages they had heard about. You can imagine them hobbling and wretched but relieved. They got a friendly welcome. They ate their fill of dried salmon and camas roots—staple foods for the Nez Perce. They luxuriated in the low-altitude warmth, taking pleasure in knowing that the last significant uncertainty of the journey was behind them. At last they had reached the Columbia River drainage. From here, the Nez Perce assured them, the rivers were navigable. No more walking. No more snowy passes between them and their long-anticipated arrival at continent's end. Lewis wrote: *"The pleasure I now felt in having triumphed over the rocky Mountains and decending once more to a level and fertile country where there was every rational hope of finding a comfortable subsistence for myself and party can be more readily conceived than expressed, nor was the flattering prospect of the final success of the expedition less pleasing."*

Pleasing yes, comfortable subsistence no. The camas roots and dried salmon supplied to them by the Nez Perce gave them serious indigestion. Clark, September 20: *"I find myself verry unwell all the evening from eateing the fish & roots too freely."* The next day: *"I am verry Sick to day and puke which relive me."* He tried to warn the main party when they arrived, but hungry men must eat—whatever the consequences and despite having to travel yet another twenty miles across the prairie to the river, where they planned to build dugouts for the onward journey. What a sight they must have made, this pitiful, intestinally distressed band of invalids. Again, Clark: *"Capt Lewis Scercely able to ride a jentle horse . . . Several men So unwell that they were Compelled to lie on the Side of the road for Some time others obliged to be put on horses."*

For more than two weeks, their health problems persisted. Camped on an island below the village of Chief Twisted Hair, they did their work between bouts of illness. Nearly all of them were incapacitated to some degree, but they had great motivation—not only to reach the ocean, but

"began to Snow about 3 hours before Day and Continud all day   the snow in The morning 4 Inches deep on The old Snow, and by night we found it from 6 to 8 Inches deep . . . I have been wet and as cold in every part as I ever was in my life, indeed I was at one time fearfull my feet would freeze in the thin mockersons which I wore" —CLARK, SEPTEMBER 16, 1805

also to escape the cause of their discomfort. The hunters had brought in only a few deer, and although they killed two horses for meat, they had no option but to consume big quantities of the troublesome camas roots.

Finally, on October 7, the canoes were launched and loaded. The Expedition's thirty-eight horses, branded with Lewis' iron, were left with three Nez Perce men who promised to look after them through the winter. Saddles and a small quantity of gear had been cached to await their return. They were armed with a map drawn by Chief Twisted Hair on white elkskin; and Twisted Hair was coming part way with them to serve as an interpreter and liaison with the tribes downstream.
It was time to go.

OBSTACLES

Despite the rigors of the Lolo Trail, Clark continued to make careful sketch maps, such as the one shown below, which covers September 11–12.

Left: John Clymer's painting, *Lewis and Clark in the Bitter Roots.*

Following page: The Clearwater River washes over its stony bed on the west side of the Continental Divide.

"We dined & suped on a skant proportion of portable soupe, a few canesters which, a little bears oil and about 20 lbs. of candles form our stock of provision, the only resources being our guns & packhorses. the first is but a poor dependance in our present situation where there is nothing upon earth except ourselves and a few small pheasants, small grey Squirrels, and a bluebird of the vulter kind about the size of a turtle dove or jay bird."—LEWIS, SEPTEMBER 18, 1805

FEEDING THE CORPS

To satisfy the ferocious appetites of their men, Lewis and Clark relied on a combination of stored provisions, freshly killed meat and fish, wild fruits and vegetables, and food purchased from various Indian tribes living along the Missouri and Columbia River systems.

Before departing, they stowed an enormous quantity of provisions on the keelboat. Clark compiled a list that tallied 3,400 pounds of flour, 3,750 pounds of corn and cornmeal, 50 kegs of salt pork, 750 pounds of salt, 560 pounds of biscuits, 112 pounds of sugar, 50 pounds of coffee, 100 pounds of lard, 600 pounds of unspecified grease, and 74 additional bushels (no weight specified) of corn and cornmeal. The list is incomplete. It leaves out items we know they carried: portable soup (which, despite Lewis' enthusiasm for this emergency ration, no one liked), honey (which, they dug out of trees near Camp Wood), some basic spices, and at least 120 gallons of whiskey.

It was a heavy load, but nowhere near enough food to fuel the Corps all the way to the Pacific and back. They obviously needed more than they could carry, and knew they would have to hunt, gather, and trade along the way. From the start, the Captains tried to husband their resources. They bought deer and other provisions from Indians and settlers along the Lower Missouri.

Hunting improved once they got well beyond the farthest white settlements. Abundant deer and black bear fed them across present-day Missouri. North of Kansas City, black bear dropped from the menu and elk was added. Then, near Sioux City, Joseph Field shot the animal they'd heard so much about—a buffalo, manna of the Great Plains nomads. Soon, roasted buffalo became the entree of choice, with rack of venison, elk cutlets, leg of pronghorn, grilled beaver tail, and fried catfish on the side. For dessert there were wild berries, cherries, plums, grapes, and apples.

During their winter with the Mandans, they alternately feasted and worried about where their next meal would come from. They participated in several major buffalo hunts but also ranged far and wide in search of deer and elk, which they packed back on horse-drawn sledges. On one week-long excursion, Lewis and a party of hunters brought back thirty-six deer and fourteen elk.

Hunting alone couldn't keep up with their keen winter appetites. They needed to buy dried corn, beans, squash, and jerky from the Mandans. Reluctant to tap their store of trade goods (they would need everything they had to acquire horses and more food farther west) they put Shields, their blacksmith, to work mending the Mandans' metal tools and pounding out new battle-axes.

There were plenty of animals to shoot the following spring, as the Corps worked its way into eastern Montana, but after the long winter the animals were lean (*"pore"* in the jargon of the time). Bison were so pore, Lewis said, that the Corps preferred to eat beaver. They soon found that while the adult bison were unpalatable, their calves were in prime shape, better than the finest veal Lewis ever tasted. By early summer, all the *"it was white & not unlike the fat of Poark, tho' the texture was more spongey and somewhat coarser. I had a part of it cooked and found it very pallitable and tender, it resembled the beaver or the dog in flavour. it may appear somewhat extraordinary tho' it is a fact that the flesh of the beaver and dog possess a great affinity in point of flavour."*—LEWIS, ON WHALE BLUBBER, JANUARY 5, 1806

animals were fat. They ate bison, deer, elk, antelope, more bison, and, once they got into the rugged cliffs of the Missouri Breaks, bighorn sheep.

On July 13 Lewis wrote *"we eat an emensity of meat; it requires 4 deer, an Elk and a deer, or one buffaloe, to supply us plentifully 24 hours."* How much meat is that? Hunters usually figure a quarter to a third of an animal's live weight is meat. A bull bison weighs 800 to 2,000 pounds; elk run 700 to 1,000; mule deer are 150 to 400. By some estimates, the men were eating about 9 pounds of meat per day.

They didn't merely roast it on a spit. Charbonneau showed them how to make six-foot sausages he called boudin blanc, or white pudding (see recipe, p. 82). Sacagawea, in turn, gathered wild licorice and the tuberous bulbs of breadroot, which Lewis called the *"whiteapple,"* and deemed *"a tastless insipid food: . . . I have no doubt our epicures would admire this root very much, it would serve them in their ragouts and gravies in stead of the truffles morella."* Sacagawea also gathered wild beans called hog peanuts, which she found in hoards collected by meadow mice.

Beyond Great Falls, they entered the broad intermountain valleys of southwestern Montana and passed out of prime buffalo country. Once again, deer, elk, and antelope became staples. Those animals remained in abundant supply to around Three Forks, where game began to thin out.

Hungry times set in around Lemhi Pass. Cameahwait and his band of Shoshones were nearly starving when the Expedition met them. Clark returned from a reconnaissance of the Salmon River gaunt. His men openly voiced their concern about starving in the mountains. The summer salmon runs were nearly finished. The Shoshones and Flatheads they encountered were headed east to the buffalo country for the winter, while the Expedition pushed on westward, eating the last of their cornmeal, flour, and detested dried soup as, day after day, the hunters came up

short. On the starvation trek over the Lolo Trail, the hunters produced about one day's ration to cover ten days of travel; they made up only part of the difference by killing several colts and a horse.

Things weren't a whole lot better on the west side of the Rockies, where they made an intestinally explosive adjustment to a diet of dried salmon, dried berries, and dried roots (camas at first and then wapato, either boiled or pounded and made into a sort of bread). The hunters brought in a trickle of venison, but otherwise, the only fresh meat was domestic dog—more than one hundred canines purchased from the various Sahaptian-and Chinookan-speaking peoples who lived along the Snake and Columbia Rivers.

Later, during their coastal winter, the hunters shot large numbers of elk but had trouble preserving the meat. It spoiled easily in the damp climate. And by then the Corps was so poor that they could not afford to buy much fresh fish from the Clatsops. All along, they sampled local cuisine and sat down to the occasional Indian banquet. It seems they weren't one bit squeamish. They ate grilled prairie dogs, found a coyote tasty, drank beer concocted by Collins from spoiled camas-root bread, chewed up a wolf, and relished the blubber from a beached whale. On the coast, they learned about eulachon, or candle fish, so named because it was so oily you could light a dried one and it would burn like a candle. In the Rockies they angled for trout, dredged it in flour, and fried it in bear grease. As for vegetables, they weren't exactly in salad country, but when they could get them, they enjoyed beans and squash, wild onions, scurf pea, thistles, watercress, and more.

In the end, they had literally eaten their way across the country on a culinary adventure that today we might call the original cook's tour of America.

October 10, 1805—It's a warm, cloudy evening at the confluence of the Snake and Clearwater rivers, and William Clark, reluctant diner, is facing down a plate of boiled dogmeat. Everyone else in camp loves the stuff, relishing it as a welcome change from the dried fish and roots that had proved such an explosive combination during the long and flatulent sojourn among the Nez Perce. But Clark feels no such joy as he chews and swallows; gazes across the quick, blue-green current of the Snake; and takes in the billowing hills of velvet brown that rise hundreds of feet above the water.

"Our diet extremely bad," he concludes.

Deep down, though, he must have felt grateful to have anything at all to eat. The Expedition had been on short rations ever since ditching their cottonwood dugouts on the far side of the Rockies. They had nearly starved on the Lolo. And in the past couple of weeks, they'd killed just eight deer while they recuperated from their alpine ordeal, built five new dugouts, and plunged down the rapids of the Clearwater River.

Now they were on the mend, gaining strength every day, their innards finally adjusting to the new diet, the current of a mighty

ON TO THE SEA

Pacific Ocean

Columbia River

Snake River

Clearwater River

NORTH

river at their backs, their canoes shuddering through miles of thundering whitewater—pitching headlong into great standing waves, slamming into boulders, splitting open, at times foundering, even sinking while nonswimmers clung to the hull and waited for a rope. They lost tomahawks to the river, along with shot pouches, bedding, and clothing, but never a man, never a canoe, never a rifle. They would have portaged more often, Clark wrote, as they continued down the turbulent Snake, if they weren't in such a hurry.

Theirs was an urgent task now, the season late, the obstacles ahead unknown. Making miles was the order of the day. But if urgency ruled their pace, a growing sense of exhilaration and triumph must have risen in their hearts. They had crossed the Rocky Mountains. In doing so, they had cleared up the essential geographic mystery of their day. Now they were poised to achieve their primary objective of standing on a Pacific beach with the whole of the North American continent behind them. Perhaps they'd meet a ship out there. A ship that would take them home or at least replenish their diminishing stock of Indian trade goods. And if it were British? Why, then they'd have the satisfaction of watching the British officers politely gnash their teeth for Old King George while the Captains told them all about the "heretofore unknown lands" of the interior.

Joyful prospects indeed. Heady and patriotic, too, for such men to know they were establishing a bold and tangible American claim to the Oregon Country.

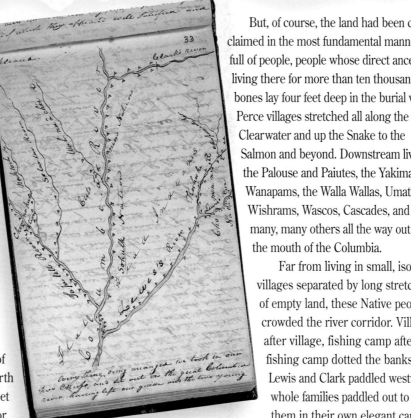

But, of course, the land had been claimed already, and claimed in the most fundamental manner possible. It was full of people, people whose direct ancestors had been living there for more than ten thousand years and whose bones lay four feet deep in the burial vaults. The Nez Perce villages stretched all along the Clearwater and up the Snake to the Salmon and beyond. Downstream lived the Palouse and Paiutes, the Yakimas and Wanapams, the Walla Wallas, Umatillas, Wishrams, Wascos, Cascades, and many, many others all the way out to the mouth of the Columbia.

Far from living in small, isolated villages separated by long stretches of empty land, these Native peoples crowded the river corridor. Village after village, fishing camp after fishing camp dotted the banks. As Lewis and Clark paddled westward, whole families paddled out to greet them in their own elegant canoes, then continued on their way—off to visit friends or to trade at neighboring villages. As the members of the Corps of Discovery wrestled their dugouts through various stretches of whitewater, they passed dozens of Indian men spearing salmon. Groups of women waded in the marshy backwaters, pulling up wapato roots with their toes as they gabbed about their families. Or they worked on

ON THE COLUMBIA
Opposite: The massive lava flows of the Columbia Plateau form stair-stepping ledges throughout the arid, eastern portion of the Columbia River Gorge. Inset journal page shows the confluence of the Snake, Columbia, and Yakima Rivers in the vicinity of the Tri-Cities area of Washington. The map at bottom shows the approximate territories of the Columbia River peoples.

Following spreads:
DOWN THE COLUMBIA
John Clymer's 1978 painting *Angry River* depicts the Corps running rapids on the Columbia River system after crossing the Rocky Mountains in late fall 1805.

Yakimas
Cascades
Chinooks
Walla Wallas
Wanapams
Wishrams
Wascos
Nez Perce

John Clymer ©1978

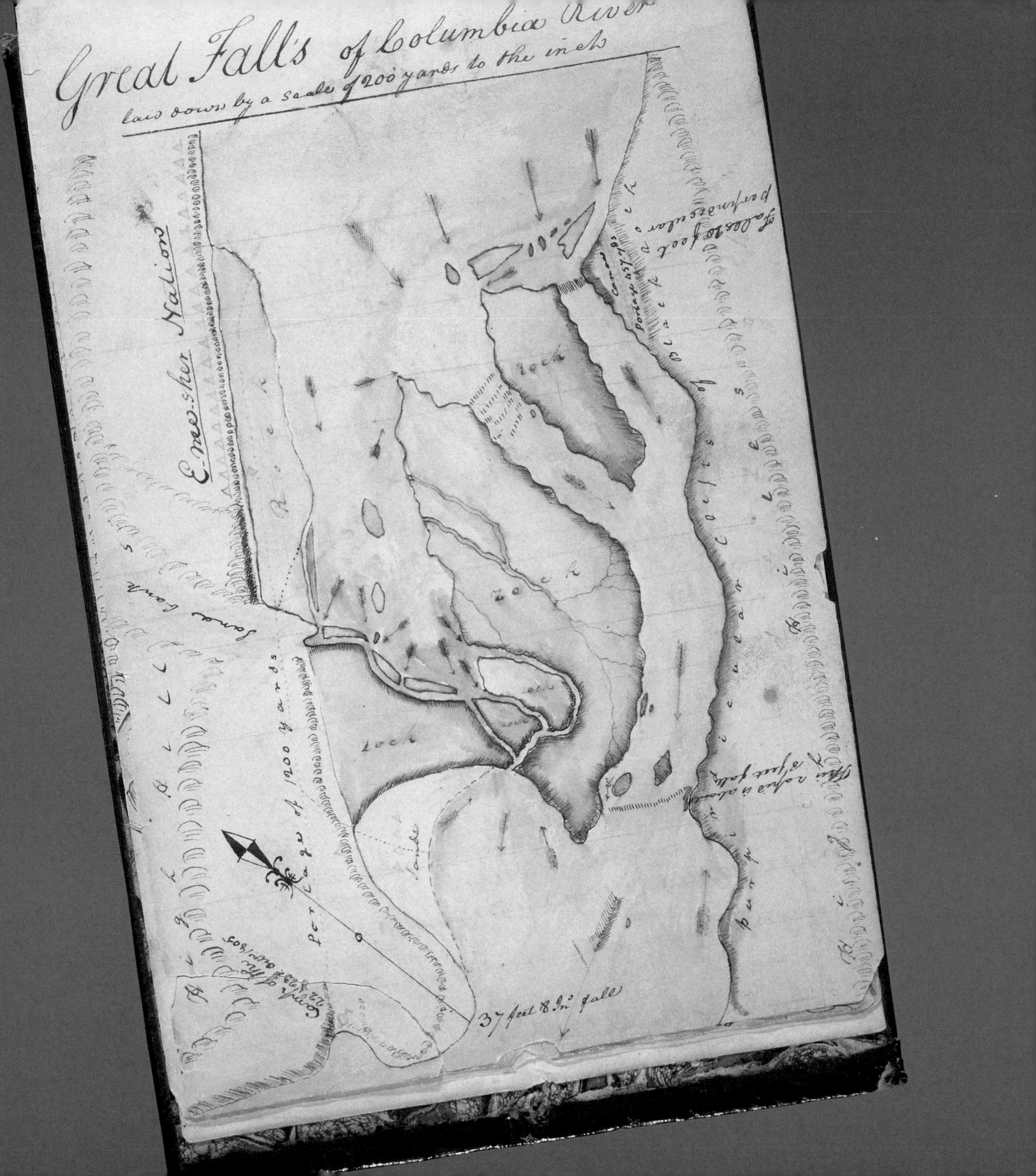

Great Falls of Columbia River

laid down by a scale of 200 yards to the inch

Eneeshur Nation

River

Portage 457 yds

Black a Creek

rock

rock

rock

rock

37 feet 8 In: fall

Portage of 1200 yards

Portage of the 22 Octer 1805

"The wife of Shabano our interpetr we find reconsiles all the Indians, as to our friendly intentions a woman with a party of men is a token of peace." —CLARK, OCTOBER 13, 1805

the banks, drying salmon on scaffolds, playing with their children, pounding the dried fish into meal, packing the meal into standardized beargrass baskets, and stacking the baskets in neat piles on the rocks and cliffs above the river. Kibitzers often gathered when the Captains paused to scout a particularly difficult set of rapids. They watched, offered advice, helped out, and sometimes swiped a knife or a shirt by way of payment or tribute.

Lewis and Clark had never experienced anything like it. Back on the Great Plains, they had gone for weeks between encounters with Indians. After leaving the Mandan villages, they had traveled for five straight months before meeting the Shoshones. Now they were seeing Indians almost every day.

At the confluence of the Snake and Columbia, it was the Wanapams and Yakimas. They marched into the Expedition's camp two hundred strong, sang, danced, and gave the men twenty pounds of fat horse meat. Salmon were so plentiful at the confluence that the Indians used the dried fish as fuel. Dogs were in abundance too: the Corps shoved off with forty in the canoes. As the Columbia led them on through grand desert canyons faced with lava cliffs, the Captains accepted baskets of berries from the Walla Wallas and scarce firewood from the Umatillas. They bought dogs and fish, roots, acorns, and sometimes firewood from the Methows, Tapanash, Wishram, and Wascos. They even traded in one of their dugouts for a fine, lightweight Indian canoe *"neeter made,"* Clark said, *"than any I have ever Seen."*

Neater made than their own, certainly, but even in their ponderous dugouts, the Corps' paddlers managed quite well, even in difficult whitewater. Their boating skills really shined, though, in the depths of the Columbia Gorge, where they entered the most dangerous section of the river. It began about six miles below the mouth of the Deschutes River at Celilo Falls and extended for roughly eighty miles, taking in such explosive landmarks as the Short Narrows, the Long Narrows, the Cascades, and dozens of other, less ferocious stretches of rocky whitewater.

Celilo Falls gave them little trouble. They portaged it in a day with the help of some locals the Captains hired to haul the baggage by horseback. The following morning, they reached the head of the Short Narrows, where a chasm of black, flat-topped cliffs squeezed the entire breadth of the Columbia into a single channel of roaring whitewater just forty-five yards wide. The Indians considered it impassable. But Clark and Cruzatte (the Expedition's best boatman) climbed onto the cliffs to see for themselves. They took in what Clark called *"the horrid appearance of this agitated gut Swelling, boiling & whorling in every direction,"* then turned to each other and shrugged. It was just big water—huge standing waves, lots of foam and eddies, with rocks safely buried far beneath the rushing surface. If they could avoid the cliff faces on either side and stay upright in the waves, then the furious current would flush them straight through.

"We passed Safe," Clark said, *"to the astonishment of all the Ind[ians]."* He did admit, though, that *"from the top of the rock [the water] did not appear as bad as when I was in it."*

It never does. Rapids always seem worse with a paddle in the water and your butt at gunwale height, the boat lifting and dropping over the waves, sweeping past rocks, tipping, righting, coming up on the next wave or set of cliffs way too fast, the adrenaline pumping and the spray in your face.

It would be a thrill to take a raft through the Short Narrows today, but it can't be done. You can't even stand on the same high rock where Clark and Cruzatte scouted the whitewater. Both the rapids and the rock lie underwater. So do the Long Narrows and the Cascades, Celilo Falls, and virtually all of the other rapids the Corps

COLUMBIA WHITEWATER
Clark's map of the Great Falls of the Columbia (facing page) shows two portage routes. The Expedition used the route along the left side of the map to portage their baggage, and used the route along the right side to portage their canoes. His smaller map (left) sketches the Cascades of the Columbia, a 10-mile stretch of rapids that began at present-day Cascade Locks and emptied into tidewater near Beacon Rock.

Pacific Ocean Cascades of the Columbia Mt. Hood Mt. Rainier Celilo Falls Short and Long Narrows Deschutes River The Dalles John Day River Columbia River Snake River

NORTH

of Discovery ran on the Snake and Columbia Rivers. They have been submerged behind a series of hydroelectric dams. So have the sites of virtually all of the Indian villages. And the salmon runs—the bountiful flood tides of protein that once sustained the tribes—have been decimated by the turbines and hundreds of miles of slackwater reservoirs.

The Corps repeated its bravura paddling performance on the Long Narrows, and then pulled over for a much-needed rest at a flat-topped promontory overlooking the river (in The Dalles). They dubbed the place Fort Rock and camped there for three days, repairing their battered canoes, drying the cargo, and hunting in the wooded foothills of Mt. Hood. Much to Clark's joy, they dropped dog from the menu and feasted on venison, geese, and steelhead trout fried in bear's oil, *"The finest fish I ever tasted."* Harbor seals bobbed in the river and would have provided the Corps with plenty of rich red meat all the way to the coast, except that the animals always sank when shot.

Soon they were underway again, gliding beyond the last of the semi-arid shortgrass hills and then slipping into the lush, western forests of the Columbia Gorge, where the drizzling climate of the Northwest Coast stalls against the Cascade Range. Rain splattered off the paddlers' backs for days on end, soaking them to the skin. Waterfalls poured from the heights. Colossal trees, ten to twelve feet in diameter, towered above their camps. Moss, ferns, vines, and tangled shrubs crowded the forest floor, and the mist was sometimes so thick that a man could not be seen at fifty paces.

As they passed into this sodden climate, the Corps also entered an entirely different Native culture. The many Chinookan peoples who lived here spoke a much different language from the Sahaptian-speakers above Celilo Falls. They built large plank houses decorated with elaborate wood carvings, practiced infant head-flattening, drove hard bargains, and paddled out from their numerous villages in gorgeous canoes that the Corps came to envy.

The farther west they traveled, the more European trade goods the men saw among the Indians—brass kettles, cutlasses, knives, guns, powder flasks, sailors' clothing. The presence of these items both cheered and distressed them. It meant they were getting closer to the coast, but it also meant that their own diminishing stock of trade goods was losing value. Prices went from outrageous to unconscionable, and the Captains liked it about as much as a North Dakotan likes paying off a New York cabbie. They felt gouged and preyed upon at every turn, and it began to dawn on them just how grim the winter might be if they didn't find a ship at the mouth of the Columbia.

Still, there were consolations. On November 2, they cleared the last of the Cascades rapids and emerged, Clark rightly noted, on water that *"had everry appearance of being effected by the tide."* The next day, they passed a steep, wooded point near Corbett, Oregon, and paddled back onto George Vancouver's map of the Columbia—seven months and roughly 2,365 miles from the Mandan villages, by Clark's reckoning. On November 5, near present-day Kalama, they spotted the Coast Ranges and spent their first night in nearly a month, Clark said, *"entirely clear of Indians."*

But the rain streamed down all the way. Temperatures dropped. Their buckskin shirts, leggings, and moccasins rotted to shreds in the dank and could not be replaced because the underbrush was too thick for the hunters to walk through. The food was awful, the whiskey long gone, the tobacco in

Snake River   Clearwater River   Three Forks

North

"the Indians left us and Crossed the river which is about 5 miles wide through the highest Sees I ever Saw a Small vestle ride, their Canoe is Small, maney times they were out of Sight before the were 2 miles off Certain it is they are the best canoe navigators I ever Saw"

—CLARK, STORMBOUND, NOVEMBER 11, 1805

alarmingly short supply. Clark's succinct summary of their condition—*"we are all wet cold and disagreeable"*—became an almost-daily refrain.

Then, on the morning of November 7, as the Corps paddled west of present-day Skamokawa, Oregon, a thick fog lifted from the river, the clouds parted, and then, amid the gleeful hoots and howls of the men, William Clark reached for a notebook and scribbled this immortal line: *"Ocian in view! O! the joy."*

The joy, indeed. It filled their hearts and carried them on for another twenty-six miles that day. It buoyed their spirits as they pitched their tattered tents in the rain, and it must have generated a calm sense of well-being and self-satisfaction as the men took their ease around the kettles of pounded fish and gazed out upon the open water.

"Great joy in camp," Clark wrote. *"We are in View of the Ocian, this great Pacific Octean which we been So long anxious to See. and the roreing or noise made by the waves brakeing on the rockey Shores (as I Suppose) may be heard disticly."*

Actually, they were still looking at the Columbia River estuary. The open ocean lay twenty miles west—no great distance, just a half-day's trip at the rate they were going. But as the Expedition paddled along the steep, rocky slopes of the north shore, the weather took a savage turn. Huge waves and brutal storms stranded them for days at a time in a series of desperate, sometimes floating camps crammed against the cliffs. Wind, thunder, hail, lightning, and rain: the elements raged on as they huddled virtually unprotected in dismal little coves that flooded with every high tide. Driftwood logs two hundred feet long and seven feet thick surged toward them on the swells. They had to sink the

COASTAL CANOES

Charles M. Russell's painting (right) showing a meeting between Indians and the Expedition on the lower Columbia River features the elegant cedar canoes of the Northwest Coast. So does Lewis' journal entry (below) for February 1, 1806, which includes sketches of three different styles of canoe.

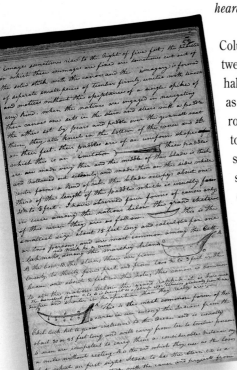

Pacific Ocean   Columbia River Estuary   "Ocian" in View   Willamette River   Columbia River   Snake River

NORTH

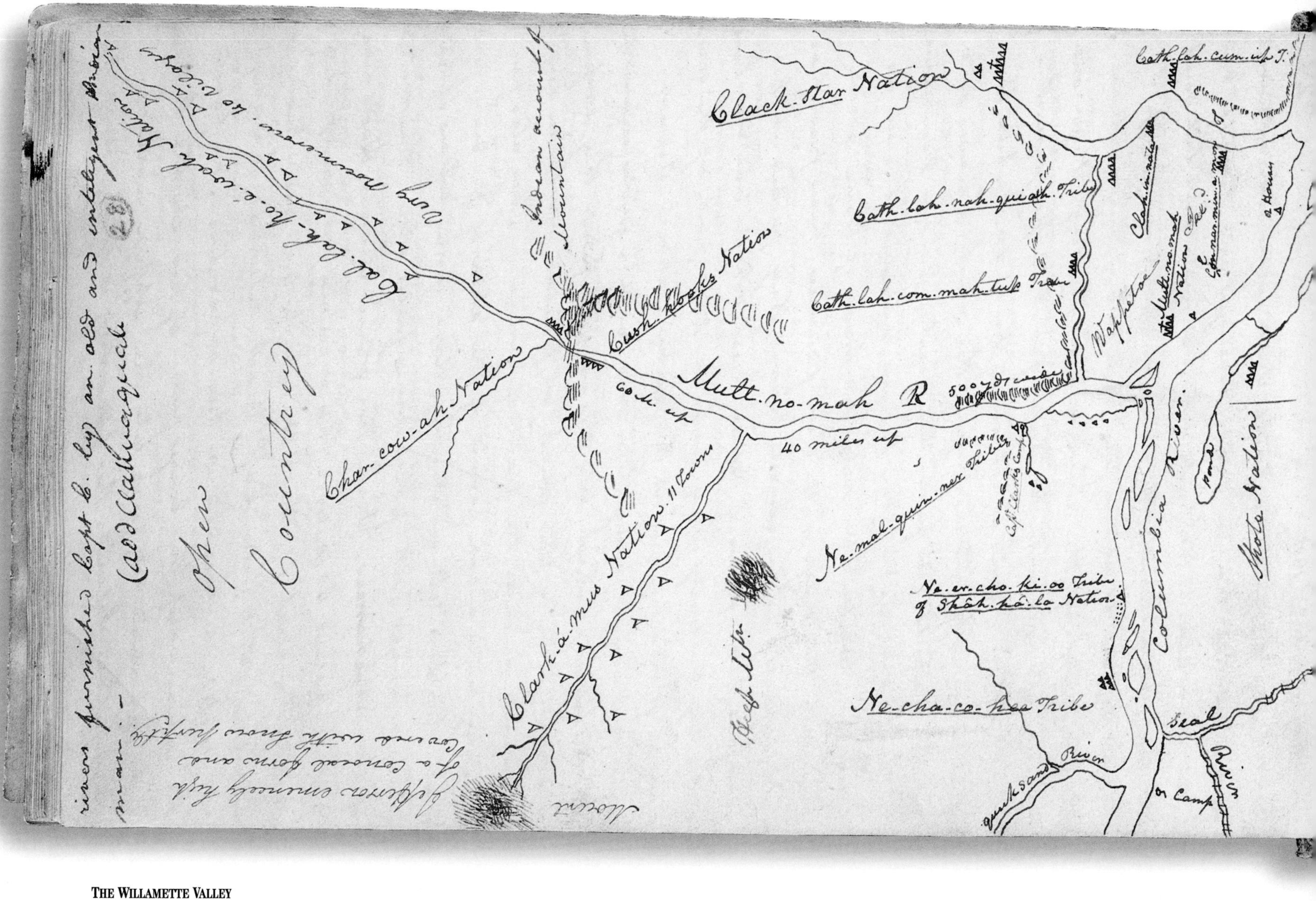

Clack Star Nation

Cath.lah.cum.ip.T.

Cath.lah.nah.qui.ah Tribe

Cath.lah.com.mah.tup Trou

Cush hooks Nation

Wappeto

Clah.ni.na.ta Nat.

Clutimat.nat.
mat Nation oJ.

Char-cow-ah Nation

Mult.no.mah R

500 yds wide

Shoto Nation

Columbia River.

60 m. up

40 miles up

Ne.mal.quin.ner Tribe

Ya.er.cho.ki.oo Tribe
of Shah.ha.la Nation

Clark.a.mus Nation 11 Towns

Ne.cha.co.hee Tribe

Quicksand River

Seal River

or Camp

THE WILLAMETTE VALLEY

Clark's map shows the confluence of the Columbia River and the Willamette (which Clark labeled the Mult-no-mah). On the westbound journey in early November 1805, the Corps passed through the area but missed seeing the mouth of the Willamette because it was obscured by a large island. They missed it again on the return voyage in early April 1806, but some Indians told them about the

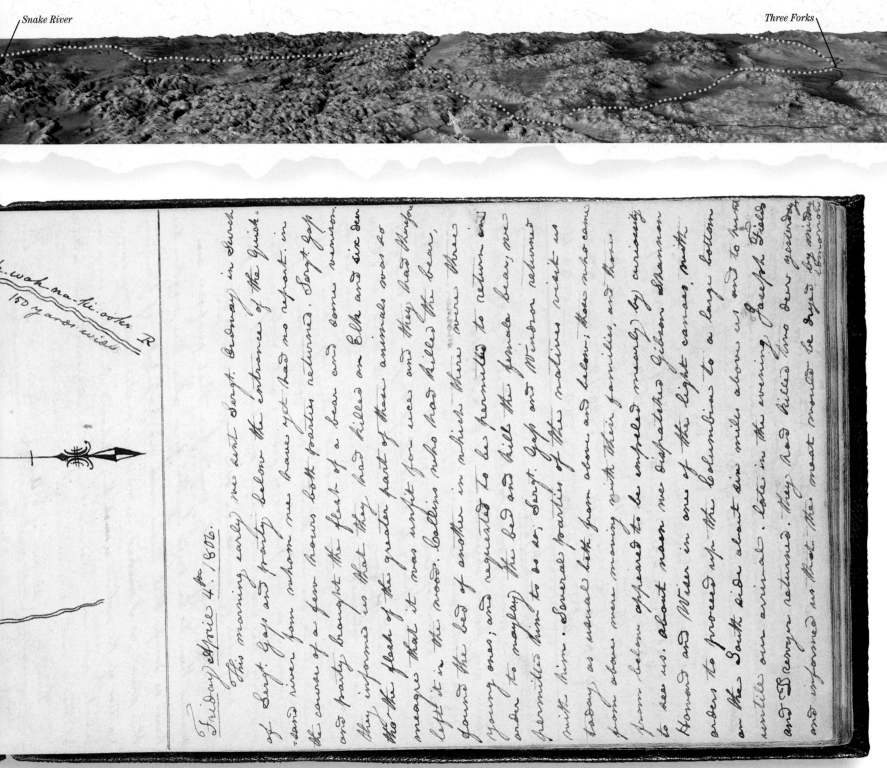

Willamette and guided Clark 10 miles up its course. *"I provailed,"* Clark wrote, *"on an old man to draw me a Sketch of the Multnomar River ang give me the names of the nations resideing on it which he readily done."* Lewis' journal entry for April 4, 1806, sketches the activities of various hunting parties he and Clark dispatched near the mouth of the Willamette to gather and dry meat for the journey up the Columbia. They had been told by Indians of a famine upriver. Following pages: Clouds form over the Columbia River.

LEWIS & CLARK

canoes under heaps of rocks to prevent the waves from battering them to splinters against the cliffs. Clothing was scarce. It had rotted away, as had their bedding, their tents, and the Captains' fine tipi. Small stones and gravel rattled down on them from the slopes, and the river water was so brackish it qualified as a laxative.

Perhaps most frustrating of all, Indians paddled casually in and out of camp through the very swells that kept the Corps of Discovery pinned to the cliffs. *"Those people left us,"* Clark wrote after a group of Cathlamets dropped by to sell fish, *"and Crossed the river (which is about 5 miles wide at this place) through the highest waves I ever Saw a Small vestles ride. Those Indians are Certainly the best Canoe navigaters I ever Saw."*

Finally, on November 15, the entire party got around Point Ellice (opposite present-day Astoria) and landed on *"a butifull Sand beech"* near a vacant Indian village. *"This I could plainly See would be the extent of our journey by water,"* Clark wrote, *"as the waves were too high at any Stage for our Canoes to proceed any further down."*

So, while Lewis led a small group to the coast on foot, Clark and most of the men camped on the beach, living like potentates (relatively speaking) in crude little huts built from planks scrounged at the village. The weather moderated. The hunters brought in fresh meat, and parties of Chinooks and Clatsops visited regularly, offering roots, fish, baskets, hats, furs, and sex. Commerce in the last category was in such great and urgent demand that the Captains had to issue bits of colorful ribbon to keep the men from trading away their knives and other valuables. *"Several Indians and Squars came this evening I beleave for the purpose of gratifying the passions of our men,"* Clark wrote at one point. *"The young women Sport openly with our men . . . maney of the women are handsom."*

O! THE JOY

While paddling on November 7, 1805, the party saw what Clark and everyone else thought was the Pacific Ocean, and that night they camped within earshot of breaking waves. However, what they saw was the turbulent Columbia River Estuary. The true ocean still lay twenty miles west. Right: Radiant sunlight silhouettes the steep slopes of the Columbia River Gorge. Following page: Impenetrable moss-laden forests along the Columbia River Estuary were so dense that at times the Expedition's hunters could not penetrate them.

Snake River

Three Forks

"It is almost incredeable to assurt the bogs which those animals Can pass through. I prosue'd this gang of Elk through bogs which the wate of a man would Shake for 1/2 an Acre, and maney places I Sunk into the mud and water up to my hips without finding any bottom on the trale of those Elk." —CLARK, DECEMBER 8, 1805

After his four-day reconnaissance of the coast, Lewis returned to camp. He'd seen neither ship nor trading post, so they'd just have to make due with what little trade goods remained. Still, if they found a good spot for a fort somewhere near the coast, they might yet see a ship, restock, and hoist a glass with people who would truly appreciate their accomplishment.

For now, though, it was time to savor the triumph among themselves. Clark, eager to make his own ramble along the coast, invited anyone who was interested to join him. Eleven men accepted, and they set off the next morning at dawn. It must have been a jolly group. Footloose, carefree, no longer racing the calendar, they spent three days strolling along the surf, beachcombing, scrambling over headlands, carving their names into trees, and admiring the mountainous swells that exploded against the black cliffs at high tide. They gawked at curious animals that had washed up on shore—a Risso's dolphin, a flounder, a ten-foot sturgeon, a whale. And they shot whatever they pleased: a California condor for science, forty-eight plover for lunch, a Columbian black-tailed deer for breakfast grilled over a driftwood bonfire.

They wandered as far north as present-day Long Beach, but perhaps it's best to leave them farther south, camped on the beach with a fire to warm them, the continent at their backs, and the sun fading west and low over the restless Pacific Ocean.

"Men appear much Satisfied with their trip," Clark wrote that evening, *"beholding with estonishment the high waves dashing against the rocks & this emence ocian."*

BOGGY GROUND

Left: The coastal forests around Fort Clatsop abounded with bogs that often stymied the Expedition's hunters as they tracked elk. Below: Detail of Fort Clatsop replica near present-day Astoria.

93

e fish which now begin to run and are
great quantities in the Columbia R.
40 miles above us by means of skiming
ping nets. on this page I have drawn
reness of them as large as life; it
fect as I can make it with my
and will serve to give a
ral idea of the fish. the
of the fins are boney but
sharp tho' somewhat pointed.
small fin on the back
ct to the tail has no
ys of bone being a
caranous pellicle.
the gills have
ach. those of the
eight each, those
are 20 and 2
that of the back
the fins are of
is of a bleuish
the the lower
part. the
behid the
second of
the purple
and
a silver
like

thin mem.
the fins next
eleven rays
abdomen have
of the pinnaani
naff formed in front.
has eleven rays. all
a white colour. the back
duskey colour and that of
part of the sides and belley
ry white. no spots on any
first bone of the gills next
eye is of a bleuis cast, and the
a light goald colour nearly white.
of the eye is black and the iris of
white. the under jaw exceeds the uper;
the mouth opens to great extent, folding;
that of the herring. it has no teeth.
the abdomen is obtuse and smooth; in this
differing from the herring, shad, anchovy;
&c of the Malacapterygiaus Order & Class
Clupea

93

R
No. 81

During the winter of 1805–06, Lewis made this sketch of a eulachon, a small marine fish related to smelt. It was an important dietary item for Northwest Indians, and was relished by the Expedition. Lewis wrote they *"are taken in great quantities in the Columbia R. about 40 miles above us by means of skiming or scooping nets. on this page I have drawn the likeness of them as large as life; it as perfect as I can make it with my pen and will serve to give a general idea of the fish . . . I find them best when cooked in Indian stile, which is by roasting a number of them together on a wooden spit ... they are so fat they require no additional sauce and I think them superior to any fish I ever tasted."*

"a Cloudy rainey morning verry early I rose and walked on the Shore of the Sea coast and picked up Several Curious Shells. I Saw Indians walking up and down the beech which I did not at first understand the Cause of, one man came to where I was and told me that he was in Serch of fish which is frequently thrown up on Shore and left by the tide, and told me [in English] the 'Sturgion was verry good' and that the water when it retired left fish which they eate" —CLARK, DECEMBER 10, 1805

When Lewis and Clark shoved off from Fort Mandan in April 1805, they hoped they might reach the Pacific in time to double back over the Rockies and spend another winter among the affable Mandans. No such luck. Instead, they passed the winter of 1805–06 several miles southwest of present-day Astoria in a small enclosure of log huts they built among the damp, mossy forests of towering Sitka spruce. Named Fort Clatsop for the Indians who lived close by, the little outpost stood fifty feet square, was gated front and back, and consisted of two rows of shed-roofed buildings that faced one another across a narrow, rectangular courtyard. Clark described the site as a *"most eligable Situation."* It was within a day's walk of the ocean, offered access to the Columbia estuary, and stood well above high tide. A nearby spring provided fresh water. There were plenty of trees for lumber and firewood. And the elk hunting was good, at least at first.

The Expedition arrived at the site on December 7 after a miserable trip across the estuary that included ten straight stormbound days in conditions far worse than any they had experienced on Point Ellice. As the men cut trees, split timbers, roofed their huts, and built chimneys, the skies opened up on them. Rain fell continuously, sometimes joined by hail and snow. Lightning flashed, thunder rolled, and the great trees swayed in ferocious winds. Still, the Corps took just over two weeks to finish their huts and were *"Snugly fixed,"* Clark reported, in time for a Christmas supper of tainted elk, spoiled fish, and a few roots.

That dreary holiday meal set the tone for the rest of the winter. Though snug in their huts, the members of the Expedition lived in Spartan circumstances, sustained by a grim diet of boiled elk, fish, roots, and the occasional dog bought from the Clatsops by way of a treat. Meat spoiled easily in the warm and sodden climate. Fires were difficult to keep lit. There was no dram of whiskey to look forward to and very little tobacco. The men came down with flu, colds, strained muscles, boils, and venereal disease. And though the Clatsops visited almost daily and provided the men with frequent sexual diversion, relations never approached the level of sincere camaraderie the Expedition had enjoyed the previous winter with the Mandans.

Work kept boredom at bay. The men hunted for elk and packed the meat and hides back through bogs and dense forests crisscrossed with enormous fallen trees. They jerked or smoked the meat, tanned the hides, and used the leather to replace all that had rotted away as they traveled down the Columbia: mocassins, leggings, shirts, bedding, tarps, ropes, packs, and other items. They chopped firewood, mounted guard, and made occasional forays to the beach near present-day Seaside, where a party of Expedition men made salt from sea water.

The Captains oversaw the men's chores and traded with visiting Indians, but they spent most of the time at their desks, writing in their journals, drawing charts and diagrams, and rummaging through notes

AT FORT CLATSOP
The tanned hide (opposite top) shows one of the plans the Captains drew up for Fort Clatsop. Clymer's painting (opposite bottom) depicts the Expedition's salt-making operation near present-day Seaside, Oregon. Above: A carved wooden bowl and a sprig of spruce. Below: An oufitted Chinookan canoe.

A COASTAL WINTER

"We would have Spent this day the nativity of Christ in feasting, had we any thing either to raise our Sperits or even gratify our appetites, our Diner concisted of pore Elk, So much Spoiled that we eate it thro' mear necessity, Some Spoiled pounded fish and a fiew roots." —CLARK, DECEMBER 25, 1805

and specimens. Clark's work focused on mapping the West from Fort Mandan to the mouth of the Columbia. His masterpiece finally substituted hard geographic fact for the vast expanse of white space and conjecture that had filled previous maps of the American West. He and Lewis pored over it, noting with satisfaction that they had fulfilled Jefferson's instructions to find the most practical and navigable route to the Pacific. True enough, but "most practical and navigable" left a lot to be desired. Clark's map would also obliterate Jefferson's hopes for a mostly water route across the continent.

Lewis kept his quill pen flying all winter, describing and sketching dozens of plants and a hundred animals. Of these, ten plants, eleven mammals, two fish, and eleven birds were new to science. He wrote at length about the various Indian peoples who lived nearby, explaining how they harvested and prepared various roots and fish; gently flattened the heads of their infants; built houses; carved canoes; designed bows and arrows, fishing tackle, and clothing. He also took a lively interest in how his own men got things done, writing, for example, a five-hundred-word description of how Drouillard baited beaver traps.

Lewis and Clark expected to remain at Fort Clatsop until April, but by early March, food had become a grave concern. The hunters had shot out the elk, and the Captains could not afford to buy much more food from the Clatsops. Their remaining stock of trade goods, they wrote, could fit easily into a large handkerchief. They decided it was time to bid adieu to the dreary walls of Fort Clatsop.

But first, Lewis tried to buy two Indian canoes. Prices were high, Lewis desperately poor. He paid for one with his own uniform coat but felt he could not afford the other. And so, in a shameful departure from his usual pattern of scrupulous honesty when dealing with Indians, Lewis ordered his men to steal the second canoe. Thus equipped, the Corps of Discovery embarked from Fort Clatsop on March 23, 1806. Before they left, the Captains posted in their quarters a list of the Expedition's members and a sketch of Clark's map of their route from St. Louis to the Pacific.

"She [Sacagawea] observed, "that She had traveled a long way with us to See the great waters, and that now that monstrous fish was also to be Seen, She thought it verry hard that She Could not be permitted to See either (She had never yet been to the Ocian)." —CLARK, JANUARY 6–10, 1806

A SEASIDE LARK

When Clark announced his plan to cross Tillamook Head (pictured at right) and see a beached whale, Sacagawea pleaded to go along, so Clark included her in the party. Clark's map shows the hiking route from their winter camp over Tillamook Head to find the beached whale in January 1806. In the following spread, Clymer's painting, *Sacagawea at the Big Water,* depicts her joy.

"we loaded our Canoes & at 1 P.M. left Fort Clatsop on our homeward bound journey. at this place we had wintered and remained from the 7th of Decr. 1805 to this day and have lived as well as we had any right to expect"

—CLARK, MARCH 23, 1806

It's late March, the weather cold and unsettled. The Expedition, driven by the pent-up energy of a hard winter, is eager to be moving. St. Louis stands three thousand miles away—up the Columbia and the Snake and the Clearwater to the Nez Perce villages, back over the mountains on the dreaded Lolo Trail, back to the boats they had hidden on the Beaverhead, and then all those long miles down the muddy Missouri. This time, at least, they know what to expect.

They left Fort Clatsop in a truculent mood—truculent enough to steal that canoe from the Clatsops. The theft stands out as unusual behavior for the generally honest and respectful Lewis and Clark. But if they felt guilty about it, they were soon on the receiving end of theft much more brazen than they ever contemplated, which only served to make them more truculent.

They were also worried. After a week of upstream travel, they met Indians coming downriver looking for food, talking about the tough winter along the upper Columbia. People were hungry. Hunting was poor and the salmon migration had not yet begun. *"This information,"* wrote Clark, *"gives us much uneasiness with respect to our*

HOMEWARD BOUND

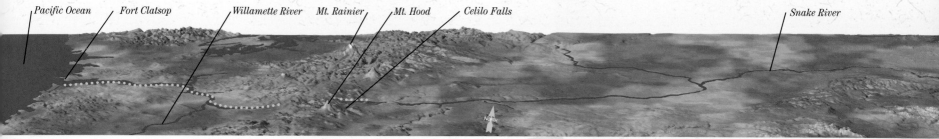

future means of Subsistence." The last thing they wanted was another cold, hungry trip over the Bitterroot Mountains. In preparation, they stopped for six days opposite the mouth of the Sandy River to hunt elk and dry enough meat to last them to the Nez Perce villages. At that point, they could rely on their horses for both food and transport—assuming, of course, that Twisted Hair had looked after them as he had promised, and that they managed to get there before the hungry Nez Perce rode east over the Lolo. That was an unpleasant thought—that they might arrive on the Clearwater with empty bellies to find no horses and no Nez Perce.

     Meanwhile, there were many Chinooks camped along the lower river waiting for the salmon migration. Pretty soon they'd be busy netting and drying, but for now, they had time on their hands. They gathered around to gawk at these odd foreigners—these well-armed but not rich white men driven by a mysterious mission and so easily provoked by petty thievery. The Corps was constantly on guard, yet it still lost things. The Indians crowded the Expedition camps. They stole brazenly, openly, as if for the fun of it, as if they enjoyed seeing the strangers lose their composure. One gang of rowdies tried to snatch John Colter's tomahawk out of his hand. Another group made off with Lewis' dog—serious business in a place where dogs could be both pets and meals—and Lewis chased after them, ready to kill the thieves. Once he stormed toward a village threatening to burn the houses if he didn't recover a stolen robe.

     The Expedition was restless, on edge, not patient, no longer charmed by the novelty of the people they met, and clearly provoked by the chasm of misunderstanding that separated their culture from that of the natives.

ROOSTER ROCK

Right: Rooster Rock bulges from the lush forests of the Columbia River Gorge near present-day Portland.

Below: Sunset over the gorge.

Clearwater River   *Lolo Pass*

"as we had no other means of passing the river we busied ourselves collecting dry timber for the purpose of constructing . . . the Indians swam over their horses and drew over their baggage in little basons of deer skins which they constructed in a very few minutes for that purpose."—LEWIS, JULY 3, 1806, CROSSING THE CLARK FORK RIVER

Missouri & Yellowstone Confluence

Marias River

ROCKY

Traveler's Rest

PACIFIC OCEAN

MOUNTAINS

RANGE

Columbia River

CASCADE

THREE FORKS
Left: Summer at Three Forks, Montana.

THE WAY HOME
Above: The map shows the divergent routes Lewis and Clark took across Montana from Traveler's Rest to the confluence of the Missouri and Yellowstone Rivers. Lewis explored the Marias River while Clark went overland and down the Yellowstone.

Pacific Ocean   Fort Clatsop   Willamette River   Mt. Rainier   Mt. Hood   Celilo Falls   Snake River

NORTH

Snake River | Clearwater River | Salmon River | Lochsa River | Lolo Pass

They decided to abandon the river above Celilo Falls and strike off overland to the Nez Perce villages. To do this, they would need a pack string beyond the falls. So while Lewis oversaw progress on the river, Clark went ahead to buy horses. It wasn't easy. He didn't have much to trade with. People were reluctant to sell. He paid exorbitant prices and more than once purchased a horse that was subsequently stolen or lost. Yet he managed. He ended up with thirteen horses of varying quality, including ten troublesome stallions. He did it with the same determination that got Lewis and the river crew safely above the falls with most of their gear and not a shot fired in anger—although there had been plenty of anger and several furious harangues directed by Lewis at the people he viewed as unprincipled low-life thieves.

Three weeks later, on May 14, the Expedition arrived at the Clearwater River near present-day Kamiah. The overland journey had been hard—the hunting poor, the weather often cold and stormy, and no timber for fires—but they'd managed to buy enough dogs to eat and fuel to cook them with, and the Indians in this part of the country had been more than decent. Instead of stealing, they had actually returned items carelessly lost or misplaced by the men. Yellept, a chief of the Walla Wallas, had greeted the Expedition effusively and insisted that they stay for three days of talking and partying. Of them Lewis wrote with evident relief, *"they are the most hospitable, honest, and sincere people that we have met with in our voyage."*

They got the same warm treatment from the Nez Perce. Twisted Hair produced most of their horses, most of them in good condition. Other men brought more horses as gifts. In return, the Captains lavished their hosts with some of the few treasures they still possessed. There was friendly talk, dancing in the evenings, agreeable women in the shadows, and some rather modest feasting. In fact, there wasn't much to eat—it had indeed been a hard winter. The Nez Perce had been forced to make stew from lichen growing on pine trees. Nor would anyone be leaving this place in the near future. The Lolo Trail was still deeply buried in snow and would

CROSSING THE LEWIS FORK
Opposite page: Clymer's painting, *The Lewis Crossing,* shows Lewis and his party rafting across the Clark Fork River just west of present-day Missoula on July 3, 1806. They are accompanied by the two young Nez Perce who had guided the Expedition east over the Lolo Trail.

"it is now the season at which the buffaloe begin to coppelate and the bulls keep a tremendious roaring we could hear them for many miles and there are such numbers of them that there is one continual roar. our horses had not been acquainted with the buffaloe they appeared much allarmed . . . when I arrived in sight of the white bear Islands . . . I sincerely belief that there were not less than 10 thousand buffaloe within a circle of 2 miles arround that place." —LEWIS, JULY 11, 1806

not be possible for weeks. This was tough news, and as Lewis put it, *"unwelcome inteligence to men confined to a diet of horsebeef and roots, and who are as anxious as we are to return to the fat plains of the Missouri and thence to our native homes."* All that hurrying up the Columbia, all that focused effort, only to be stopped in their tracks.

The men tried to curb their frustration. On May 17, Lewis noted that the river was rising and welcomed it as a sign that snow was melting in the high country: *"that icy barier which seperates me from my friends and Country, from all which makes life esteemable.— patience, patience—"*

LEWIS IN BLACKFEET COUNTRY
On the return trip from the Pacific, Lewis again explored the Marias River. His reconnaissance penetrated deeply into Blackfeet territory. This portrait (below) of the Blackfeet warrior Iron Shirt was painted by Karl Bodmer during the 1830s.

CAMP DISAPPOINTMENT
Following page: Lewis' exploration of the Marias ended here, along Cut Bank Creek, near present-day Browning, Montana.

It took a lot of patience. They waited nearly four weeks. From their position in the relatively warm river valley, it was hard for them to accept that the high country could still be snowed in; that there could be flowers down here and winter up there. But they took the advice of the Nez Perce and stayed put. They spent their time hunting—mostly deer and bear—bartering for food, looking after their horses, and socializing with the Indians.

At last, when the river had fallen six feet from its high water mark, they loaded their horses. The Nez Perce told them it was still too early, but they went anyway. They left the river on June 10, rode across Weippe Prairie, and on the 15th started into the mountains. Two days later, wallowing in deep snow and unable to find the path, they gave up and turned back to Weippe. On the 24th, they set off again, this time in the company of three young Nez Perce who not only knew the way but also knew where the snow melted first—the places where they could camp dry and the horses would find grass. On most of the trail, snow still lay deep, but it was dense enough to support the weight of horses. Lewis and Clark were continually impressed with how well the Indians knew the route. They could be on snow for long distances, seeing no sign of the trail, and when they got to a bare patch of ground, there was the beaten path in front of them. They knew where to go and where to camp, and this time they made the crossing in only six days, with no hardship and a steaming reward—a thorough soak in the hot springs at Lolo Creek. Proceeding on, they arrived at the green, mosquito-humming meadows of Traveler's Rest on the last day of June.

At this point, they did a remarkable thing for men in a hurry—a thing that shows dedication to their mission, even if it seems a bit foolish to us. They split up the party according to a complicated plan they had devised back at Fort Clatsop. Lewis would take a detachment directly to Great Falls on the Nez Perce route. There, he would leave three men to prepare for portaging while he and six volunteers explored the extent of the Marias River to locate the northern boundary of the Louisiana Territory.

While he was doing that, Clark and the rest of the men would retrace their outbound route back to the Beaverhead River where, in August of the previous year, they had left their canoes and some baggage. Reclaiming the equipment, they would float downriver to Three Forks. From there, about half the men would continue with the boats to Great Falls to join Lewis' three men. They would accomplish the portage and head downstream to a rendezvous with Lewis at the mouth of the Marias. The other half would go with Clark, riding overland to the Yellowstone River where at the first opportunity they would build canoes and float down to the Missouri. Somewhere near the confluence, sometime near the end of July, the entire Corps expected to reunite. Or rather, most of the Corps. There was one other twist. When Clark set off down the Yellowstone in canoes, he would send Sgt. Nathaniel Pryor and two men on a separate mission. Taking the best horses, they would head overland to the Mandan villages carrying a letter to a North West Company trader named Hugh Heney. Lewis wanted Heney to convince some Sioux chiefs to travel downriver with the Expedition, and then proceed to Washington to meet and be impressed by Jefferson. Heney would need advance notice, hence the need to send out a fast land party.

This plan is amazing for several reasons. First is the apparent folly of breaking up their strength just as they were entering Blackfeet territory. They apparently thought it was worth the risk, although having had no experience with that tribe, they also had no grounds for assessing the risk. Would it have changed their minds to know how fiercely the Blackfeet protected their turf over the next few decades? To know that two of the Expedition's men—Drouillard and John Potts—would die at the hands of the Blackfeet some years later? Perhaps. But they already knew how their

SKIRMISH WITH THE BLACKFEET
Previous page: Somewhere along this drainage of Montana's Two Medicine River, Lewis and his small party met a band of young Blackfeet warriors, camped with them, and fought a short battle the next morning when the Blackfeet tried to steal their rifles and horses. Lewis and his men killed two Blackfeet and fled south to the Missouri.

Snake River   Traveler's Rest   Bitterroot Valley   Beaverhead River   Three Forks

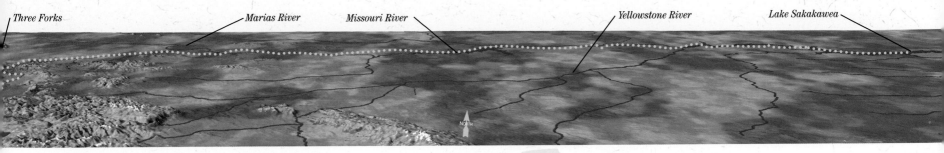

friends the Nez Perce and Shoshones feared the Blackfeet, and that knowledge did not dissuade them. It's probable that after being so lucky in so many previous encounters with Native people, the Captains simply underestimated the danger or overestimated their diplomatic prowess.

Perhaps more amazing is that after so much time in the field, having suffered so much hardship, practically aching from the desire to get home, they still had the energy and the will to explore new country. Any traveler who has been away from home for months or years has felt the overwhelming urge to pick up the pace when at last your destination is in sight. No distractions. No hesitation. No additional chores. For Lewis and Clark, coming over the Rockies must have felt like the final turn back to the barn. All they needed to do was collect their things from caches on the Beaverhead and at Great Falls and sail downstream with the wind at their backs.

Instead, they adopted a complicated plan fraught with danger. Accordingly, in the cool morning of July 3, they parted company. Clark with twenty-one men and Sacagawea started up the Bitterroot Valley. Lewis with his nine men went the other way, north to present-day Missoula, then east up the Blackfoot River. Lewis must have enjoyed knowing where he was going: back to the plains in the blooming warmth of summer; back to buffalo country, where the hunting was better than superb. Yet he did worry about the Blackfeet. For the first day, they were accompanied by their Nez Perce guides, but those young men had no intention of continuing to the plains and made no secret of their concern for the Expedition. Before parting, they came across the tracks of a strong Hidatsa war party that had recently come through. The Nez Perce shook their heads. *They said that they were confident that the Pahkees [Hidatsas] would cut us off,"* Lewis wrote. He was sad to see his friends go, but he figured he could deal with whatever arose—he and his well-armed, well-mounted party.

Or rather, his once well-mounted party. That all changed when they arrived at Great Falls and seven of their horses vanished overnight, stolen by unseen Indians. Suddenly Lewis had too few mounts to accomplish the Marias expedition as he had planned it. It was a serious setback, and if any part of him really wanted to abandon the trip north, this was the time to yield to circumstance. After all, he had arrived safely on the big water highway

home. Buffalo were again plentiful. The canoes with ten more men would be here shortly, and the pirogues lay hidden downstream. With his partner off on a risky reconnaisance of his own (on that day, July 15, Clark reached the Yellowstone near present-day Livingston, Montana) a prudent Lewis might have said, "Enough! Let's git while the gittin's good."

He should have, and we can't help but wonder what drove him to pursue his Marias exploration with only Drouillard and the two Field brothers. They rode north, trying to keep their heads down, through country thick with signs of the Blackfeet, *"who rove through this quarter of the country and as they are a vicious lawless and reather an abandoned set of wretches I wish to avoid an interview with them if possible."* He had no doubts that the encounter would be a bad one, maybe a disaster.

On July 22, a Tuesday, they camped along Cut Bank Creek ten miles east of what is now Glacier National Park. The weather was overcast, and although Lewis could see that the Marias did not rise north of the 50th parallel, as he'd hoped, he still wanted to make his celestial observation. He wanted proof. So for two days he stubbornly waited for the sky to clear. It did not. He waited another day, and then another, and finally on Saturday, he gave up, and the four men started back toward the Missouri.

By that time, they had been in Blackfeet country more than eleven days with no contact, but in this open place where anyone could see for miles, it was inevitable that eventually they would run into the lords of the northern plains. First sighting: thirty horses at the base of a low hill. Above them, on the crest, a group of men. How many warriors? No way to tell. The Blackfeet had already spotted Drouillard, who was riding apart from Lewis. They were watching Drouillard intently. They hadn't yet detected Lewis and the Fields brothers, but Lewis was not about to abandon his man. Instead, he rode directly toward the strangers. They approached each other warily and spoke through sign language. The Blackfeet (there were only eight of them) seemed receptive and agreed to make camp with the white men. Late into the night, they talked and smoked. Lewis spoke of

PRIZED HORSES

Horses were greatly prized by all Indians who lived among the Rockies or out on the Great Plains. Stealing enemies' horses was considered a valorous deed, and few tribes were better at it than the Crow. Lewis and Clark each had horses stolen from them on the return trip. They never saw who took them under the cover of night, but it was probably Crow Indians.

his journey, of his contacts with other tribes in the region, and of the American desire to bring everyone together in a grand trading network. Things seemed friendly enough when Lewis, having arranged a guard rotation with his comrades, finally lay down to sleep.

It was a mistake, and it came near to costing him his life. What would his Nez Perce friend Twisted Hair have thought, had he seen Lewis at this point? First, telling the Blackfeet about his plans for commerce, something which would provide their enemies with rifles. Second, lying down among these infamous warriors and closing his eyes. And third, sleeping past dawn.

And so it happened that Lewis woke to the furious yelling of the Field brothers and Drouillard fighting for their rifles. Joseph Field had been awake, on guard, but he was only one, and the Indians had made a daring attempt for all four weapons. The whites reacted with the fury of desperation; they knew what would happen to them if they lost their rifles and horses. The eight Blackfeet, perhaps because they had less at stake, behaved more defensively, with less adrenaline. One died with Reubin Field's knife in his heart. A second fell with Lewis' bullet in his belly. The others fled.

The whites ended up with most of the horses and all of the baggage. In a flash, they loaded up and set off on a wild rush back to the Missouri, riding all that day, most of the night, and all the next day—about one hundred miles in total, all the while looking back over their shoulders for avenging Blackfeet, preparing to defend themselves on the riverbank if the boats weren't there. But the boats were there. With the incredible good luck that this Expedition so often experienced, they hit the Missouri just as five canoes, the white pirogue, and fourteen of their pals hove into view (two others came by horseback later that day). It doesn't happen any neater in the movies. They swatted their horses' rumps and jumped into the boats. A quick stop at the mouth of the Marias a few miles farther to reclaim the second pirogue and some goods from a cache, and they were off. Down the river, swiftly and safe. Safe by a hair.

"A GANGUE OF BUFFALOW"
Right: John Clymer's painting illustrates an August 1, 1806, incident involving Clark's reconaissance party on the Yellowstone River, not far from modern Glendive. An enormous herd of bison crossing the river obliged Clark's party to land and wait a half-hour for the animals to pass. Clark wrote: *"this gangue of Buffalow was entirely across [the river] and as thick as they could swim . . . I took 4 of the men and killed 4 fat Cows for their fat and what portion of their flesh the Small Canoes Could Carry."*

"we arrived at a Boiling Spring . . . this Spring contains a very considerable quantity of water, and actually blubbers with heat for 20 paces below where it rises it has every appearance of boiling, too hot for a man to endure his hand in it 3 seconds. I directt Sergt. Pryor and John Shields to put each a peice of meat in the water of different Sises. the one about the Size of my 3 fingers Cooked dun in 25 minits the other much thicker was 32 minits before it became Sufficiently dun." —CLARK, JULY 7, 1806, IN MONTANA'S BIG HOLE VALLEY

After the Captains split up at Traveler's Rest in early July 1806, Clark headed south through the Bitterroot Valley, backtracking the route they had followed the previous September. He and his party traveled efficiently, slowed only by streams and rivers that thundered out of the mountains in spring flood. Near the head of the Bitterroot, they diverged from their 1805 route and took a different path. Instead of crossing to the Salmon River, they followed a well-traveled Indian route southeast over the Continental Divide to the Big Hole Valley. This put them again in country familiar to Sacagawea. She pointed out the short route back to Camp Fortunate, where they recovered their hidden canoes and set off down the Beaverhead River.

The Shoshone woman again proved helpful when they reached Three Forks. Here, Sgt. Ordway and nine men continued downstream to meet Lewis' party near Great Falls. Clark took all the horses, ten men, Sacagawea, and her baby up the Gallatin toward the Yellowstone. *"The indian woman who has been of great Service to me as a pilot through this Country recommends a gap in the mountain more South which I shall cross."* She also told him that buffalo had been common in these valleys a few years earlier. Fearful of the Blackfeet, her people would not go out on the plains for more than a few days at a time; instead, they scoured the mountain valleys for game, and buffalo had become scarce.

At present-day Livingston, Montana, they met the Roche Jaune, or Yellowstone River. Big and silty-green, it held enough water to float canoes, but the trees were too small for dugouts. So they stayed on horseback. The rocky terrain made the

CLARK DESCENDS THE YELLOWSTONE

animals footsore; Clark ordered them fitted with buffalo-hide moccasins. He made notes on rock types, vegetation, and the navigability of streams. He mentioned that the prairie had been stripped by swarms of grasshoppers. But he missed the land that sixty-seven years later would become Yellowstone National Park. Two days of riding would have put him at Mammoth Hot Springs, yet he makes no mention of their existence. This is odd, considering that during winter in the Mandan villages he had heard about the Falls of the Yellowstone; why not the geysers?

The Crow Indians might have told them, had they ever met a Crow. They passed log forts that Sacagawea said might have been built by Crows. Clark noted smoke from what he took to be signal fires. He prepared a speech in case there was a council, yet there never was. Still, the Crows

"Sergt. Pryor informed me that it would be impossible for the two men with him to drive on the horses after him without tireing all the good ones in pursuit of the more indifferent to keep them on the Course. that in passing every gangue of buffalow Several of which he had met with, the loos horses as Soon as they saw the Buffalow would imediately pursue them and run around them . . . This disposition in the horses is no doubt owing to their being frequently exercised in chasing different animals by their former owners the Indians . . . for which purpose they train all their horses." —CLARK, JULY 24, 1806

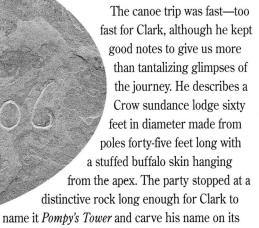

were nearby, and had other priorities, as Clark's party learned when they found large trees and settled in to build canoes. That night, someone made off with half of their horses. Five days later, Sgt. Pryor and his overland party would lose the remaining herd. It was good that they could take to the river.

The canoe trip was fast—too fast for Clark, although he kept good notes to give us more than tantalizing glimpses of the journey. He describes a Crow sundance lodge sixty feet in diameter made from poles forty-five feet long with a stuffed buffalo skin hanging from the apex. The party stopped at a distinctive rock long enough for Clark to name it *Pompy's Tower* and carve his name on its face. Downriver, he dug up a dinosaur rib. Wildlife was boggling in its abundance, to the point that Clark says no one will believe him so he'll be silent on the topic, but he can't stop writing about bison, deer, elk, bighorn, pronghorn, wolves, grizzlies, beaver, geese, swallows, and others in such numbers that he begins to sound incredulous himself. The grunts of rutting buffalo were so loud and close to camp that the party couldn't sleep without getting up to shoo them away. Yet buffalo annoyance was nothing compared to the hordes of mosquitoes that made life miserable and sleep impossible once they hit the Missouri.

Through it all, Clark kept his careful mapping notes and concluded on August 3, 1806, *"The distance from the Rocky Mountains at which place I struck the River Rochejhone to its enterance into the Missouri 837 Miles 636 Miles of this distance I decended in 2 Small Canoes lashed together."* Swatting mosquitoes, he recommended the Yellowstone as a travel route and called it a *"delighfull river."*

CLARK'S SIGNATURE
During his reconnaissance of the Yellowstone River in the summer of 1806, Clark carved his name onto a prominent sandstone formation overlooking the river. He dubbed the formation *"Pompy's Tower,"* after Sacagawea's son. Today the tower is called Pompey's Pillar and still bears Clark's name (above) in the rock.

Left: The Yellowstone River runs fast and clear at spring flood.

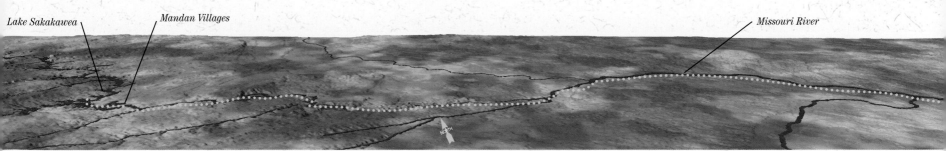

Meanwhile, back on the Yellowstone, Clark and his party were having a much less eventful time. They had traveled on horseback down the river for five days until they came to a grove of cottonwood trees large enough to make dugouts. It took several days to build two boats, which they joined together like a catamaran for stability. On July 24, the craft was ready. Waving farewell to Sgt. Pryor and his three comrades as they set off on their overland mission to the Mandan villages, Clark shoved off into swift current. They flew: sixty-nine miles the first day, fifty-eight the next.

On August 3, they reached the Missouri. The mosquitoes were terrible, so they left a note for Lewis and kept going, slowly. Five days later, a surprise drifted into view from upstream. It was Sgt. Pryor and his three comrades, hailing them from two wobbly bull-boats. Chagrined, they told about how on their second night out they had lost all their horses to Crow Indians. They never saw the burglars. There was no confrontation. They just became overnight pedestrians. Well, hell: Shouldering their gear, they had walked back to the Yellowstone, built the skin boats, and hurried after Clark.

SWELTERING HEAT

Opposite: Leaving the plains behind, the Corps continued east on the last leg of their journey.

Lewis sailed in four days later, on August 12, with stories of adventure and narrow escape. Ironically, almost comically, it was he who had suffered the worst physical injury of the Expedition. His own man, the one-eyed, near-sighted Cruzatte, had mistaken him for an elk and shot him in the buttocks. Poor Cruzatte was mortified and denying everything. Lewis was flat on his belly in the canoe, saying all was well and he'd be back on his feet soon enough.

Now there was little to do but ride the river, the now-familiar home-flowing river. They spent three days at the Mandan villages and convinced the chief,

Sheheke, to accompany them eastward. They paid off Charbonneau, gave the young and valuable Sacagawea a grateful goodbye, and granted John Colter an early discharge. Colter, evidently, had been smitten by the West. He wanted to turn around and go back. The others might be eager to get home, but Colter had met a pair of trappers headed upriver and decided to join them. Why not be among the first to tap the riches he'd seen?

For the rest of them, it was onward, downstream, sliding south and east through the green abundance of late August, feasting on game, wild plums, and berries—and then, to their great delight and culinary relief, imported niceties. They began meeting parties coming upriver, keelboats loaded with trade goods, whiskey, and news of the past two years, including the entertaining rumor that the Expedition had met with disaster and everyone was dead. Not so, they happily declared, and by the way, is that a whiskey keg? They drank, listened to the news, basked in the admiring gaze of the rookies, and hurried on. By now, they didn't even take time to hunt. They could live on wild fruit, the men agreed. Let's get on home.

And there we leave them, riding high on the breast of the Missouri. There was much yet to come—writing the official report, drawing the great map of the Northwest, attending triumphal parties and happy reunions. Soon Lewis would be governor of the Louisiana Territory. Clark would be busy in the fur trade and embarking on a long, successful career. He would serve as Superintendent of Indian Affairs and as governor of the Missouri Territory long after his friend Lewis' tragic death, in 1809, apparently from a self-inflicted bullet.

But those events lay well in the future. Sailing through the rich Iowa summer, at the end of their great Expedition, they were as good as kings.

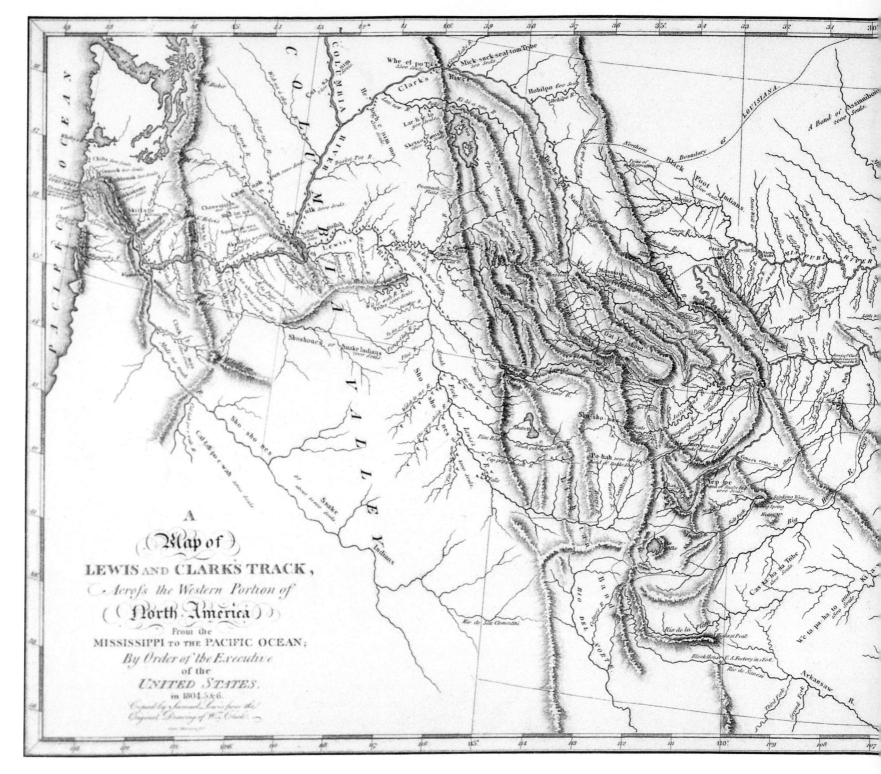

CLARK'S MASTERPIECE

Clark's map of western North America shows the Expedition's route from the mouth of the Missouri River to the mouth of the Columbia. The map was based on hundreds of compass bearings and calculated

distances Clark laid down daily in his "Courses & Distances" tables as well as on the dozens of large scale maps he sketched throughout the voyage. But the map also shows enormous swaths

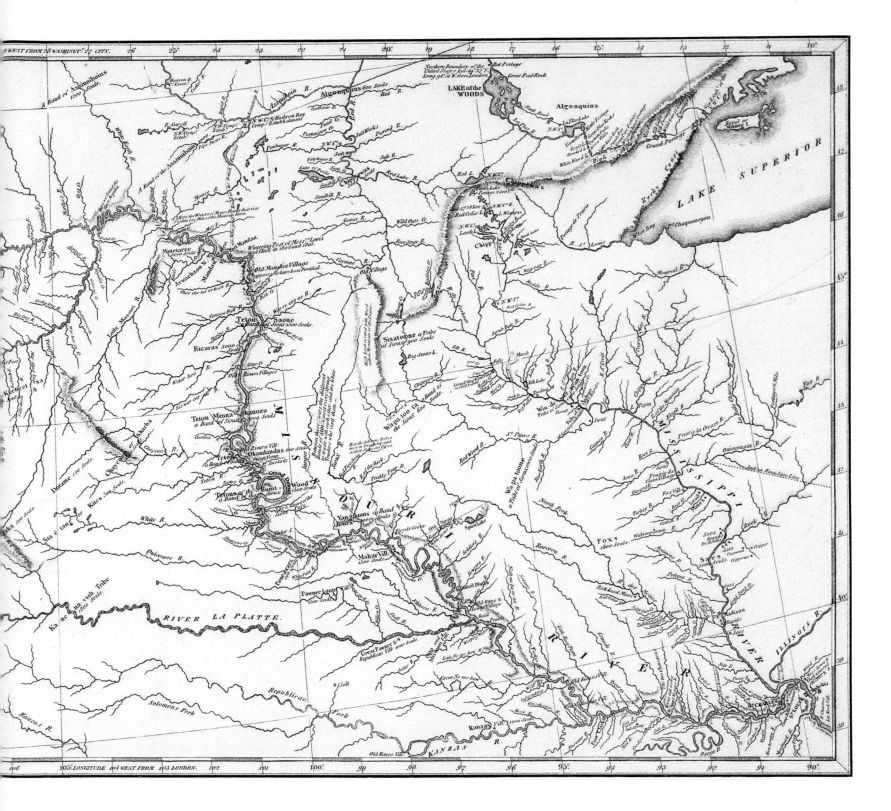

of territory Clark never saw. For those regions, he relied on numerous interviews he and Lewis conducted with various Indians, French boatmen, and traders. It was perhaps the single most important document the Expedition produced.

Captain Meriwether Lewis (1774–1809). Born on a Virginia plantation, Lewis was a slave owner who joined the army in 1794 and served in the Ohio Valley and the Old Northwest Territory. There, he befriended and served briefly under Clark. In 1801, President Jefferson appointed him his personal secretary. In 1803, Jefferson formally gave him command of the Expedition. After returning in triumph from the West, he became governor of the Louisiana Territory. There, political, personal, and financial difficulties led to deep emotional problems. He killed himself on the Natchez Trace in Tennessee.

Second Lieutenant William Clark (1770–1838). A Virginian and younger brother to the Revolutionary War hero George Rogers Clark, he moved with his family to Kentucky at age fourteen. He joined the army in 1792, fought in the Northwest, and rose to the rank of captain. He left the army after four years to attend to family business. Lewis offered him co-command of the Expedition. Both were appalled when Army red tape led to his commissioning as a second lieutenant—a fact both leaders kept from the men. After the Expedition, Clark served as governor of the Missouri Territory but spent most of the rest of his life in charge of Indian relations west of the Mississippi.

Sergeant Charles Floyd (1782–1804). The only man to die during the Expedition, Floyd was a Kentuckian who kept a journal of the voyage until a few days before his death on August 20, 1804, of an apparent ruptured appendix, near present-day Sioux City, Iowa.

Sergeant Patrick Gass (1771–1870). The Expedition's leading carpenter, Gass was born in Pennsylvania and enlisted in the army in 1799. He joined the Expedition in January 1804 and was promoted to sergeant after Floyd's death. His journal of the voyage was published in 1807. He lost an eye during the War of 1812. He married when he was sixty and died in West Virginia thirty-nine years later. He was the last known survivor of the Expedition.

Sergeant John Ordway (c.1775–c.1817). Born in New Hampshire and an army regular before the Expedition, Ordway was one of the party's most consistent journalists. After the voyage, he accompanied Lewis to Washington, D.C., with a delegation of Indians. In 1809 he settled in Missouri, grew wealthy, and got married. By 1817, Ordway and his wife were dead.

Sergeant Nathaniel Hale Pryor (1772–1831). Born in Virginia, Pryor moved to Kentucky with his parents when he was eleven and joined the Expedition at the age of thirty-one. After the voyage, he obtained an officer's commission, eventually rose to the rank of captain, and fought in the Battle of New Orleans. After the War of 1812, he became a trader among the Osage Indians, married an Osage woman, and lived with the tribe until he died.

Private John Boley (dates unknown). A Pennsylvanian, Boley was a member of the return party, which turned back from the Mandan villages in the spring of 1805. Upon his return, he joined Zebulon Pike's expedition to the upper Mississippi in 1805 and also accompanied Pike in 1806 to the Southwest and the Rockies. He settled near St. Louis.

Private Willim E. Bratton (1778–1841). A hunter and blacksmith for the party, Bratton was born in Virginia but moved to Kentucky when he was twelve. He joined the Expedition when he was twenty-four. After the voyage he served in the War of 1812, and lived in Kentucky, Missouri, Ohio, and Indiana.

Private John Collins (?–1823). Frequently drunk and disobedient during the early months of the Expedition, Collins, a Maryland native, stole a hog from a farmer during the winter of 1803–04 and was court-martialed for stealing whiskey from the common supply in 1804. Other skills seem to have outweighed Collins' shortcomings, though, since the Captains included him in the Corps' permanent party from the start. Later, he joined William Ashley's trapping venture to the upper Missouri and was killed during Ashley's battle with the Arikara.

Private John Colter (1775–1813). One of the Expedition's most dependable hunters, Colter was a Virginia native who moved to Kentucky as a youth with his parents. Returning from the Rockies in 1806, he got permission to leave the Expedition at the Mandan Villages to work as an independent trapper for Manuel Lisa's Missouri River Fur Company. During the four years that followed, Colter wandered all over the mountains and was apparently the first white to see Yellowstone. In 1808 he escaped, naked, from the Blackfeet near Three Forks after his trapping partner (fellow Expedition veteran John Potts) was killed. Colter died of jaundice after marrying and settling in Missouri.

Private Pierre Cruzatte (dates unknown). Half Omaha and half French, one-eyed and nearsighted, Cruzatte was a master boatman whose fiddle playing enlivened the party's camps throughout the voyage. While hunting on the return journey, he apparently mistook Lewis for an elk and shot his commander in the butt.

Private John Dame (1784–?). A member of the return party, Dame was born in New Hampshire.

Interpreter George Drouillard (?–1810). The Expedition's premier hunter and fluent in Plains Indian sign language, Drouillard was half Shawnee and half French-Canadian. After the Expedition, he joined Manuel Lisa's fur company and in 1810 helped establish Lisa's ill-fated trading post at Three Forks, where he was killed by Blackfeet.

Privates Joseph Field (c.1772–1807) and **Reubin Field** (c.1771–1823?). Two more Virginians who moved to Kentucky at an early age, the Field brothers were among the first recruits for the Expedition and were considered among the finest hunters in the party. Both were with Lewis during his 1806 fight with the Blackfeet. Joseph died within a year of returning from the voyage. Reubin settled in Kentucky and married.

Private Robert Frazer (?–1837). Probably a Virginian, Frazer kept a journal throughout the voyage, but the journal was never published and is apparently lost. His map of the West, however, survives. After the Expedition, he settled in Missouri.

Private George Gibson (?–1809). Born in Pennsylvania, Gibson occasionally played fiddle for the party and served as a sign language interpreter. He died in St. Louis.

Private Silas Goodrich (dates unknown). The Expedition's best fisherman, Goodrich was a native of Massachusetts. After the voyage, he reenlisted in the army. Clark says he was dead by 1825–28.

Private Hugh Hall (c.1772–?). Born in Massachusetts, Hall joined the army in 1798 and was transferred to the Expedition in 1803. He was court-martialed with Collins in 1804 for stealing whiskey and was last seen by the Captains in St. Louis in 1809, when he borrowed money from Lewis.

Private Thomas Proctor Howard (1779–?). Another Massachusetts native, Howard was enough of a tippler for Clark to note during the winter of 1803–04 that he *"never Drinks water."* After the Expedition, Howard continued serving in the army.

Private Francois Labiche (dates unknown). Part Omaha, part French, and perhaps part African, Labiche was an experienced boatman and Indian trader

EXPEDITION ROSTER

whose interpretive skills were highly valued by Lewis. After the Expedition, he settled in the St. Louis area.

Private Hugh McNeal (dates unknown). A Pennsylvanian, McNeal made the entire voyage and continued serving with the army after the Expedition.

Private John Newman (c.1785–1838). Expelled from the Expedition in October 1804 for uttering *"expressions of a highly criminal and mutinous nature,"* Newman was sent back to St. Louis from the Mandan Villages in the spring of 1805. The specifics of his misdeed are unknown but may have been connected with Moses Reed, who had deserted and had been recaptured in August of that year. After the Expedition, Newman trapped on the Missouri during the 1830s and was killed by the Yankton Sioux.

Private John Potts (1776–1808?). A German native, Potts joined Manuel Lisa's fur-trapping company after the Expedition. He was killed by the Blackfeet near Three Forks when he and Colter were ambushed.

Private Moses B. Reed (dates unknown). Originally a member of the permanent party, Reed deserted in August 1804, was captured, court-martialed, and expelled from the party. He was sent back to St. Louis from the Mandan villages in the spring of 1805 and dropped out of sight.

Private John Robertson (c.1780–?). A New Hampshire native, Robertson got in trouble for drinking during the winter of 1803–04 and was designated as a member of the return party.

Private George Shannon (1785–1836). Youngest member of the Expedition, Shannon was born in Pennsylvania and moved with his family to Ohio in 1800. He was lost for two weeks during the autumn of 1804 and nearly starved. After the Expedition, he was wounded by the Arikara in 1807 during Nathaniel Pryor's mission to return the Mandan chief Sheheke to his people. In 1810, he helped Nicholas Biddle prepare a history of the Expedition, studied law, practiced in Kentucky, and was elected a U.S. senator from Missouri.

Private John Shields (1769–1809). The Expedition's blacksmith, gunsmith, and a skilled carpenter, Shields, thirty-four in 1803, was the oldest known member of the permanent party. The Captains traded on his crucial blacksmithing talents for corn and other provisions from the Mandans during the winter of 1804–05. After the Expedition, he trapped in Missouri with Daniel Boone, a relative, and settled in Indiana.

Private John B. Thompson (dates unknown). Little is known of Thompson except that he seems to have had some experience as a surveyor, which might have led Clark to refer to him as *"a valuable member of our party."*

Private Ebenezer Tuttle (1773–?). A Connecticut native, Tuttle was a member of the return party.

Corporal Richard Warfington (1777–?). Placed in charge of the return party, Warfington turned back for St. Louis with the keelboat in the spring of 1805. His group returned with invaluable materials destined for President Jefferson: maps, dispatches, journals, and specimens of plants and animals, including a live prairie dog and four live magpies.

Private Peter M. Weiser (1781–?). Born and reared in Pennsylvania, Weiser made the entire voyage with Lewis and Clark, then joined Manuel Lisa's fur-trading company on the Missouri. Clark listed him as *"killed"* by 1825–28. He may have been killed by Blackfeet near Three Forks or in some other fur-era skirmish.

Private William Werner (dates unknown). A discipline problem during the long, boring winter of 1803–04, Werner was a member of the permanent party. After the Expedition, he settled in Virginia.

Private Isaac White (c.1774–?). A Massachusetts native, White was a member of the return party.

Private Joseph Whitehouse (c.1775–?). A Virginia native who moved to Kentucky with his family as a boy, Whitehouse was one of the party's journalists. A skin-dresser by trade, he often acted as a tailor for the other men. After the Expedition he was arrested for debt, served in the army during the War of 1812, deserted in 1817, and dropped from sight of the historic record.

Private Alexander Hamilton Willard (1778–1865). A blacksmith who assisted Shields during the Expedition, Willard was convicted of sleeping on guard duty July 12, 1804. After the voyage, he worked as a government blacksmith for the Sauk and Fox Indians, and later for the Delawares and Shawnees. He served in the War of 1812, lived in Missouri and Wisconsin, had twelve children, and emigrated to California in 1852 at the age of seventy-four.

Private Richard Windsor (dates unknown). Often assigned hunting duties during the Expedition, Windsor remained in the army after the voyage and served until 1819. During the 1820s, he lived in Illinois.

York (c.1770–?). Clark's slave and companion from childhood, York is given no other name in the Journals or in any primary document. He carried a gun and shouldered a full share of duties with the other Expedition members. Clark reluctantly freed him in 1811, and York ran a freight-wagon business in Tennessee and Kentucky. Clark wrote that the business failed and that York decided sometime before 1832 to rejoin him in St. Louis but died of cholera on the way.

Sacagawea (c.1788–1812?). A crucial liaison and indispensable interpreter to her native people, the Lemhi Shoshone, Sacagawea was a valued member of the Expedition who at times helped guide the party through southwestern Montana. As a girl, she had been kidnapped by a Hidatsa raiding party at Three Forks around 1800. In 1804, she was sold as a wife to Toussaint Charbonneau, and the two were living among the Hidatsas when the Corps of Discovery arrived at the Mandan Villages in the autumn of the same year. During the trip to the Pacific and back, her presence with a baby reassured many tribes of the Expedition's peaceful intentions. Little is known about her life after the Expedition. The best evidence indicates she died in 1812 in South Dakota. Clark lists her as dead by 1825–28.

Toussaint Charbonneau (c.1758–?). A French-Canadian trader living among the Hidatsas, Charbonneau served as an interpreter and celebrated chef for the Expedition. After the voyage, he worked for Manuel Lisa in the Missouri River Fur Company and performed diplomatic errands between the Missouri River tribes and the United States during the War of 1812. He joined an 1815 expedition to Santa Fe, where the Spanish briefly imprisoned him. He worked as an interpreter during Prince Maximilian's steamboat journey up the Missouri during 1834–35, remained on the U.S. government payroll as an interpreter until 1839, and died in his eighties.

Jean Baptiste Charbonneau (1805–1866). Son of Charbonneau and Sacagawea, the boy was nicknamed *"Pomp"* or *"Pompy"* by Clark, who offered to educate the child and who seems to have taken him into his St. Louis home when the boy was about six. In 1823, Jean Baptiste caught the eye of Prince Paul of Wurttemburg, who took him to Europe for six years. He later returned to the mountains and became a fur trapper and then guide for explorers and soldiers. He settled in California and died in Oregon while on his way to Montana.

INDEX

p 1 *Lewis and Clark at the Bitterroots,* John F. Clymer, 1967, courtesy Mrs. Clymer and the Clymer Museum of Art.

pp 2–3 Missouri River, Glasgow, Montana, Wayne Mumford.

pp 4–5 Missouri River, Glasgow, Montana, Wayne Mumford.

pp 6–7 *A Herd of Bison Crossing the Missouri River,* William Jacob Hays, Sr., 1863, oil on canvas, 3.60, Buffalo Bill Historical Center, Cody, Wyoming, Gertrude Vanderbilt Whitney Trust Fund Purchase.

pp 8–9 *The Lost Greenhorn,* Alfred Jacob Miller, 1866, oil on canvas, 9.70, Buffalo Bill Historical Center, Cody, Wyoming, gift of the Coe Foundation.

p 10 Meriwether Lewis, Charles Willson Peale, c. 1807, Independence National Historical Park Collection; William Clark, Charles Willson Peale, c. 1810, Independence National Historical Park Collection; roster of men, WA Mss 304, Beinecke Rare Book and Manuscript Library, Yale University.

p 11 Letter of credit, 4 July 1803, ink on paper, 1804 L/A 731, Jefferson Papers, Missouri Historical Society, St. Louis; Jefferson's code, LC-MS-27748-203, Library of Congress.

pp 12–13 Clark's elkskin-bound journal, 26 October 1805, ink on paper, Objects 109, Clark Family, Missouri Historical Society, St. Louis.

p 14 Memorandum of articles, WA Mss 303, Item 4, Beinecke Rare Book and Manuscript Library, Yale University.

pp 14–15 Topographical sketch, WA Mss 303, Item 2, Beinecke Rare Book and Manuscript Library, Yale University.

pp 16–17 Confluence of the Marias and Missouri Rivers, Wayne Mumford.

p 18 *Captain Meriwether Lewis,* Charles B. J. F. Saint-Mémin, c. 1807, watercolor on paper, neg. 51322, © Collection of The New-York Historical Society.

pp 18–19 Pine Butte Swamp Preserve, Montana, Wayne Mumford.

p 20 Sumac and thimbleberry, Wayne Mumford.

p 21 *Raven Blanket—Nez Perce,* E. S. Curtis, folio plate 259, Dartmouth College Library.

pp 22–23 Lolo Trail near Snowbank Camp, Idaho, Wayne Mumford.

p 23 Bob Scriver's *Explorers of the Marias,* Wayne Mumford.

pp 24–25 Long and Short Narrows of the Columbia, Codex H: 2-3. vol. 5, p. 330, American Philosophical Society.

p 25 Clark's field notes, WA Mss S-879, Rev. of Doc. 4, Beinecke Rare Book and Manuscript Library, Yale University.

p 26 Clark's compass and chain, Missouri Historical Society, St. Louis.

pp 30–31 *Lewis and Clark, 1804* by L. Edward Fisher, commissioned by the Missouri Bankers Association, print photographed by Kevin Halle.

pp 32–33 *Evening Light on Mississippi River as Viewed from Louis Point,* Mississippi Palisades State Park, Carroll County, Illinois, © Willard Clay.

p 34 Clark's field notes, WA Mss S-879 William Clark's Field Notes—Rev. of Doc. 7, Beinecke Rare Book and Manuscript Library, Yale University.

pp 34–35 *Evening Bivouac on the Missouri,* Karl Bodmer, courtesy of Joslyn Art Museum, Omaha, Nebraska, gift of Enron Art Foundation.

p 36 *Lewis and Clark at St. Charles, May 21, 1804,* Charles A. Morganthaler, courtesy of the St. Charles County Historical Society.

p 37 Cottonwood trees, Montana, Wayne Mumford.

pp 38–39 Flathead Valley, Montana, Wayne Mumford.

pp 40–41 Lupine near Red Lodge, Montana, Wayne Mumford.

p 42–43 White-tailed deer *(Odocoileus virginianus),* Wayne Mumford.

p 44 Queen Anne pistol, courtesy Springfield Armory, Springfield, Massachusetts; M.1815 Harpers Ferry Rifle, USDA Collection IDAS112, courtesy of USDA Forest Service, Clearwater National Forest.

pp 45-47 Lewis & Clark air rifle (Lukins gun), transparency, 88.083, Stewart Collection, VMI Museum, Lexington, Virginia.

p 45 Lewis' branding iron imprint on leather, color transparency, #OrHi100065, Oregon Historical Society; Lewis' branding iron, #OrHi10061, Oregon Historical Society; Clark's compass and case, Lewis & Clark Collection, 95-3550, Smithsonian Institution.

p 46 Composition of Lewis and Clark artifacts: Lewis watch, Clark watch fob compass, Lewis telescope, and two Clark journals, David Schultz, 1995, Voorhis Collection, Missouri Historical Society, St. Louis.

pp 47 Clark's compass and chain, Missouri Historical Society, St. Louis; Clark's elkskin-bound field journal, 1805, ink on paper, Objects 109a, William Clark Papers, Missouri Historical Society, St. Louis.

pp 48-49 Storm clouds near Glasgow, Montana, Wayne Mumford.

pp 50–51 Farm and clouds on the high plains, © Willard Clay.

p 52 Deerskin painting of plains tribes, c. 1900, #1115, courtesy Don McQuiston, Spirit of Native America Collection, San Diego Museum of Man.

p 53 Grasslands and farms on the high plains, © Willard Clay.

pp 54–55 Missouri River near Glasgow, Montana, Wayne Mumford.

pp 56–57 Pronghorn antelope, Wayne Mumford.

p 58 Grouse, Wayne Mumford.

p 59 Prairie dog *(Cynomys ludonacianus),* Wayne Mumford.

p 62–63 Prairie near Wilton, North Dakota, Wayne Mumford.

p 63 Missouri meadowlark, Wm. E. Hitchcock after Audubon, 1844, hand-colored lithograph, RBC, QL674.A9 1840, vol. VII, Library of Congress.

p 64 Buffalo-hide shield (Crow, eastern Montana, c. 1830), #573, courtesy Don McQuiston, Spirit of Native America Collection, San Diego Museum of Man; *Sioux Warrior Charging,* P.K. & Catlin, 1829, lithograph, RBC, SF277.A6, Library of Congress; *Traveaux-Piegan,* E. S. Curtis, folio plate 193, Dartmouth College Library.

p 65 *Pehriska-Ruhpa, Moennitarri Warrior in the Costume of the Dog Danse,* Rene Rollet after Bodmer, 1840, hand-colored aquatint and etching, RBC, Atlas. E165.W64, Library of Congress.

p 66 *Le Soldat du Chene, an Osage Chief,* Charles de Saint-Mémin, 1805, RBC, E77.M1304, Library of Congress; Mahas Queen, 1809, engraving, *from The Travels of Capts. Lewis and Clark,* RBC, F592.6 1809, Library of Congress; *Moveable Skin Lodges of the Kaskias,* Young and Delleker 1823 after T. R. Peale 1823, engraving, RBC, F592.J3, Library of Congress.

p 67 *Buffalo Hunt, Under the White Wolf Skin,* George Catlin (from his North American Indian Portfolio), c. 1845, Santa Barbara Museum of Natural History.

p 68 *Funeral Scaffold of a Sioux Chief near Fort Pierre,* after Karl Bodmer, engraving, Joslyn Art Museum, Omaha, Nebraska, gift of Enron Art Foundation; *Painted Lodges-Piegan,* E. S. Curtis, folio plate 186, Dartmouth College Library.

p 69 *Peace Pipe,* John F. Clymer, 1979, courtesy Mrs. Clymer and the Clymer Museum of Art.

pp 70 *The Old Cheyenne,* E. S. Curtis, folio plate 672, Dartmouth College Library.

p 71 *Offering of the Mandan Indians,* Karl Bodmer, hand-colored aquatint print from Prince Maximilian's *Travels in the Interior of North America,* c.1839–1842, Santa Barbara Museum of Natural History; *Osage Warrior,* Charles B. Fevret de Saint-Mémin, c. 1804, watercolor, courtesy the Henry Francis du Pont Winterthur Museum.

p 72 Bison skull, courtesy Don McQuiston, Spirit of Native America Collection, San Diego Museum of Man; Mandan Chief Mato-Tope, Karl Bodmer, engraving, 1845, RBC AP2.G73, vol. XXVI, Library of Congress; *Mandan Earth Lodges,* Karl Bodmer, pencil on paper, Joslyn Art Museum, Omaha, Nebraska, gift of Enron Art Foundation.

p 73 *Interior of a Mandan Earth Lodge,* Karl Bodmer, Joslyn Art Museum, Omaha, Nebraska, gift of Enron Art Foundation.

p 74 *Rain-Making Mandan,* George Catlin, c.1855-1870, oil on cardboard on bristol board, 24.86, Buffalo Bill Historical Center, Cody, Wyoming, gift of Paul Mellon; *The Land of the Atsina,* E. S. Curtis, 1908, folio plate 169, Dartmouth College Library.

p 75 *Ready for the "Okipe" Buffalo Dance-Mandan,* E. S. Curtis, from *The North American Indian,* vol. 5, Dartmouth College Library; *Crow's Heart–Mandan,* E. S. Curtis, from *The North American Indian,* vol. 5, Dartmouth College Library; Buffalo Dance (Mandan), George Catlin, 1845, RBC, NE 2527.CA, Library of Congress.

pp 76–77 Buffalo hide, © 1995 Brian Seed and W. S. Nawrocki, photo by Hillel Burger, T1908 A.11, Peabody Museum, Harvard University; peace pipe, photo by Hillel Burger, T599, Peabody Museum, Harvard University.

p 77 Saddle blanket and leggings c. 1835, NA.403.164 and NA.202.440, Buffalo Bill Historical Center, Cody, Wyoming, Chandler-Pohrt Collection; *Offering the Buffalo Skull-Mandan,* E. S. Curtis, from *The North American Indian,* vol. 5, Dartmouth College Library.

pp 78–79 *Mih-Tutta-Hang-Kusch, Mandan Village,* Karl Bodmer, Joslyn Art Museum, Omaha, Nebraska, gift of Enron Art Foundation.

pp 80–81 Missouri River sunrise near Mandan, North Dakota, Wayne Mumford.

p 82 *American Bison, or Buffalo,* J. T. Bowen after Audubon, 1845, hand-colored lithograph, RBC, QL715.A9, vol. II, Library of Congress.

p 83 *As It Was In the Old Days,* E. S. Curtis, folio plate 652, Dartmouth College Library.

pp 84-85 Makoshika Badlands, Montana, Wayne Mumford.

p 86 Sacajawea—Shoshone Princess & Mascot of the Lewis & Clark Expedition, shown on horseback, © Henry Altman 1905, CN024513, Oregon Historical Society.

p 87 Madison River near Three Forks, Montana, Wayne Mumford.

p 88 Grouse feather courtesy of John Santori, photographed by Kevin Halle; Heath Cock or Cock of the Plains, William Clark, March 2, 1806, ink on paper, Voorhis #2, Clark Papers, Missouri Historical Society, St. Louis.

pp 88–89 Native grouse, Wayne Mumford.

CREDITS

p 90 Sheet 19: April 7–14,1805, Clark-Maximilian maps, Joslyn Art Museum, Omaha, Nebraska, gift of Enron Art Foundation.

pp 90–91 Sheet 20: April 14–28, 1805, Joslyn Art Museum, Omaha, Nebraska, gift of Enron Art Foundation.

p 92 Route about May 19–24, 1805, WA Mss 303, Item 21, Beinecke Rare Book and Manuscript Library, Yale University; Route about May 7–13, 1805, WA Mss 303, Item 17, Beinecke Rare Book and Manuscript Library, Yale University.

pp 92–93 Route about April 20–30, 1805, WA Mss 303, Item 17, Beinecke Rare Book and Manuscript Library, Yale University; Route about May 24–30, 1805, WA Mss 303, Item 23, Beinecke Rare Book and Manuscript Library, Yale University.

p 93 Route about May 11–19, 1805, Wa Mss 303, Item 20, Beinecke Rare Book and Manuscript Library, Yale University; Route about May 19–25, 1805, WA Mss 303, Item 14-6, Beinecke Rare Book and Manuscript Library, Yale University.

pp 94–95 Missouri River, Loma, Montana, Wayne Mumford.

pp 96–97 White Cliffs of the Missouri River, Montana, Wayne Mumford.

p 97 Sheet 21: April 28–May 7, 1805, Clark-Maximilian maps, Joslyn Art Museum, Omaha, Nebraska, gift of Enron Art Foundation.

p 98 Formations, White Cliffs, Missouri River, Montana, Wayne Mumford.

pp 98–99 *Attack of the Grizzly Bear,* George Catlin, 1845, RBC, NE 2527.C4 1845, Library of Congress.

p 101 *At the Water's Edge-Piegan,* E. S. Curtis, folio plate 195, Dartmouth College Library.

pp 102–103 Draught of the falls and portage of the Missouri River, Codex E: 132-133, vol. 4, p. 360, neg. 966, American Philosophical Society.

p 104 Handsom Falls of the Missouri River, William Clark, c. July 3, 1805, ink on paper, L/A 461, Clark Family Papers, Voorhis #1, Missouri Historical Society, St. Louis.

p 105 Great Falls, Montana, Wayne Mumford.

pp 106–107 Great Falls, Montana, Wayne Mumford.

p 108 Sacagawea Spring near Missouri River, Montana, Wayne Mumford.

p 109 Belt Creek portage, Missouri River, Montana, Wayne Mumford.

pp 110 Cottonwoods, Pompey's Pillar, Montana, Wayne Mumford.

pp 112–113 Sunrise, Trapper Peak near Darby, Montana, Wayne Mumford.

pp 114–115 Gates of the Mountains, Montana, Wayne Mumford.

pp 116–117 Three Forks, Montana, Wayne Mumford.

pp 118–119 *Up the Jefferson,* John F. Clymer, 1978, courtesy Mrs. Clymer and the Clymer Museum of Art.

pp 120–121 *In the Land of the Sioux,* E. S. Curtis, folio plate 95, Dartmouth College Library.

p 121 Shoshone man, ©1988 David Stoecklein/The Stock Solution.

pp 122–123 Horse Prairie, Red Butte, Montana, Wayne Mumford.

pp 124–125 Lemhi Pass, Montana/Idaho border, Wayne Mumford.

p 125 *The Blackfoot Country,* E. S. Curtis, folio plate 636, Dartmouth College Library.

p 126 "Method of Head-Flattening and Adults with Skull Deformities (Chinook Indians)," William Clark, c. 30 January 1806, ink on paper, L/A 187a, Clark Family Papers, Voorhis #2, Missouri Historical Society, St. Louis.

p 127 Leaf of an evergreen shrub, William Clark, 12 February 1806, ink on paper, L/A 646, Clark Family Papers, Voorhis #2, Missouri Historical Society, St. Louis; Head of a braut, Codex J: 181, vol. 6, p. 419, neg. 940, American Philosophical Society; Shoshone smoking pipe, Codex F: 99, vol. 5, p. 82, American Philosophical Society.

p 128–129 Lemhi River Valley, Idaho, Wayne Mumford.

p 129 Lewis' monkey flower, Wayne Mumford.

pp 130–131 Salmon River near North Fork, Idaho, Wayne Mumford.

p 132 River's Edge at Lemhi Pass, Wayne Mumford.

pp 132–133 Clark's elkskin-bound journal, William Clark, 30 September 1805, ink on paper, L/A 750c, MHS Archives, Clark Family Papers.

pp 134–135 Bitterroot River, Montana, Wayne Mumford.

pp 136 Lolo Trail near Snowbank Camp, Idaho, Wayne Mumford.

p 137 Shoshone fish war, Codex F: 147, vol. 5, p. 136, American Philosophical Society; Maple leaf, Oregon, Wayne Mumford.

pp 138–139 Packer Meadows, Glade Creek, Montana/Idaho border, Wayne Mumford.

p 139 Subalpine fir *(Abies lasioscarpa),* Wayne Mumford.

pp 140 Bitterroot Mountains near Powell, Idaho, Wayne Mumford.

p 141 Pinecone, Wayne Mumford.

pp 142–143 *Lewis and Clark at the Bitterroots,* John F. Clymer, 1967, courtesy Mrs. Clymer and the Clymer Museum of Art.

p 143 Route from Traveler's Rest toward Lolo Trail, William Clark, September 11–12, 1805, ink on paper in elkskin-bound journal, L/A 506, Clark Family Papers, Missouri Historical Society, St. Louis.

pp 144–145 South Fork, Clearwater River near Kooskia, Idaho, Wayne Mumford.

p 146 Carved wood spoon, 19th century, Jerry Taylor, courtesy Maryhill Museum of Art, Goldendale, Washington; white salmon trout, Codex J: 133, vol. 6, p. 422, neg. 940, American Philosophical Society.

pp 148–149 Columbia River near Wishram, Washington, Wayne Mumford.

pp 150 Near Wishram, Washington, Wayne Mumford.

p 151 Confluence of Snake and Columbia Rivers (with Indian group), Codex H: 33, vol. 5, p. 299, American Philosophical Society.

pp 152–153 *Angry River,* John F. Clymer, 1978, courtesy Mrs. Clymer and the Clymer Museum of Art.

pp 154 Great Falls of the Columbia River, William Clark, 2–23 October 1805, 1805 L/A 522e, Clark Family Papers, Voorhis #4, Missouri Historical, St. Louis.

p 155 Great Rapids of the Columbia River, Codex H: 4, vol. 5, p. 370, neg. 705, American Philosophical Society.

p 156 Columbia River Bottoms, Oregon, Wayne Mumford.

p 157 Mt. Hood near Wishram, Washington, Wayne Mumford.

p 158 Lewis' journal entry, February 1, 1806, Codex J: 52, vol. 6, p. 264, neg. 940, American Philosophical Society.

pp 158–159 *Lewis and Clark on the Lower Columbia,* Charles M. Russell, 1905, watercolor, gouache, and graphite on paper, 1961.195, Amon Carter Museum, Fort Worth, Texas.

pp 160–161 Great Rapids of the Columbia River, Codex H: 4, vol. 5, p. 370, neg. 705, American Philosophical Society.

pp 162–163 Columbia River, Lewis & Clark Wild Refuge, Skamokawa, Washington, Wayne Mumford.

p 164 Surf, Wayne Mumford.

pp 164–165 Columbia River near Skamania, Washington, Wayne Mumford.

pp 166–167 Moss, Mt. Hood National Forest, Oregon, Wayne Mumford.

pp 168–169 Spruce bog, Fort Canby State Park, Washington, Wayne Mumford.

p 169 Historic Fort Clatsop near Astoria, Oregon, Wayne Mumford.

pp 170 Leaves, Wayne Mumford.

p 170–171 *Eulachon,* Codex J: 93, vol. 6, p. 343, neg. 871, American Philosophical Society.

p 172 Carved wood bowl, 19th century, Jerry Taylor, Maryhill Museum of Art, Goldendale, Washington; spruce branch, Wayne Mumford; outfitted Chinookan canoe, Wayne Mumford.

p 173 Sketch plan of Fort Clatsop, William Clark, December 7, 1805, ink on leather, L/A 419, Clark Family Papers, Missouri Historical Society, St. Louis; *The Salt Makers,* John F. Clymer, 1975, courtesy Mrs. Clymer and the Clymer Museum of Art.

p 174 Clark's draft, January 6–10, 1806, route to the whale site, Courtesy American Philosophical Society.

pp 174–175 Tillamook Head, Ecola State Park, Oregon, Wayne Mumford.

pp 176–177 *Sacajawea at the Big Water,* John F. Clymer, 1974, courtesy Mrs. Clymer and the Clymer Museum of Art.

pp 178–179 Rainbow over Crazy Mountains, Montana, Wayne Mumford.

p 180 Blue Mountains and Columbia River, Oregon, Wayne Mumford.

pp 180–181 Rooster Rock near the Columbia River, Oregon, Wayne Mumford.

pp 182–183 Three Forks, Montana, Lewis & Clark campsite 27–29 July 1806, Wayne Mumford.

p 184–185 *The Lewis Crossing,* John F. Clymer, 1968, courtesy Mrs. Clymer and the Clymer Museum of Art.

p 186 *Mehkshéhme-Sukáhs, Piegan Blackfeet Chief,* Karl Bodmer, Joslyn Art Museum, Omaha, Nebraska, gift of Enron Art Foundation.

p 186–187 Camp Disappointment/Cut Bank Creek, Montana, Wayne Mumford.

p 188 Fight site, Two Medicine River, Montana, Wayne Mumford.

p 190 Horses at Big Hole Valley, Montana, Wayne Mumford.

pp 192–193 *Captain Clark-Buffalo Gangue,* John F. Clymer, 1978, courtesy Mrs. Clymer and the Clymer Museum of Art.

pp 194–195 Yellowstone River, Montana, Wayne Mumford.

p 195 Clark's Signature, Pompey's Pillar, Montana, Wayne Mumford.

p 196 Ruby Range, Jefferson River Valley, Montana, Wayne Mumford.

pp 198–199 Lewis and Clark: "Tracks" map from Nicholas Biddle, 1814, restrike from original plates, Friends of the Library printing, neg. 910, American Philosophical Society.

Journal excerpts are from *The Journals of the Lewis & Clark Expedition,* Gary E. Moulton, editor, published by University of Nebraska Press, c1983–1991. Author annotations are in brackets. Listing of flora and fauna first recorded by Lewis and Clark are cited from *Lewis and Clark: Pioneering Naturalists* by Paul Russell Cutright, University of Illinois Press, Chicago, 1969.

One hundred twenty-two species and subspecies of animals were observed and recorded by the explorers in the Corps' journals during the Expedition.

Fish

July 24, 1804 Channel catfish—*Ictalurus punctatus* Raf. Taken from Missouri at Camp White Catfish, just above mouth of Platte River.

Aug. 25, 1804 Blue catfish—*Icatalurus furcatus* Lesueu River. Taken from Missouri near mouth of Vermillion River, Clay Co., South Dakota on north, Dixon Co.; Nebraska on south.

Nov. 11, 1805 White sturgeon—*Acipenser transmontanu* Richardson. On the Pacific coast just north of Cape Disappointment, Pacific Co., Washington.

June 11, 1805 Goldeye—*Amphiodon alosoides* Raf. Above junction of Marias River with Missouri, Chouteau Co., Montana.

June 11, 1805. Sauger—*Stizostedion Canadense* Smith. Pulled from Missouri above the mouth of Marias River, Chouteau Co., Montana.

June 13, 1805 Cutthroat trout—*Salmo clarkii* Richardson. Discovered and described by Lewis at Great Falls, Cascade Co., Montana.

Feb. 24-25, 1806 Eulachon; candle fish—*Thaleichthys pacificus* Rich. Described by Lewis and drawn by Clark at Fort Clatsop.

March 13, 1806? Starry flounder—*Platichthys stellatus* Pallas. Referred to by Lewis at Fort Clatsop, Clatsop Co., Oregon.

March 13, 1806? Steelhead trout—*Salmo gairdneri* Richardson. Described by Lewis at Fort Clatsop.

April 26, 1806 Columbia River chub—*Myolcheilus lateralis* Agassiz and Pickering. Taken from Columbia below mouth of Umatilla River, Benton Co., Washington.

April 29, 1806 Northern squawfish—*Ptychocheilus oregonensis* Richardson. Encountered by Lewis at the mouth of Walla Walla River, Walla Walla Co., Washington.

July 16, 1806 Mountain sucker—*Pantosteus platyrhynchus* Cope. Taken from Yellowstone River just east of present-day Livingston, Park Co., Montana.

Reptiles and Amphibians

May 18, 1804? Plains horned toad—*Phrynosoma cornutum* Harlan. Lewis sent Jefferson a specimen from St. Louis.

August 5, 1804? Bull snake—*Pituophis sayi sayi* Schlegel. Described by Lewis near mouth of Niobrara River, Bon Homme Co., South Dakota, on north, Knox Co., Nebraska on south.

June 15, 1805 Prairie rattler—*Crotalus viridis viridis* Rafinesque. Described by Lewis at Great Falls, Cascade Co,m Montana.

June 25, 1805? Water terrapin—*Pseudomys troosti elegansi* Wied. Noted by Lewis at great Falls, Cascade Co., Montana.

July 23, 1805 Western hog-nosed snake—*Heterodon nasicus nasicus* Baird and Girard. Discovered by Lewis not far from present-day Townsend, Broadwater Co., Montana.

July 24, 1805 Western garter snake—*Thamnophis ordinoides vagrans* Baird and Girard. Discovered by Lewis near present-day Townsend, Broadwater Co., Montana.

March 11, 1806? California newt; warty salamander—*Triturus torosus torosusi* Rathke. Discovered at "grand rapids," namely Cascades; described by Lewis at Fort Clatsop.

March 28, 1806 Northwestern garter snake—*Thamnophis sirtilas concinnus* Hallowell. Found on Deer Island above Cowlitz River, Cowlitz Co., Washington.

March 29, 1806? Western frog—*Rana pretiosa pretiosa* Baird and Girard. Noted by Lewis near mouth of Lewis's River, Cowlitz or Clark Co., Washington, on north, Columbia Co., Oregon on south.

April 24, 1806 Western fence lizard—*Sceloporus occidentalis* Baird and Girard. Encountered by Lewis near Present-day Roosevelt, Kickitat Co., Washington.

April 25, 1806 Northern Pacific rattler—*Crotalus viridis oreganus* Holbrook. Killed near present-day Roosevelt, Klickitat Co., Washington.

May 29, 1806 Pigmy horned toad—*Phrynosoma douglassi douglassi* Bell. Described by Lewis at Camp Chopunnish, Idaho.

May 30, 1806 Columbian toad—*Bufo boreas boreas* Baird and Girard. Observed by Lewis at Camp Chopunnish, Clearwater River, Idaho Co., Idaho.

May 30, 1806 Pacific tree frog—*Hyla regilla* Baird and Girard. Observed by Lewis at Camp Chopunnish, Idaho Co., Idaho.

July 29, 1806 Soft-shelled turtle—*Amyda spinifera spinifers* Lesueu River. Caught by Clark where Tongue River empties into Yellowstone at present-day Miles City, Custer Co., Montana.

Birds

Aug. 5, 1804 Least tern—*Sterna albifrons antillarum* Lesson. Fully described by Lewis on Missouri, Washington Co., Neb. on west, Harrison Co., Iowa on east.

Sept. 12, 1804 Prairie sharp-tailed grouse—*Pedioecetes phasianellus campestris* Ridgway. Discovered by Lewis and Clark in South Dakota Charles Mix Co. On north of Missouri, Gregory Co. on south.

Sept. 16, 1804 Black-billed magpie—*Pica pica hudsonia* Sabine. Discovered near the site of present-day Chamberlain, South Dakota Lyman Co. on west of Missouri and Brule Co. on east.

Oct. 17, 1804 Nuttall's poor-will—*Phalaenoptilus nuttallii nutallii* Audubon. Discovered by Lewis and Clark just below the mouth of Cannonball River, North Dakota, Sioux Co., on west and Emmons Co. on east.

April 10, 1805 Prairie horned lark—*Eremophila alpestris leucolaema* Coues. Noted by Lewis at Fort Mandan, McLean Co., North Dakota.

April 11, 1805? Norther flicker—*Colaptes auratus luteus* Bangs. Reported by Lewis at Fort Mandan, McLean Co., North Dakota.

April 14, 1805 Montana horned owl—*Bubo virginianus occidentalis* Stone. Discovered by Lewis. Camped that night in Montrail Co., North Dakota.

May 5, 1805 Hutchins's goose—*Branta canadensis hutchinsii* Richardson. Seen by Lewis above the mouth of Poplar River, Montana. Roosevelt Co. on north, McCone Co. on south.

May 9, 1805 Western willet—*Catoptrohporus semipalmatus inornatus* Brewste River. Discovered and fully described by Lewis. Expedition camped that night above present-day Fort Peck Dam, Valley Co., Montana.

June 4, 1805 McCown's Longspur—*Rhynchophanes mccownii* Lawr. Discovered by Lewis on Marias River, Chouteau Co., Montana.

June 5, 1805 Sage grouse—*Centrocercus urophasianus urophasianus* Bonap. Discovered by Lewis on Marias River, Chouteau Co., Montana.

June 8, 1805 Pale goldfinch—*spinus tristris pallidus* Mearns. Discovered on Marias River, Montana.

June 10, 1805? White-rumped shrike—*Lanius ludovicianus excubitorides* Swainson. Described by Lewis at mouth of Marias River, Chouteau Co., Montana.

June 22, 1805 Western meadowlark—*Sturnella neglecta neglecta* Audubon. Discovered by Lewis at Great Falls, Cascade Co., Montana.

June 23, 1805 Long-billed curlew—*Numenius americanus americanus* Bechstein. Observed by Lewis at Great Falls, Montana.

June 25, 1805? Brewer's blackbird—*Euphagus cyanocephalus* Wagler. Mentioned by Lewis at Great Falls, Cascade Co., Montana.

June 30, 1805? Pacific *nighthawk*—*Chordeiles minor hesperis* Grinell. Mentioned by Lewis at Great Falls, Cascade Co., Montana.

July 20, 1805 Lewis' woodpecker—*Asyndesmus lewis* Gray. Discovered by Lewis north of Helena, Lewis and Clark Co., Montana.

July 21, 1805 Richardson's blue grouse—*Dendragapus obscurus richardsonii* Douglas. Discovered by Lewis north of Helena, Lewis and Clark Co., Montana.

Aug. 1, 1805 Pinon jay—*Gymnorhinus cyanocephalus* Wied. Discovered by Lewis on Jefferson River, Montana, Madison Co., on south and Jefferson Co. on north.

Aug. 22, 1805 Clark's nutcracker—*Nucifraga columbiana* Wilson. Discovered by Clark near present town of Tendoy on Lemhi River, Lemhi Co., Idaho.

Sept. 20, 1805 Black-headed jay—*Cyanocitta stelleri annectens* Baird. First seen by Lewis on this date on the Lolo Trail. Described by Lewis March 4, 1806, at Fort Clatsop.

Sept. 20, 1805 Oregon ruffed grouse—*Bonasa umbellus sabini* Douglas. First noted by Lewis on Lolo Trail; described at Fort Clatsop March 3, 1806.

Sept. 20, 1805 Franklin's grouse—*Canachites canadensis franklinii* Douglas. Discovered by Lewis on Lolo Trail, Idaho. Described at Fort Clatsop.

Oct. 20, 1805 Double-crested cormorant—*Phalacrocorax auritus auritus* Lesson. Observed by Lewis and Clark on Columbia below mouth of Umatilla River Klickitat Co., Washington, on north and Morrow Co., Oregon on south.

Nov. 29, 1805? Western common crow—*Corvus brachyrhynchos hesperis* Ridgway. Reported by Clark at Tongue Point near present-day Astoria, Oregon.

Jan. 3, 1806? Oregon jay—*Perisoreus conadensis obscurus* Ridgway. Referred to by Lewis at Fort Clatsop.

March 1, 1806? Columbian sharp-tailed grouse—*Pedioecetes phasianellus columbianus* Ord. Described by Lewis at Fort Clatsop.

March 3, 1806? American raven—*Corvus corax sinuatus* Wagler. Mentioned by Lewis at Fort Clatsop. Different from subspecies *C. c. Principalis* known to Lewis and Clark in the East.

March 3, 1806? Dusky horned owl—*Bubo virginianus saturatus* Ridgway. Seen on the Kooskooskee in Idaho Co., Idaho. Described by Lewis at Fort Clatsop.

ANIMAL LISTING

March 3, 1806? Northwestern crow—*Corvus caurinus* Baird. Described by Lewis at Fort Clatsop.

March 4, 1806? Western pileated woodpecker—*Dryocopus pileatus picinus* Bangs. Referred to by Lewis at Fort Clatsop.

March 4, 1806? Western winter wren—*Troglodytes troglodytes pacificus* Baird. Noted by Lewis at Fort Clatsop.

March 7, 1806? Bonaparte's gull—*Larus philadelphia* Ord. Described by Lewis at Fort Clatsop.

March 7, 1806? Glaucous-winged gull—*Larus glaucescens* Neumann. Described by Lewis at Fort Clatsop.

March 7, 1806 Pacific loon—*Gavia arctica pacifica* Lawrence. Described by Lewis at Fort Clatsop.

March 7, 1806? Pacific fulmar—*fulmarus glacialis rodgersii* Cassin. Described by Lewis at Fort Clatsop.

March 7, 1806? Western gull—*Larus occidentalis occidentalis* Audobon. Described by Lewis at Fort Clatsop.

March 7, 1806? Western grebe—*Aechmophorus occidentalis* Lawrence. Described by Lewis at Fort Clatsop.

March 8, 1806? Lesser Canada goose—*Branta candensis leucopareia* Brandt. Described by Lewis at Fort Clatsop.

March 9, 1806? Whistling swan—*Olor columbianus* Ord. Described by Lewis at Fort Clatsop.

March 10, 1806? Red-necked grebe—*Podiceps grisegena holbollii* Reinhardt. Described by Lewis at Fort Clatsop.

March 15, 1806? White-fronted goose—*Anser albifrons frontalis* Baird. Described by Lewis at Fort Clatsop.

March 28, 1806? Ring-necked duck—*Aythya collaris* Donovan. Described by Lewis above Fort Clatsop.

April 5, 1806? Harris's woodpecker—*Dendrocopos villosus harrisi* Audubon. Referred to by Lewis above mouth of Willamette River, Multnomah Co., Oregon.

April 7, 1806 Mountain quail—*Oreortyx pictus pictusi* Douglas. Discovered and described by Lewis above the mouth of Washougal River, Multnomah Co., Oregon on south and Clark Co., Washington on the north.

June 6, 1806 Western tanager—*Piranga ludiviciana* Wilson. Discovered and described by Lewis at Camp Chopunnish on Clearwater River Idaho.

June 15, 1806 Cabanis's woodpecker—*Dendrocopos villosus hyloscopus* Cabanis and Heine. Seen by Lewis on Lolo Trail, Idaho Co., Idaho.

June 15, 1806 Broad-tailed hummingbird—*selasphorus platycercus platycercus* Swainson. Discovered by Lewis just west of Hungry Creek on Lolo Trail, Idaho.

July 1, 1806? Western mourning dove—*Zenaidura macroura marginella* Woodhouse. Mentioned by Lewis where the Lolo Creek empties into Bitterroot River, Missoula Co., Montana.

Aug. 7, 1806 Forster's tern—*sterna forsteri* Nuttall. Seen by Lewis on Missouri just above mouth of Yellowstone River, North Dakota. Williams Co. on north and McKenzie Co. on south.

Mammals

May 19, 1804 White-tailed deer—*Dama virginianus macroura* Rafinesque. Lewis and Clark killed their first deer just above St. Charles, Missouri, St. Charles Co. on north, St. Louis Co. on south.

May 30, 1804 Plains gray wolf—*Canis lupus nubilus* Say. First observed near site of present Leavenworth, Kansas, and from there commonly seen to the western limits of its range.

May 31, 1804 Eastern wood rat—*Neotoma floridana*

Ord. Discovered below the mouth of Osage River, Missouri, Osage Co. on south, Callaway Co. on north.

July 3, 1804 Missouri beaver—*Castor canadensis missouriensis* V. Bailey. First mentioned near Iatan, Platte Co., Missouri, and from there on frequently. Most abundantly in the region of Three Forks, Montana.

Sept 14, 1804 White-tailed jackrabbit—*Lupus townsendii campanius* Hollister. Discovered by Lewis and Clark near present-day Chamberlain, South Dakota.

June 13, 1804 Raccoon—*Procyon lotor hirtus* Nelson and Goldman. First encountered near Chariton River, Missouri. And again on Oct. 21, 1805 on Columbia above John Day River.

Sept. 14, 1804 Pronghorn—*Antilocapra americanan americana* Ord. Discovered by Lewis and Clark near mouth of Ball Creek, Lyman Co., South Dakota.

Sept. 15, 1804 Desert cottontail—*Sylvilagus audubonii baileyi* Merriam. Encountered near the mouth of White River, South Dakota.

Sept. 17, 1804 Mule deer; black-tailed deer—*Dama hemionus hemionus* Rafinesque. Discovered below the present-day site of Chamberlain, South Dakota.

Sept. 18, 1804 Coyote—*Canis latrans latrans* Say. Collected first specimen near site of present-day Chamberlain, South Dakota.

Nov. 9, 1804 Long-tailed weasel—*Mustela frenata longicauda* Bonaparte. Obtained at Fort Mandan. Shipped a white weasel to Jefferson on April 7, 1805.

April 7, 1805 Northern bobcat—*Lynx rufus pallescens* Merriam. Lewis and Clark shipped the skin of a Loucirvia from Fort Mandan to Jefferson.

April 7, 1805 Short-tailed shrew—*Blarina brevicauda brevicauda* Say. A tin box containing "mice" and other natural history specimens shipped from Fort Mandan.

April 9, 1805? Pocket gopher—*Thomomys talpoides rufescens* Wied. Described by Lewis above mouth of Knife River, North Dakota.

April 26, 1805 Audubon's mountain sheep—*Ovis canadensis auduboni* Merriam. Seen by J. Field at mouth of Yellowstone River, McKenzie Co., North Dakota Lewis and Clare met *O. c. canadensis* farther west.

April 29, 1805 Grizzly bear—*Ursus horribilis horribilis* Ord. Killed first grizzly just below Big Muddy Creek (Martha's River of Lewis and Clark), Montana, Roosevelt Co. on north, Richland Co. on south.

May 3, 1805 Yellow-haired porcupine—*Erethizon dorsatum epixanthum* Brandt. Discovered by Lewis and Clark at the mouth of Porcupine (now Poplar) River, Montana, Roosevelt Co. on north, Richland Co. on south.

May 10, 1805 Shiras's moose—*Alces alces shirasi* Nelson. Lewis reported seeing several near mouth of Milk River, Montana. Also noted by Lewis on July 7, 1806 near Lewis and Clark Pass, Lewis and Clark Co., Montana.

May 25, 1805 Two subspecies of striped skunk—*mephitis mephitis hudsonica* Richardson. Lewis and Clark discovered this subspecies above the mouth of Musselshell River, Fergus Co., Montana.

July 2, 1805 Bushy-tailed wood rat—*neotoma cinerea cinerea* Ord. Discovered by Lewis and Clark at Great Falls, Cascade Co., Montana.

July 6, 1805 Swift fox—*Vulpes velox velox* Say. Discovered by Lewis at Great Falls, Cascade Co., Montana.

July 8, 1805 Thirteen-lined ground squirrel—*Spermophilus tridecemlineatus pallidus* J.A. Allen.

Discovered and described by Lewis at Great Falls, Cascade Co., Montana.

Aug. 3, 1805 Mountain lion—*Felis concolor missoulensis* Goldman. Killed by Fields on Jefferson River between Three Forks and Twin Bridges, Montana.

Aug. 20, 1805 Ermine—*Mustela erminea invicta* Hall. Reproted by Lewis while among the Shoshoni on Lemhe River, Lemhe Co., Idaho.

Sept. 7, 1805 Black-tailed prairie dog—*Cunomyus ludovicianus ludovicianus* Ord. First collected by Lewis and Clark in Boyd Co., Nebraska.

Oct. 23, 1805 Harbor seal—*Phoca vitulina richardii* Gray. First seen at Narrows of Columbia, more than 100 miles from Pacific. Identified then as sea otters, though Lewis and Clark later admitted mistake.

Nov. 19, 1805 Columbian black-tailed deer—*Dama hemionus columbianus* Richardson. Discovered by Clark north of Cape Disappointment, Pacific Co., Washington.

Nov. 20, 1805 Sea otter—*Enhydra lutris nereis* Merriam. Lewis and Clark apparently first saw sea otter furs while encamped on Baker's Bay, north side of Columbia estuary, Pacific Co., Washington. They never did see a live sea otter River.

Dec. 2, 1805 Roosevelt's elk—*Cervus canadensis roosevelti* Merriam. Lewis and Clark killed the first Roosevelt's elk at the mouth of Columbia at Tongue Point near present-day Astoria, Oregon.

Feb 26, 1806? Mountain beaver—*Aplodontia rufa rufa* Raf. Described by Lewis at Fort Clatsop.

Feb. 21, 1806? Great-tailed fox—*Vulpes fulva macroura* Baird. Referred to by Lewis at Fort Clatsop.

Feb. 21, 1806? Oregon bobcat—*Lynx rufus faciatus* Raf. Described by Lewis at Fort Clatsop.

Feb. 22, 1806 Mountain goat—*Oreamnos americanus americanus* Blainville. Lewis wrote first description at Fort Clatsop. Seen Aug. 24, 1805 in Lemhi Co., Idaho.

Feb. 25, 1806? Douglas's squirrel—*Tamiasciurus douglasii douglasii* Bachman. Described by Lewis at Fort Clatsop.

Feb. 25, 1806? Townsend's chipmunk—*Eutamias townsendii townsendii* Bachman. Alluded to by Lewis at Fort Clatsop.

Feb. 25, 1806? Richardson's red squirrel—*Tamiasciurus hudsonicus richardsoni* Bachman. Described by Lewis at Fort Clatsop.

Feb. 25, 1806 Western gray squirrel—*Scirrus griseus griseus* Ord. Described by Lewis at Fort Clatsop.

Feb. 26, 1806? Townsend's mole—*Scapanus townsendii* Bachman.Referred to by Lewis at Fort Clatsop.

Feb. 26, 1806? Western badger—*Taxidea taxus neglecta* Mearns. Described by Lewis at Fort Clatsop.

April 2, 1806 Yellow-bellied marmot—*Marmota flaviventris avara* Bangs. Observed by Lewis on the north side of Columbia above mouth of John Day River, Klickitat Co., Washington.

April 16, 1806 Oregon pronghorn—*Antilocapra americana oregona* V. Bailey. Encountered on Columbia just below Ceilo Falls, Klickitat Co., Washington.

May 27, 1806 Columbian ground squirrel—*Spermophilus columbianus columbianus* Ord. Described by Lewis at Camp Chopunnish.

One hundred seventy-eight species of plants were documented and gathered during the exploration.

March 26, 1804 Osage orange—*Maclura aurantiaca* Nutt. St. Louis, Missouri. Lewis sent specimens to Jefferson

June/ July 1804? Pomme blanche; prairie apple—*Psoralea esculenta* Pursh. Most likely Lower Missouri.

July/ Aug. 1804? Lance-leaved psoralea—*Psoralea lanceolata* Pursh. Possibly collected between the Platte and Vermillion.

Aug. 17, 1804 Broad-leaved gum-plant—*Grindelia squarrosa* (Pursh) Dunal. Near old Omaha Indian village and Omaha Creek, Dakota Co., Nebraska.

Aug. 25, 1804 Large-flowered clammyweed—*Polanisia trachysperma* T. & G. At or near mouth of Vermillion River, Clay Co., South Dakota.

Sept. 2, 1804 Rabbit brush—*Bigelowia douglasii* Gray. South Dakota. Big Bend.

Sept. 4, 1804 Silvery buffalo-berry—*Shepherdia argentea* Nuttall. Mouth of Niobrara River, Don Homme Co., South Dakota on north, Knox Co., Nebraska, on south.

Sept. 5, 1804 Wood's rose—*Rosa woodsii* Lindl. Above mouth of Niobrara, South Dakota, Bon Homme Co., on north, Knox Co., Nebraska, on south.

Sept. 15, 1804 Cut-leaved sideranthus—*Amellus spinulosus* Pursh. White River, Lyman Co., South Dakota.

Sept. 15, 1804 Linear-leaved wormwood—*Artemisia dracunculoides* Pursh. South Dakota, near mouth of White River, Lyman Co. South Dakota.

Sept. 18, 1804 Missouri milk vetch—*Astragalus missouriensis* Nutt. South Dakota, just below Big Bend of Missouri.

Sept. 21, 1804 Aromatic aster—*Aster oblongifolius* Nuttall. South Dakota, just above Big Bend, Lyman Co.

Sept 21, 1804 Bushy atriplex—*Atriplex canescens* Pursh James. Big Bend South Dakota.

Sept. 21, 1804 Few-flowered psoralea—*Psoralea tenuiflora* Pursh. Just above Big Bend, Lyman Co., South Dakota on south, Hughes Co. on north.

Oct. 1, 1804 Hoary sagebrush—*Artemisia cana* Pursh. South Dakota, above mouth of Cheyenne River, Dewey Co.

Oct. 1, 1804 Long-leaved mugwort—*Artemisia longifolia* Nuttall. South Dakota, above mouth of Cheyenne River.

Oct. 1, 1804 Squaw bush—*Rhus triobata* Nuttall. Near mouth of Cheyenne River, South Dakota, Sully Co. on east, Dewey or Stanley Co. on west.

Oct. 12, 1804 Indian tobacco—*Nicotiana quadrivalvis* Pursh. Upper Arikara villages, appx 15 miles above mouth of Grand River, Corson Co, South Dakota.

Oct. 17, 1804 Silver-leaf psoralea—*Psoralea argophylla* Pursh. Southern North Dakota near mouth of Cannonball River, Emmons Co. to the east and Sioux and Morton Cos. to the west.

May 20, 1805 Brittle opuntia—*Opuntia fragilis* (Nutt.) Just below mouth of Musselshell River, Garfield Co., Montana on south and Phillips Co. on north.

June 6, 1805 Tansy—*Tanacetum nuttalli* T. & Nutt. Noted by Clark on Teton River, Chouteau Co., Montana.

June 18, 1805 White squaw currant—*Ribes cereum* Douglas. Described by Lewis at Great Falls, Cascade Co., Montana.

July 23, 1805 Leafy or Dwarf thistle—*Cirsium drummondii* T. & G. Boradwater Co., Montana, north of Three Forks.

July 23, 1805 Geyer's onion—*Allium geyeri* S. Wats. Central Broadwater Co., Montana, near Three Forks.

Aug 3, 1805 Western paper birch—*Betula occidentalis* Hooker. Jefferson River, Madison Co., Montana.

Aug. 13, 1805 Rocky Mountain maple—*Acer glabrum* Torrey. Lemhi River, Lemhi Co., Idaho.

Aug. 13, 1805 Western red baneberry—Actaea arguta Nuttall. Lemhi River, Lemhi Co., Idaho.

Aug. ? 1805 Lewis' monkey flower—*Mimulus lewisii* Pursh. Portage hill; perhaps Lemhi Pass.

Sept. 3, 1805 Lyall's angelica—*Angelica lyallii* Wats. North Fork of Salmon River, Lemhi Co., Idaho.

Sept. 4, 1805 Sitka mountain ash—*Pyrus sambucifolia?* (var. *pumila* Sargent). Lost Trail Pass from North Fork of Salmon, Lemhi Co., Idaho to Ross's Hole, Ravalli Co., Montana.

Sept. 14, 1805 Western larch—*Larix occidentalis* Nuttall. Bitterroot Mountains, Idaho.

Sept. 15, 1805 Subalpine fir—*Abies lasiocarpa* Hook. Lolo Trail, Bitterroot Mountains. Idaho.

Sept. 16, 1805 Engelmann spruce—*Picea engelmannii* Parry. Noted by Lewis and Clark on Lolo Trail Bitterroot Mountains, Idaho Co., Idaho.

Sept. 16, 1805 Whitebark pine—*Pinus monticola* Douglas. Described by Lewis at Fort Clatsop.

Sept. 20, 1805 Common snowberry—*Symphoricarpos albus laevigatus* (Fernald) Blake. Noted by Lewis on westward transit of Lolo Trail, Idaho.

Sept. 20, 1805 Wavy-leaved or Sitka alder—*Alnus sinuata* (Regel). Lolo Trail, Idaho Co., Idaho.

Sept. 20, 1805 Western red cedar; Western arbor vitae—*Thuja plicata* Donn. First observed on Lolo Trail.

Sept. 21, 1805 Common matchweed; Broomwed—*Solidago sarothrae* Pursh. Just above Big Bend, South Dakota, Hughes Co., on north and Lyman Co., on south.

Sept. 25, 1805 Pacific yew—*Taxus brevifolia* Nutall. Lolo Trail.

Oct. 1, 1805 Ponderosa Pine—*Pinus ponderosa* Douglas. Canoe Camp near present-day Orofino, Lewis Co., Idaho.

Oct. 12, 1805 Netleaf hackberry—*Celtis reticulata* Torrey. Snake River near Riparia, Whitman Co., Washington

Oct. 12, 1805 Peach-leaved willow—*Salix amygdaloides* Anderss. Noted by Lewis on Snake River near present town of Riparia, Whitman Co., Washington.

Oct. 22, 1805 California hazelut—*Corylus californica* (DC) Rose. Columbia near mouth of Deschutes River.

Oct. 30, 1805 Vine maple—*Acer circinatum* Pursh. Great Rapids of Columbia River, Washington and Hood River Co., Oregon.

Oct. 16, 1805 Many-spined opuntia—*Opuntia polyacantha* Haworth. Sanke River, Washington Franklin Co., on north and Walla Walla Co. on south.

Oct. ? 1805 Dull Oregon grape—*Berberis nervosa* Pursh. The Narrows below Celilo Falls.

Oct. ?, 1805 Oregon white-topped aster—*Aster oregonus* Nuttall. Snake River, southeast Washington.

Nov. 1, 1805 Madrone—*Arbutus menziesii* Pursh. Cascades of the Columbia.

Nov. 6, 1805 White alder—*Alnus rhombifolia* Nutt. Mouth of Cowlitz River, Cowlitz, Co., Washington.

Nov. 30, 1805 California rhododendron—G. Don. Noted by Lewis and Clark near present-day Astoria, Oregon.

Nov. 30, 1805 Oregon ash—*Fraxinus latifolia* Benth. South side of Columbia near present-day Astoria, Oregon

? ? 1805 Narrow-leaved purple coneflower—*Echinacea angustifolia* DC. Fort Mandan, McLean Co., North Dakota.

Jan. 20, 1806 Salal—*Gaultheria shallon* Pursh. Fort Clatsop, on Lewis and Clark River, Clatsop Co., Oregon.

Jan. 22, 1806 Western bracken—*Pteridium aquilinum pubescens* Underw. Described by Lewis at Fort Clatsop.

Jan. 24, 1806 Chinook licorice—*Lupinus littoralis* Doug. Described at Fort Clatsop.

Jan. 27, 1806 Evergreen Huckleberry—*Vaccinium ovatum* Pursh. Fort Clatsop on Lewis and Clark River, Clatsop Co., Oregon.

Jan. 28, 1806 Oregon crab apple—*Pyrus fusca* Rafinesque. Described by Lewis at Fort Clatsop.

Feb. 2, 1806 Blue elderberry—*Sambucus glauca* Nuttall. Described by Lewis at Fort Clatsop.

Feb. 4, 1806 Sitka spruce—*Picea sitchensis* (Bong.) Carr. Described by Lewis at Fort Clatsop.

Feb. 5, 1806 Mountain hemlock—*Tsunga mertensiana* (Bong.) Carr. Described by Lewis at Fort Clatsop.

Feb. 6, 1806 Grand fir—*Abies grandis* Lindley. Fort Clatsop, Clatsop Co. Oregon.

Feb. 6, 1806 Western white pine—*Pinus monticola* Douglas. Described by Lewis at Fort Clatsop.

Feb. 7, 1806 Blue huckleberry—*Vaccinium membranaceum* Dougl. Described by Lewis at Fort Clatsop.

March 13, 1806 Edible thistle; Shanataque—*Cirsium edule* Nuttall. Fort Clatsop, Clatsop Co., Oregon.

March 15, 1806 Oregon wood-sorrel—*Oxalis oregona* Nuttall. Noted at Fort Clatsop.

March 25, 1806 Lyall's nettle—*Urtica lyallii* S. Wats. Noted by Lewis two days' travel above Fort Clatsop.

March 25, 1806 Pacific blackberry—*Rubus vitifolius* Cham. & Sch. Noted by Lewis to days' travel above Fort Clatsop.

March 25, 1806 Straggly gooseberry—*Ribes divaricatum* Douglas. Noted by Lewis on lower Columbia near Puget's Island.

March 26, 1806 Oregon white oak—*Quercus garryana* Douglas. Below mouth of Cowlitz River, Cowlitz Co., Washington on north, Columbia Co., Oregon on south.

March 26, 1806 Red alder—*Alnus rubra* Bongard. Between Puget's Island and Cowlitz River, Washington.

March 27, 1806 Red flowering currant—*Ribes sanguineum* Pursh. Near mouth of Cowlitz River, Cowlitz, Co., Washington.

March 27, 1806 Salmonberry—*Rubus spectabilis* Pursh. Near mouth of Cowlitz River Cowlitz Co., Washington, on north, Columbia Co., Oregon, on south.

April 1, 1806 Slender toothwort—*Dentaria tenella* Pursh. Near mouth of Sandy River (Quicksand River of Lewis and Clark). Multnomah Co., Oregon.

April 8, 1806 Canyon gooseberry—*Ribes menziesii* Pursh. Below Beacon Rock and Lower Cascades. Skamania Co., Washington, on north, and Multnomah Co., Oregon, on south.

April 10, 1806 Bigleaf maple—*Acer macrophyllum* Pursh. Cascades below Wind River, Oregon.

PLANT LISTING

April 10, 1806 Mission bells; Rice root—*Fritillaria lanceolata* Pursh. Brant Island just above Beacon Rock. Skamania Co., Washington, on north and Multnomah Co., Oregon, on south.

April 10, 1806 Wetern wake-robin—*Trillium ovatum* Pursh. Lower Cascades above Beacon Rock. Skamania Co., Washington, on north, Multnomah Co., Oregon, on south.

April 11, 1806 Oregon grape—*Berberis aquifolium* Pursh. Cascades of Columbia

April 14, 1806 Menzies' larkspur—*Delphinium menziesii* DC. On day's journey below The Dalles, Wasco Co., Oregon.

April 15, 1806 Pestle parsnip—*Smyrnium nudicaule* Pursh. Rock Fort Camp, The Dalles, Wasco Co., Oregon.

April 15, 1806 Saskatoon serviceberry—*Amelanchier alnifolia* (Nutt.)—Nuttall. Mouth of Mill Creek (Rock Fort Camp), The Dalles, Wasco Co., Oregon.

April 15, 1806 Thimbleberry—*Rubus nutkanus velutinus* Brew. Rock Fort Camp, The Dalles, Wasco Co., Oregon.

April 16, 1806 Dark-leaved mugwort—*Artemisia ludoviciana* Nutt. Rock Fort Camp, Wasco Co., Oregon.

April 16, 1806 Golden currant—*Ribes aureum* Pursh. Below Celilo Falls, Klickitat Co., Washington.

April 17, 1806 Large-headed clover—*Trifolium macrocephalum* (Pursh) Poiret. Rock Fort Camp, The Dalles, Wasco Co., Oregon.

April 17, 1806 Linear-leaved phacelia—*Hydrophllum lineare* Pursh. Rock Fort Camp, The Dalles, Wasco Co., Oregon.

April 17, 1806 Narrow-leaved collomia—*Collomia linearis* Nutt. Rock Fort Camp, The Dalles, Wasco Co., Oregon.

April 17, 1806 Slender popcorn flower—*Plagiobothrys tenellus* (Nutt.) Gray. Rock Fort Camp, The Dalles, Wasco Co., Oregon.

April 17, 1806 Small-flowered collinsia—*Antirrhinum tenellum* Pursh. Rock Fort Camp, The Dalles, Wasco Co., Oregon.

April 17, 1806 Uropappus—*Microseris macrochaeta* (Gray) Schultze-Bip. Rock Fort Camp, The Dalles, Wasco Co., Oregon.

April 20, 1806 Sagebrush—*Artemisia tridentata* Nutt. Narrows of the Columbia below Celilo Falls.

April 20, 1806 Wild hyacinth—*Brodiaea grandiflora* Pursh. Celilo Falls, Klickitat Co., Washington.

April 25, 1806 Gairdner's Yampah; Fennel—*Perideridia gairdneri* (H. & A.) Mathias. Between Celilo Falls and mouth of Walla Walla River, Benton Co., Washington.

April, 29, 1806 Black hawthorn—*Crataegus douglasii* Lind. Mouth of Walla Walla River, Walla Walla Co., Washington.

April 30, 1806 Spring birch—*Betula fontinalis* Sargent. Walla Walla River, Walla Walla Co., Washington.

May 6, 1806 Biscuit root; Lewis' lomatium—*Peucedanum simplex* Nuttall. Above mouth of Potlatch River (Colter's Creek) on Clearwater, Nez Perce Co., Idaho.

May 6, 1806 Fetid rayless goldenrod—*Bigelowia graveolens* Gray. Above mouth of Potlatch (Colter) River on Clearwater, Nez Perce Co., Idaho.

May 6, 1806 Lewis' syringa—*Philadelphus lewisii* Pursh. Just above Potlatch River (Coulter's Creek) on south side of Clearwater, Idaho.

May 7, 1806 Showy phlox—*Phlox speciosa* Pursh. On the south side of the Clearwater below Camp Chopunnish.

May 8, 1806 Yellow bell—*Fritillaria pudica* (Pursh) Spreng. Above Potlatch River, Nez Perce Co., Idaho.

May 8, 1806 Yellow fawn lily—*Erythronium grandiflorum* Pursh. South side of Clearwater above Potlatch River, Nez Perce Co., Idaho.

May 17, 1806 Mariposa lily—*Calochortus elegans* Pursh. Camp Chopunnish, on Clearwater River, Idaho Co., Idaho.

May 20, 1806 Cascade pentstemon—*Penstemon serrulatus* Menzies. Camp Chopunnish on Clearwater River, Idaho Co., Idaho.

May 29, 1806 Cascara sagrada—*Rhamnus purshiana* DC. Camp Chopunnish on Clearwater River, Idaho.

May 29, 1806 Ocean spray—*Spiraea discolor* Pursh. Camp Chopunnish, Clearwater River, Idaho Co., Idaho.

May 30, 1806 Tolmie's onion—*Allium tolmieri* Baker. Camp Chopunnish, Idaho Co., Idaho.

May ? 1806 Sugar bowls—*Clematis hirsutissima* Pursh. Possibly on Clearwater below Camp Chopunnish.

June 1, 1806 Ragged robin; Beautiful Clarkia—*Clarkia pulchella* Pursh. Camp Chopunnish, Idaho Co., Idaho.

June 1, 1806 Western wallflower—*Erysimum asperum* (Nutt.) DC. Camp Chopunnish, Idaho Co., Idaho.

June 5, 1806 Giant rye grass—*Ellymus condensatus* Presl. Camp Chopunnish, Idaho Co., Idaho.

June 5, 1806 Large mountain brome grass—*Bromus marginatus* Nees. Camp Chopunnish, Idaho Co., Idaho.

June 5, 1806 Narrow-leaved skullcap—*Scutellaria angustifolia* Pursh. Camp Chopunnish, Clearwater River, Idaho Co., Idaho.

June 5, 1806 Orange honeysuckle—*Lonicera ciliosa* (Pursh) DC. Camp Chopunnish. On June 16, Lolo Trail, Hungry Creek, Idaho Co., Idaho.

June 5, 1806 Silky lupine—*Lupinus sericeus* Pursh. Camp Chopunnish, on the Clearwater River, Idaho.

June 6, 1806 Oregon sunshine—*Actinella lanata* Pursh. Camp Chopunnish, near Kamiah, Idaho Co., Idaho.

June 9, 1806 Rayless camomile—*Santolina suaveolens* Pursh. Camp Chopunnish, on the Clearwater River, Idaho Co., Idaho.

June 9, 1806 Virgate phacelia—*Phacelia heterophylla* Pursh. Camp Chopunnish, Idaho Co., Idaho.

June 10, 1806 Blue bunch wheatgrass—*Festucca spicata* Pursh. On the plains of the Columbia, Weippe Prairie, Idaho or Clearwater Co., Idaho.

June 10, 1806 Cluster rose—*Rosa pisocarpa* A. Gray. Noted by Lewis between Camp Chopunnish and Weippe Prairie.

June 10, 1806 Common lomatium—*Peucedanum utriculatum* C. & R. Lewis and Clark travelled from Camp Chopunnish to Weippee Prairie, Idaho and Clearwater Cos., Idaho.

June 10, 1806 Cut-leaved daisy—*Erigeron compositus* Pursh. Probably Camp Chopunnish, May 14 to June 10, 1806.

June 10, 1806 Hair-grass—*Aira brevifolia* Pursh. plains of Columbia near Kooskooshee River.

June 10, 1806 Nootka rose—*Rosa nutkana* Presl. Noted by Lewis en route from Camp Chopunnish to Weippe Prairie, Idaho.

June 12, 1806 Narrowleaf cottonwood—*Populus angustifolia* James. Described by Lewis on north bank of Missouri between Marias River and Great Falls. Chouteau Co., Montana.

June 12, 1806 Tassels—*Geum triflorum* Pursh. Weippe Prairie, Clearwater Co., Idaho.

June 12, 1806 Western snakeweed—*Polygonum bistortoides* Pursh. Weippe Prairie, Clearwater Co., Idaho.

June 14, 1806 Clustered swertia—*Swertia fastigiata* Pursh. Weippe Prairie, Clearwater Co., Idaho.

June 14, 1806 Northern sun-cup—*Oenothera heterantha* Nuttall. Weippe Prairie, Clearwater Co., Idaho.

June 15, 1806 Bear grass; Western turkey-beard—*Xerophyllum tenax* (Pursh) Nutt. Just east of Weippe Prairie, Clearwater Co., Idaho.

June 15, 1806 Petioled wake-robin—*Trillium petiolatum* Pursh. Left Weippe Prairie, attempting to cross Britterroots, Clearwater Co., Idaho.

June 16, 1806 Northwest crimson columbine—*Aquilegia formosa* Fischer. Lolo Trail, Idaho.

June 16, 1806 Oregon boxwood—*Pachistima myrsinites* (Push) Rafinesque. Lolo Trail (Hungry Creek), Idaho Co., Idaho.

June 16, 1806 Sticky currant—*Ribes viscossissimum* Pursh. Hungry Creek on Lolo Trail, Idaho Co., Idaho.

June 16, 1806 Yellow-flowering pea—*Lathyrus ochroleucus* Hooker. Lolo Trail, Idaho.

June 23, 1806 Camas—*Camassia quamash* (Pursh) Greene. Weippe Prairie, Clearwater Co., Idaho.

June 24-29, 1806 Sticky Laurel; Mountain balm—*Ceanothus velutinus* Dougl. ex Hook. Bitterroots.

June 25, 1806 California false hellebore—*Veratrum californicum* Durand. Hungry Creek, Lolo Trail, Idaho Co., Idaho.

June 26, 1806 Lewis and Clark's synthyris—*Synthyris missurica* (Raf.) Penn. Hungry Creek. Lolo Trail, Idaho Co., Idaho.

June 26, 1806 Scarlet gilia—*Cantua aggregata* Push. Hungry Creek. Lolo Trail, Idaho Co., Idaho.

June 27, 1806 American Jacob's ladder—*Polemonium caeruleum* A. Gray. On Lolo Trail, Idaho.

June 27, 1806 Buckbrush; Chapparal—*Ceanothus sanguineus* Pursh. Lolo Trail, Idaho Co., Idaho.

June 27, 1806 Linear-leaved montia—*Claytonia linearis* Dougl. ex Hook. On Lolo Trail, Idaho Co., Idaho

June 27, 1806 Long-tailed wild ginger—*Asarum caudatum* Lindley. Lolo Trail, Idaho Co., Idaho.

June 27, 1806 Western spring beauty—*Claytonia lanceolata* Pursh. Divide between N. Fork of Clearwater and Lochsa Rivers, Idaho Co., Idaho.

June 28, 1806 Western huckleberry—*Vaccinium occidentale* A. Gray. Described by Lewis as "whortleberry." Lolo Trail.

June 30, 1806 Mountain lady's slipper—*Cypripedium montanum* Dougl. At or near Lolo Hot Springs, Lolo Creek, Missoula Co., Montana.

June ? 1806 Shrubby pentstemon—*Gerardia fruticosa* Pursh. Probably Lolo Trail, Idaho Co., Idaho.

July 1, 1806 Bitterroot; Rock rose—*Lewisia rediviva* Pursh. Mouth of Lolo (Traveler's Rest) Creek, Missoula Co., Montana.

July 1, 1806 Narrow-petaled stonecrop—*Sedum stenopetalum* Pursh. At mouth of Lolo (Traveler's Rest) Creek, Missoula Co., Montana.

July 1, 1806 Owl's clover—*Orthocarpus tenuifolius* (Pursh) Benth. Mouth of Lolo (Traveler's Rest) Creek, Missoula Co., Montana.

July 1, 1806 Silver oxytrope—*Oxytropis argentala* Pursh. At Bitterroot River at mouth of Lolo Creek.

July 1, 1806 Small-headed clover—*Trifolium microcephalum* Pursh. Mouth of Lolo (Traveler's Rest) Creek, Missoula Co., Montana.

July 4, 1806 Large monkey flower—*Mimulus lluteus*

Pursh. On Blackfoot River above present-day Missoula, Missoula Co., Montana.

July 5, 1806 Western blue-flag—*Iris missouriensis* Nuttall. Blackfoot or Steens' Prairie. Lewis and Clark Co., Montana.

July 6, 1806 Antelope brush—*Purshia tridentata* (Pursh) DC. Blackfoot or Stevens' Prairie just west of Lewis and Clark Pass, Lewis and Clark Co., Missouri.

July 6, 1806 Great-flowered gaillardia—*Gaillardia aristata* Pursh. One day's travel west of Lewis and Clark Pass, Lewis and Clark Co., Montana.

July 6, 1806 Lousewort—*Pedicularis scopulorum* Gray? Approaching Lewis and Clark Pass, on headwaters of Blackfoot River, Montana.

July 6, 1806 Silverberry—*Elaeagnus argentea* Pursh. Blackfoot or Stevens' Prairie of today. One day's journey west of Lewis and Clark Pass.

July 7, 1806 Balsam root—*Buphthalmum sagittatum* Pursh. Lewis and Clark Pass, Lewis and Clark Co., Montana.

July 7, 1806 Glaucous zygadene—*Zygadenus elegans* Pursh. Crossing the Continental Divide at Lewis and Clark Pass, Lewis and Clark Co., Montana.

July 7, 1806 Involucred fly-honey-suckle—*Lonicera involucrata* (Rich.) Banks. Lewis and Clark Pass, Montana.

July 7, 1806 Silvery lupine—*Lupinus argenteus* Pursh. On headwaters of Blackfoot River near Lewis and Clark Pass.

July 9, 1806 Lewis' wild flax—*Linum lewissi* Pursh. Sun River approaching Great Falls, Cascade Co., Montana.

July 17, 1806 Scapose primrose—*Oenothera caespitosa* Nutt. Great Falls to Teton (Tansy) River. Cascade and Teton Cos., Montana.

July 20, 1806 Greasewood—*Sarcobatus vermiculatus* (Hook.) Torrey. Just below forks of the Marias River, Glacier Co., Montana.

July 20, 1806 Nuttall's atriplex—*Atriplex nuttallii* Wats. Below forks of Marias River, between Pondera and Toole Cos., Montana.

July 20, 1806 Red false mallow—*Cristaria coccinea* Pursh. Near forks of Marias River, probably Glacier Co., Montana.

July 28, 1806 White-margined spurge—*Euphorbia marginata* Pursh. Most likely the Marias River.

Aug. 10, 1806 White milkwort—*Polygala alba* Nuttall. At or near mouth of Little Muddy River (White Earth River of Lewis and Clark), North Dakota Williams Co. on north of Missouri, McKenzie Co. on south.

Aug. 29, 1806 Pink cleome—*Cleome serrulata* Pursh. Near entrance of Vermillion River, Clay Co., South Dakota.

Sept. 16, 1806 Lodgepole pine—*Pinus contorta* Douglas. Noted by Lewis and Clark on Lolo Trail.

? 1806 Nuttall's or Mountain dogwood—*Cornus nuttallii* Audubon. Mouth of Sandy River, Multnomah Co., Oregon.

? ? 1806 Plains cottonwood—*Populus deltoides occidentails* Rydb. Encountered regularly in High Plains country.

? ? 1806 Black cottonwood—*Populus trichocarpa* Torr. & Gr. Possibly on Clearwater.

? ? ? Inland cord-grass—*Spartina gracilis* Trinius. Not tagged. No locale. No date.

? ? ? Needle and thread grass—*Stipa comata* Trin. & Rupert. Not tagged. No locale. No date.

Arcane terms and creative spellings were taken verbatim from the Expedition journals.

Appaloosa: a distinctive breed of horse developed by the Nez Perce Indians by selectively breeding for speed, strength, and endurance; characterized by their spotted coats.

Beer: brewed by Private John Collins from *"wet molded & Sowered"* bread made from camas root and presented to the Corps of Discovery on October 22, 1805.

Bier: a mosquito net used for sleeping, issued to each member of the Expedition, without which, Lewis reported, life would have been insupportable.

Blunderbuss: a bell-mouthed weapon resembling a large shotgun that fired buckshot; one was mounted on the bow of each pirogue.

Bowpiece: a small cannon mounted on a swivel at the bow of the keelboat; it fired a one-pound ball or the equivalent in smaller projectiles—musket balls, rocks, nails, and whatever else was at hand.

Brains: animal brains were used by the Expedition for tanning leather for shirts, leggings, moccasins, and other articles.

Brarow: badger.

Breadroot: a wild root also known as white apple, pomme blanche, pomme de prairie, Hankee, and prairie turnip; it was a staple of the plains tribes.

Bearking Squerrells: Ordway's name for prairie dogs.

Burning glass: magnifying glass, one of the many presents Lewis and Clark handed out to various Indian leaders; it could be used to start fires by focusing the sun's rays.

Camp Dubois, or **Camp Wood**: winter quarters 1803–04, located on the east bank of the Mississippi opposite the mouth of the Missouri along present-day Wood River.

Carcajue: wolverine.

Castorium: strong-scented oil obtained from the perineal glands of the beaver and used by trappers to attract beavers; Lewis described the scent as *"a strong rank disagreeable smell, and not unlike train oil."* Train oil was whale oil.

Chopunnish River: North Fork Clearwater River.

Cordelle: the technique of hauling a boat upriver by tow-rope; also refers to the tow-rope itself.

Dunghill fowl: chicken.

Espontoon: a wooden spear measuring six feet or longer with a metal blade. Issued to infantry officers as symbols of authority, and carried by both Lewis and Clark, espontoons were useful as rifle rests, walking sticks and weapons. Lewis saved his life along the Marias River by jamming it into the slick mud as he slid toward the edge of a cliff.

Eulachon, or **candlefish**: a small estuarine fish common along the Pacific Coast, collected as a food source; so full of oil that when dried and threaded with a cotton wick, it would burn like a candle.

Fish Creek: North Fork of the Salmon River.

Flap: loincloth.

Frisen: Clark's spelling of frizzen, the metal part of a flintlock mechanism which when struck by the hammer-mounted flint produces a spark to ignite gunpowder in the pan.

Gig: to fish with a spear equipped with a detachable, barbed point, commonly used along the Columbia River drainage to catch salmon, and also used by the Expedition.

Grows: one of Clark's variations of grouse.

Gumbo: clay derived from glacial till and shale; very plastic, slippery, and sticky when wet.

Hackmatack: western larch, a deciduous conifer that grows in moist forests west of the Continental Divide.

Holy Grass: sweetgrass, burned ceremonially by plains and mountain tribes.

Jerky: meat cut in strips and dried in the sun or over a fire.

Kooskooskee River: Clearwater River.

Lewis' River: Salmon River.

Liquor: spirits stocked and carried by the Expedition, including whiskey and brandy. The Expedition drank the last of its supply on July 3, 1805, after making their portage around Great Falls.

Medical problems: the Expedition experienced disorders including abcesses, boils, dysentery, ague, fever, goiter, malaria, frostbite, rheumatism, colds and sore throats, headache, snakebite, sunstroke, fatigue, appendicitis, colic, poisoning, venereal disease, dislocated shoulder, pleurisy, snowblindness, sore eyes, diarrhea, malnutrition, scurvy, sore feet, toothache, inflamed pelvis, gonorrheal infection, bruises, infected finger, strained back, skin disease, stomach problems, sea sickness, cuts, syphilis, muscle strain, influenza, paralysis, broken arm, gunshot wound (in Lewis' posterior), sunburn, infectious conjunctivitis.

Medical procedures: both Captains and some of the men treated various ailments by methods including lancing, amputation (of an Indian boy's frostbitten toes), heat treatment, shoulder relocation, bleeding, greasing, purging, sweating, obstetrics, steam baths, cold baths, poultices, cleaning, and dressing.

Medicinal supplies: the Expedition carried or acquired along the way medicines including laxatives, walnut bark, purgatives, saltpeter, tail of rattlesnake, diuretics, laudanum, zinc sulphate, lead acetate, astringent, mineral water, Peruvian bark, sulphuric acid, emetic, essence of peppermint, jalap, mercury, potassium nitrate, alcohol, camphor, castile soap, liniment, potassium bitartrate, salve, and chocolate drink.

Musquitor: mosquito, also musquetor, musqutor, musqutoe, misquetor, musquetoe, musquitoe, musketoe.

Pemmican: dried meat, usually buffalo, pounded into loose fibers and mixed with rendered fat and sometimes dried berries; a staple preserved food of the plains tribes.

Pirogue: an open boat powered by oars, sail or towrope; the Expedition used two pirogues as far as Great Falls.

Poggamoggan: a stone-headed battle hammer observed by Lewis among the Shoshones.

Polecat: skunk.

Portable soup: dried or concentrated soup, bought in Philadelphia by Lewis as an emergency ration; truly a last-resort item in the larder, and generally disdained by the men, the last of it was consumed on the Lolo Trail hunger march.

Quamash or **Pas-she-co**: the edible bulb of the camas lily and staple food of the Nez Perce and other mountain tribes; it was new to science when Lewis and Clark were introduced to it.

River Which Scolds All Others: Indian name for Milk River.

Rochejhone: Clark's spelling of the Roche Jaune or Yellowstone River.

Rush's pills: remedy and general cure-all provided by Dr. Benjamin Rush of Philadelphia; said to have a powerful laxative effect, each pill consisted of ten grains of mercurous chloride and fifteen grains of jalap.

Setting pole: long pole used to push a boat upriver by the boat's occupants.

Small wolf of the prairie: coyote.

Tiger cat: bobcat.

Wapato: *Sagittaria latifolia*, also called arrowhead; aquatic plant found in quiet backwaters of rivers in the Columbia drainage; its nourishing root, bought from Indians along the river, sustained the Expedition during the fall of 1805.

GLOSSARY

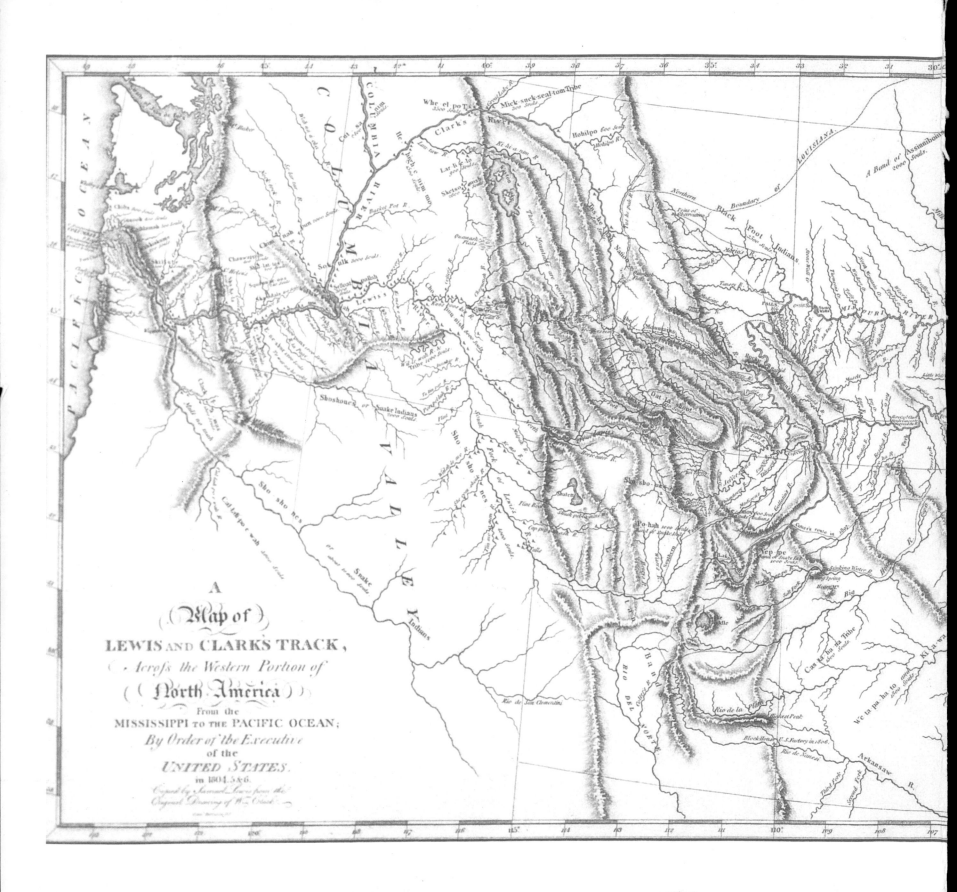

A

Map of

LEWIS AND CLARK'S TRACK,

Across the Western Portion of

North America

From the

MISSISSIPPI TO THE PACIFIC OCEAN;

By Order of the Executive

of the

UNITED STATES.

in 1804, 5 & 6.

Copied by Samuel Lewis from the
Original Drawing of Wm Clark.